# FAITH AND FOLLY
## IN
## SHAKESPEARE'S ROMANTIC COMEDIES

# Faith and Folly
in
## Shakespeare's Romantic Comedies

*R. Chris Hassel, Jr.*

THE UNIVERSITY OF GEORGIA PRESS
ATHENS

Set in 11 on 13 point Intertype Garamond
Printed in the United States of America

Library of Congress Cataloging in Publication Data

Hassel, Rudolph Chris, 1939–
    Faith and folly in Shakespeare's romantic comedies.
    Bibliography.
    Includes index.
        1. Shakespeare, William, 1564–1616—Comedies.
    2. Shakespeare, William, 1564–1616—Religion and
    ethics.   3. Christianity in literature.   I. Title.
PR2981.H35            822.3'3            79-4565
            ISBN 0-8203-0474-3

FOR SEDLEY, BRYAN, AND PAUL

# Contents

# ACKNOWLEDGMENTS

Such a book always owes debts to teachers, scholars, and friends. The staffs of the Vanderbilt and Folger libraries, the Vanderbilt University Research Council, and my typists Elaine Goleski, Donna Stinson, Jean Floyd, and Dot Deathridge, have all contributed to this work. So have my students. In addition to the many scholars who have made their expertise available to me through their publications, I would like to thank in particular Frank Manley and Paul Hunter for their early encouragement; J. Leeds Barroll and Robert G. Hunter for their useful conversations with me; Roy Battenhouse, R. M. Frye, and Robert West for their generous suggestions; and Sam Longmire for his tireless ear and Shandean good humor. I also gratefully acknowledge the following permissions I have received to reprint in this book portions of my previously published work: "Antonio and the Ironic Festivity of *The Merchant of Venice*," *Shakespeare Studies* 6 (1972): 67–74; "Frustrated Communion in *The Merchant of Venice*," *Cithara* 13 (1974): 19–33; "Love versus Charity in *Love's Labour's Lost*," *Shakespeare Studies* 10 (1977), 17–41; *Renaissance Drama and the English Church Year*, Lincoln: University of Nebraska Press, 1979, copyright © 1979 by the University of Nebraska Press; "Sacraments and the Intentional Ambiguity of *Much Ado about Nothing*," *Anglican Theological Review* 58 (1976): 330–45 (600 Haven Street, Evanston, Illinois); "St. Paul and Shakespeare's Romantic Comedies," *Thought* 46 (1971): 371–88; "Shakespeare's Comic Epilogues: Invitations to Festive Communion," *Jahrbuch der Deutschen Shakespeare-Gesellschaft West* 106 (1970): 60–69.

## PREFACE

# The Critical Background

IN A TIME of increasing critical attention to Christian patterns in Shakespeare's plays, the romantic comedies seem again to have assumed their traditional rearward position. The chapters that follow will try to demonstrate this to be a glaring oversight. We have just begun to understand how the conventions, the forms, and the characteristic tonalities of these plays may be indebted to the Christian culture in which they were written and performed. But Shakespeare also specifically and informedly alludes in his romantic comedies to familiar Pauline and Erasmian paradoxes concerning the reversals of folly and wisdom. These allusions would surely have led his audience to understand and enjoy their pertinence to Shakespeare's unique comic vision. They can still function this way today. This approach will try to offer fresh (but never idiosyncratic) interpretations of each of the comedies, and a new understanding of their interrelationships. It also hopes to convey a richer sense of the profundity of Shakespearean comedy, and a clearer awareness of its indebtedness to and exploitation of the milieu of Christian humanism out of which it grew and in which it can profitably be understood. Before we begin to develop such a thesis, however, we need to examine its general critical context.

Earlier Shakespeareans and historians of ideas like Alfred Harbage, E. M. W. Tillyard, Richmond Noble, Frank Kermode, Nevill Coghill, and Walter Clyde Curry all assumed that Shakespeare possessed considerable biblical knowledge and incorporated a basically Christian perspective into his secular works.[1] Despite this background, few Shakespeareans since G. Wilson Knight have studied Christian patterns in Shakespeare's romantic comedies.[2] Part of this reticence lies in the tenacious assumption that Shakespeare's early comedies are not to be taken seriously as reflectors of their age or their creator. More influential, however, is the skepticism of R. M. Frye and other respected Shakespeareans who doubt the existence of extensive structural and reinforcing Christian patterns in any of Shakespeare's plays.[3] Generally speaking, this skepticism has not been directed toward the romantic comedies, an oversight that may partly explain its unusual persistence. Still, Frye's considerable experience in the interpretation of Christian patterns in Renaissance literature obliges us to consider his four major reservations concerning such an approach to Shakespeare. They do not finally prove, together or singly, that such patterns cannot be convincingly demonstrated; rather, they suggest only that such demonstrations are yet to come.

Basically, R. M. Frye and I agree on "Shakespeare's dramatically masterful and theologically appropriate use of Christian doctrine" (p. 272), and that is a crucial area of agreement. In fact, Frye would probably accept, at least theoretically, most of the specifically allusive material that I will discuss. We differ mainly in the extent to which Christian doctrine may consciously or unconsciously have permeated Shakespeare's art. Further, neither Frye nor I would expect to determine precisely what Shakespeare believed, nor would we argue that he is overtly dogmatic or allegorical in his treatment of Christian doctrine. Therefore, Frye's thesis of Shakespeare's "sane and informed secularism" (pp. 7, 41), rightly understood, does not run counter to what I hope to demonstrate. Frye is careful to say that he neither uses *secular* "as a pejorative term" nor implies in it "any positive rejection of Christianity or antagonism to it" (p. 7). Like Frye, I assume that Shakespeare's plays are primarily concerned with this world. Still, a "sane and informed secularism" in the English Renaissance would almost certainly have included regular church attendance, awareness of and familiarity with a uniform Anglican doctrine and liturgy, and involvement in the major issues of the day, many of which were doctrinal or sectarian even while they were also political or aesthetic. When Frye mentions his first major reservation, the lack of explicit evidence of Shakespeare's theological reading (p. 12), he may underestimate this widespread and universal cultural influence.

A familiarity with religious commonplaces would have been especially likely in Renaissance England because of the official pressures to attend services severely monitored for uniformity of doctrine and procedure and conducted according to the *Book of Common Prayer*. Horton Davies describes some of these well-known coercive measures in *Worship and Theology in England:*

> The three Tudor Books of Common Prayer were a coerced formulary of worship intended for "soul control"—that is, to force the parson and people in a direction predetermined by their sovereign and Council. The blasphemous fact is (and it held wherever the doctrine of *cuius regio, ejus religio* was accepted) that Almighty God was to be honoured by a form of worship reinforced by the strongest temporal penalties. Every minister declining to use the Prayer Book or using other forms of worship was subject to an ascending series of punishments, ending, for the third offense, in deprivation and life imprisonment. Any lay person depraving the book or obstructing the use of it was subject to heavy penalties. Absence from church on Sundays or holy days was punishable by a fine of 12 pence for each offense, the sum to be levied by the churchwardens for the use of the poor of the parish. The later Elizabethan Acts against Recusants and Puritans contained even stiffer penalties, including imprisonment and in extreme cases, death.[4]

Though his ecumenical bias is showing, the pressures Davies describes are quite real. There would have been reluctant hearers, to be sure. But such pressures for uniformity and regular church attendance, plus a widespread liturgical education, would probably have guaranteed that some texts—most notably ones like the Lord's Prayer, the General Confession, key passages from Morning Prayer and Communion, favorite sections of homilies, significant biblical passages, and familiar liturgical responses and refrains—were almost universally known. The publication during Elizabeth's reign of such official Anglican documents as the *Book of Common Prayer* (1559), *Certaine Sermons or Homilies* (1563, 1587), the Bishops' Bible (1568–72), and Nowell's *Catechism* (1570), also attests to that pressure for uniformity. So do the various acts and proclamations of Parliament against Puritans and recusants, prescribing required church attendance, suspension of due process, fines, persecutions, and similar repressive measures.

Behind this pressure, of course, lies its corollary, the frenzied nonconformity of the Reformation and the Counter-Reformation. England had just become Protestant in 1559; Lutheran and Reformed churches in Germany and Switzerland were only officially secure in the 1530s;

Calvin was still threatened by civil suits into the 1570s; and the French Huguenots were being massacred well after that date. As Williston Walker makes clear, Protestants in the late sixteenth century debated almost every issue that had originally separated them from Catholics.[5] The Marprelate tracts; the intensified persecution of dissenters after 1583; the four competitive translations of the New Testament (Great Bible, Genevan, Bishops', and Rhemish); the reams of polemical marginal notes, appendices, prefaces, and indexes, and the confutations and defenses all indicate the vitality of English doctrinal controversy during the last decades of the century. In this light we can be reasonably confident that Shakespeare could have exploited the most familiar of these doctrines and controversies in his plays, assured that his audience would recognize them and understand their relevance. That likelihood is enhanced when close analogy and overt allusion in several of the comedies invite and direct the informed response of Shakespeare's audience to that relevance.

R. M. Frye also objects that the ethical values espoused by the plays are as demonstrably pagan as Christian (pp. 94–95). Three responses may be made to that position. First, Renaissance thinkers like Pico and Ficino certainly dabble in pagan thought, but usually only to incorporate it into the Christian system. Second, as Battenhouse has suggested to me, "traditional thought discussed ethics under the rubric of moral theology, since ethics had to do with the moral implications of theology." Third, and most important to this study, Shakespeare's comic ethos is demonstrably and uniquely Christian. The paradoxes concerning Christian faith and Christian folly that I plan to discuss are not merely general ethical patterns but widely accepted or highly controversial aspects of Christian doctrine. Simultaneously, their source, usually Pauline but sometimes also Erasmian, is often directly alluded to in the plays. In fact, Shakespeare seems consistently to have alluded to the widely known and "important" doctrinal commonplaces and controversies of his age to elucidate, enrich, and make more familiar his innovative and sometimes esoteric comic interests.

Frye further requests precedents for the operation of these patterns (pp. 64–65). As Cormican suggests, it is unlikely that another Shakespeare would have come along in his own or another age.[6] But there is ample precedent, both literary and dramatic, for the patterns I plan to discuss. O. B. Hardison and many other literary critics and historians agree that a major forerunner of Elizabethan romance and drama is the medieval ethical and religious drama and narrative. Both the ethic and the religion of those predecessors are primarily Christian, though Platonic, Ovidian, and other influences are also important.[7] Besides the liturgical drama of the Mass and the liturgy, and besides the secular drama which grew out of those forms, we have Christian moralities like *Everyman* and *The Castle of Perseverance*;[8] spiritual, allegorical drama in the romantic, comic mode of Lyly (*Endymion* is an example); and rich Christian influence variously permeating such late sixteenth- and early seventeenth-century "moralities" as *Dr. Faustus, Macbeth, Friar Bacon and Friar Bungay,* and *Othello.* Even Ben Jonson, with his classical comic perspective, incorporates Christian morality into his Roman form,[9] albeit generally with less charity and less edification than characterize Shakespeare's comic vision. Like most of the works of Shakespeare's contemporaries in epic, romance, songs and sonnets, and even literary criticism, as well as drama, Shakespeare's comedies, tragedies, and histories are to some degree a prism through which the doctrinal and liturgical patterns of his age are refracted. Unlike much of this precedent, they are not a platform from which these beliefs are homiletically enunciated. Nor, therefore, need such Christian patterns as theme, nuance, figura, or dramatic configuration be as close to the surface as Frye insists.

Frye's final reservation concerns the lack of witnesses to Christian doctrine in Renaissance plays. Indeed, the Renaissance had no tradition of close analysis of its contemporary literature, though the Bible and the classics had begun to receive such attention. Further, both Meres and the sixteenth-century commentators who delight in discovering Christian analogies in pagan literature would probably have assumed their presence in a Christian poet to be too obvious to mention. Despite these drawbacks, however, at least two witnesses have emerged. First, Griffin Higgs and fellow Oxonians choose the *Tragedy of Phylomela* to be performed at Oxford on the religious festival of Holy

Innocents', 1607, because the play "would well have fitted the day by reason of the murder of Innocent Itis." [10] Even more impressive, the anonymous author of *The Stage Acquitted* late in the century argues that the dramatic performances on holy days at the courts of Elizabeth, James I, and Charles I were specifically pertinent to their liturgical occasions, "a diversion which tended to the confirmation of the Doctrine of the Day" (p. 56). He then discusses in some detail how apposite one of the Epiphany masques, *Britannia Triumphans*, was to its festival occasion (pp. 63–64). By answering another of Frye's reservations, such testimony allows the study to be judged solely on the basis of its own doctrinal and hermeneutical validity. That is a requirement that every study must satisfy.

In recent years critics have begun to encourage a reexamination of the Christian doctrinal and liturgical patterns that may inform and shape many of Shakespeare's plays. O. B. Hardison in *Christian Rite and Christian Drama* illustrates this more recent climate when he invites nonsectarian, nonevangelical, scholarly investigations of Christian cultural influences on the form and vision of Renaissance drama: "For better or for worse, modern Western drama is the product of a Christian, not a pagan culture. Its forms, its conventions, and its characteristic tonalities are shaped by this fact." [11] Even more encouraging is a comment by Paul A. Jorgensen in his recent book, *Our Naked Frailties*. In response to R. M. Frye, he describes an approach to Shakespeare that is almost precisely what I propose in this study:

> Critics have become needlessly inhibited since the appearance of Roland Mushat Frye's *Shakespeare and Christian Doctrine*. . . . Although Frye's thesis is that critics have read too much Christian symbolism into Shakespeare, his book actually serves the more valuable purpose of pointing out and clarifying the extensive amount of Christian doctrine in the plays which lends itself to symbolic interpretation. Shakespeare's contemporaries indulged guiltlessly in this activity as they did in Biblical allegory, converting history into poetry in Sidneyan fashion; and the Geneva Bible that Shakespeare used was full of marginal notes explaining what a particular Scriptural statement or episode stood for. What the critics must now do is make Christian interpretation as accurate as they can (wherever possible giving Renaissance commentary) and try to demonstrate that the

interpretation lends itself to the central dramatic purpose of the play.[12]

Hardison warns the critic against too literal an understanding of the relationship between such inherited cultural patterns and the comic form of a "secular" writer like Shakespeare. But he adds that while ritual patterns and comic patterns, doctrine and drama, are never to be considered identical, they might often be analogous, and their relationship discernible.[13] Combined with recent general studies of relationships between Christianity and comedy,[14] these comments are at once a comforting and a sobering assurance that scholars should once again consider this area of research and interpretation respectable and potentially productive.

# CHAPTER I

# Faith and Folly
# in Shakespeare's Romantic Comedies

WE WILL CONSIDER in this first chapter some of the general influences of liturgical, Pauline, and Erasmian paradoxes concerning
faith and folly on Shakespeare's comic vision and comic form. Because overt verbal allusion offers the most widely acceptable evidence
that Shakespeare invited an informed response to these doctrinal patterns, the rest of the study will concentrate much more heavily, though
not exclusively, on that kind of evidence. Conveniently, the earliest
of these plays are also the most explicit and self-conscious in their use
of and allusions to doctrinal and controversial material. For that reason we can proceed more or less chronologically through these plays
at the same time as we encounter an increasing subtlety in their use of
the comic-Christian reversal of wisdom and folly, much as Shakespeare's audience could have done as they shared his emerging comic
vision.[1] Surveying these later chapters will be a useful way to begin
this one.

Of the six mature romantic comedies, *Love's Labor's Lost* is easily
the richest in the number and the thematic aptness of its doctrinal
allusions. The doctrinal controversy of "love" versus "charity" to
which it repeatedly alludes also exercises a persistent if subtle structural influence on the play, one which continues into the later plays.
After many potentially humbling experiences, the lords finally need
a formal penance to discover the wisdom of folly; their own merit
proves insufficient for comic grace. The play's focus on comic and
Christian folly is balanced in the next chapter by a consideration of
how several Pauline or Erasmian allusions are apposite to *A Midsummer Night's Dream*. Each of them invites the audience to connect
the play's rather esoteric interest in the imagination with the more
familiar realm of religious faith. Demonstrating such unquestionable
allusions to well-known doctrinal controversies and passages in St.

Paul and Erasmus in these first two mature romantic comedies establishes a solid foundation for the rest of the study. By isolating and analyzing Shakespeare's early, self-conscious use of analogies between religious and romantic faith and folly, we can consider the more complex reversals of folly and wisdom in the four later comedies in greater interpretive depth, without having to reestablish its obvious doctrinal context again and again.

The next three chapters study the subtler but still persistent interaction of faith and folly in *Much Ado about Nothing, As You Like It,* and *Twelfth Night.* In Benedick, Beatrice, and Claudio folly and a lack of faith are almost identical, and their simultaneous acknowledgment of imperfect eyesight and foolish behavior signify their achievement of comic and romantic faith. In *As You Like It* Rosalind, Orlando, and the rest discover and celebrate their own follies through elaborately conventional behavior; the play shares their celebration and their discovery by exposing and enjoying the great folly of art's feignings, the rituals of lovers, and their equally noble and silly attempts to express the inexpressible. The title of *Twelfth Night* obviously invites comparison with the Christian festival of Epiphany as well as the season of misrule that surrounds it. Mutual motifs of self-love and edifying humiliation suggest that acknowledged folly is a thematic interest close to the center of play and festival. Feste's role as fool and curate is an especially interesting connection between its comic and Christian motifs. So are his repeated allusions to Erasmian and Pauline commonplaces.

The final chapter considers *The Merchant of Venice,* that intriguing outlaw among the romantic comedies, in the light of the thematic and formal expectations established by the other discussions. It also looks at the play in light of the doctrinal controversy about the nature and efficacy of Communion to which it intriguingly alludes. True to its rich but recalcitrant nature, its exceptionality is an important final indication of the importance of my thesis. For its ambiguity must relate in large measure to its Christian characters' failures to achieve Shakespeare's persistent definition of comic wisdom—the humble acknowledgment of their own imperfections—before their festive return to Belmont. In fact, the play's self-conscious Christians, with their ambiguous mixture of righteousness and self-righteousness, combine with its many ironic suggestions of Shylock's frustrated Communion and its Shrovetide setting to provide us with one of our most important illustrations of the crucial place of the Pauline and Erasmian reversals of folly and wisdom in Shakespearean comedy.

This brief survey conforms to a growing awareness among critics that major differences between "the forms, the conventions, and the characteristic tonalities" of Shakespearean and satiric comedy are partly attributable to Christian cultural influences.[2] Shakespeare's comic perspective posits an ideal of humility, self-knowledge, and forgiveness. The satiric perspective posits an ideal of perfection, and derides all failures to achieve it. Ridicule, gulling, even physical punishment warn the audience to recognize and avoid the same absurdities, but they seldom cure the afflicted. In sharp contrast, Shakespearean comedy tries to lead the inevitably flawed characters through exposure and humiliation to a humble awareness and acknowledgment of their common folly. Such a treatment suggests that folly is not reprehensible but forgivable, not monstrous but universal. The bondage to be escaped in Shakespearean comedy is not folly, which is inescapable, but the refusal to acknowledge it. Acknowledging his folly liberates the wise fool from excessive reason, complete self-determination, and arrogant self-righteousness. Through this paradox the witty but uncompassionate ideal of the satiric form, the Lovewit or the Brainworm, could well become in the Shakespearean form the most severely flawed. In satiric comedy the wise expose the foolish; in Shakespearean comedy the foolish expose the wise. Behind that familiar Shakespearean comic paradox lie several Pauline and Erasmian commonplaces.

The distinctive endings of the two forms especially emphasize the Christian dimensions of Shakespearean comedy. In satiric comedy the ending celebrates the purging of folly and the punishment of its bearers. The society polarizes, sometimes graphically on the stage, into the wise and the foolish, the perfect and the flawed, the judges and the judged. There is little sympathy for the scapegoats, and less belief that they belong in decent human society. The audience must identify with the self-righteous wits in order to celebrate the play's characteristic ritual of ridicule, punishment, and expulsion for the betterment of ideal personality and society. In Shakespearean comedy the wholesale perception of universal folly—inevitably imperfect action and knowledge—results in an inclusive communion of fools. Enlightened men and women thus delight in and are relieved by their deliverance from the self-directed and exclusive ideal of the satiric tradition. Humility produces love and faith, which asks for forgiveness and forgives. The audience joins the characters in a concluding festival of shared faith and common folly, a festival which may bear extensive analogies to Christian communion in its celebration of the wisdom of humility and the wonder of undeserved grace.

Obviously Shakespeare's comedy is neither liturgical drama nor Pauline homiletics. It is far more complex than that in both makeup and effect, clearly "secular" in R. M. Frye's meaning of the term. But Shakespeare's unique comic vision evidences epistemological and ethical values attributable to prominent Pauline and Erasmian commonplaces and to the persistent general influence of the liturgical experiences so universally shared by Shakespeare and his contemporaries. His comic attitudes towards romantic faith and folly are informed by Pauline and Erasmian paradoxes to which the comedies often explicitly allude. And his festive epilogues invite the audience to participate in a ritualistic act of theatrical communion which celebrates these paradoxes in a spirit analogous to the experience of Christian Communion. The rest of this chapter explores each of these general parallels in greater detail, before the study moves on to their specific and more readily verifiable operation in the six mature romantic comedies.

## i. Faith and Folly in the Anglican Liturgy

As this discussion of Shakespeare's unique comic vision already suggests, the thematic pattern that proves most important in this study is the paradoxical reversal of folly and wisdom in comedy and in Christianity. As the lover's humble acceptance of his inevitably imperfect actions becomes a measure of his fitness for festive revelry, so does his humble acceptance of the limits of his mind. This imperative that the comic characters become aware of their unavoidable imperfection and then celebrate that awareness is also so central to the common liturgical experience of all Renaissance Christians as to warrant closer study. Shakespeare and his audience would almost certainly have understood so consistent a comic assertion and celebration of universal human imperfection, with its resultant need for personal forgiveness, edification, humility, and grace, as inescapably Christian and therefore reassuringly familiar. They were, after all, expected to acknowledge the same awareness about themselves each time they accepted the sacrament of Holy Communion.

The most prominent parts of the *Book of Common Prayer,* like the Catholic rites which lie behind them,[3] repeatedly assert the doctrine of the imperfection of man. The Kyrie pleads with God and Christ to "have mercy upon us"; the entire Order for Communion centers upon the communicant's errors and his need for forgiveness; the Lord's Prayer, like Christ's sermon on the mount which contains it, assumes that all men have sins to be forgiven and sins to forgive. The Great Litany opens with the repeated plea, "have mercy upon us miserable synners"; asks that the "Good Lorde delyver us" from a long list of offenses of the flesh, the world, and the devil; contains the versicle, "O Lorde deale not with us after our synnes," and the response, "Neither rewarde us after our iniquities"; and ends with the petition, "Thoughe we be tyed and bounde with the chayne of our synnes, yet let the pitifulness of thy great mercy lose us." Throughout the liturgy statement after statement stresses the universality of sin and the hopelessness of redemption without the grace of God. "A general confession" in the Morning Prayer service provides one of the most direct of hundreds of illustrations of this basic doctrinal assumption: "We have erred and straied from thy waies, lyke lost shepe. . . . We have left undone those thinges whiche we ought to have done, and we have done those thinges which we ought not to have done, and there is no health in us." "If we say that we have no synne, we deceyve ourselves, and there is no truthe in us."[4] Collects, the Ministration of Baptism, pertinent hymns and homilies, and the catechisms[5] all stress the imperfection of man and urge that he humbly confess it. Catholics and

Protestants alike would know from the persistent reiteration of this idea that "the most nearly perfect man is he who is most aware of his imperfections."[6]

This humbling acknowledgment of one's membership in the community of error is equated in liturgy and doctrine to the ability to believe, to forgive, and to love. William Fulke in *A Comfortable Sermon of Faith* assures us of the first association: "Yea, we may plainly perceive that true faith is alway joyned with great humility."[7] Many of Shakespeare's lovers can only believe transcendentally in their beloved after they have attained a similar humility about the inevitable follies of their actions and their knowledge. In liturgy as in Shakespearean comedy, then, faith and folly are intricately bound together through humility. But the Lord's Prayer also connects humility with the forgiveness of error in others: "forgeve us our trespasses, as we forgeve them that trespasse against us." John Marbeck similarly explains how the act of forgiveness is almost sacramental: the acknowledgment of shared error confirms one's faith and betokens his supernatural forgiveness: "Forgiving . . . our brethren . . . [is] a plaine and infallible token to certifie therewith our conscience, that we have through faith in Jesus Christ for remission of our sins. For if we can finde in our hearts, unfainedlie to forgive unto our bretheren their trespasses: it is a most infallible token, that our sinnes are cleane washed awaie & quite forgiven." Finally, knowing and acknowledging our sins is testimony to our love. Of Mary Magdalene, Marbeck says: "She hath knowen hir sins most, whereby she hath most loved me, and thou hast lesse loved me, because thou hast lesse knowen thy sinnes."[8] To love, forgive, or believe, we must first humbly acknowledge our membership in flawed humanity.

As the catechism, the *Book of Common Prayer,* and Marbeck illustrate, the humble acknowledgment of error is accompanied by the plea for grace. The litany stresses this plea with dramatic repetitiveness: "From all evil and mischief, from synne, from the craftes and assaultes of the Devil, from thy wrath, and from everlasting dampnation: Good lorde, delyver us"; "spare us, good Lorde"; "have mercye upon us miserable synners." The haunting Kyrie, so often and so beautifully interpreted musically, performs the same educative func-

6

tion, stressing as it does the need for mercy: "Lorde have mercy upon us, Christe have mercy upon us, Lorde have mercy upon us."[9] The Renaissance Christian would have had an inescapable sense of the relationship between the faithful admission of folly and the achievement of grace and wisdom. In the Communion service, the mediator of that grace is liturgical. In comedy the mediator can either be a fool, a priest or priestlike father, or a redemptive maiden. In either event the result of this mediation is a paradoxical but joyous festivity.

Modern theorists have focused on this paradox as the central relationship between comedy and Christianity. William F. Lynch finds St. Paul's "I glory in my infirmities" to be central to the comic perspective, reminding man to embrace his persistent finiteness. V. A. Kolve in discussing laughter and the comic suggests that the medieval mind often distrusted laughter, but could associate it with edification and humility. In fact, a common motif of the Corpus Christi plays was the exposure of absurdity through laughter. Such a perspective on universal human absurdity can be profoundly comic, if it affirms the rightness of God's universe. Nathan Scott agrees when he discusses the joy of finitude. Because of its "materialism," its sense of man's finiteness, his historicity and its own, "the Christian imagination is enabled to rejoice in the quiddities . . . of existence in a way that accords very closely with the path taken by the comic vision." At the core of this accord is the shared pattern of joy through humiliation: "The joy of comedy is a great joy, but it is a joy which can sometimes come only after great humiliation." As O. B. Hardison suggests, the Mass itself reflects this basically comic paradox, moving as it does from adversity to prosperity through grace.[10] Milton's *Paradise Lost,* no less than Dante's *Divine Comedy,* attests to the vigor of the paradox of the fortunate fall in the Catholic and Protestant traditions.

John Hollander's concept of the "morality of indulgence" helps us intensify these connections between the comic and Christian welcoming of shared error and shared forgiveness. He suggests that the comic audience and characters are bombarded with such a surfeit of human folly that they finally come to accept it as their own even as they become satiated with its excess.[11] This theatrical experience finds its analogy in the social festivals of disorder, which simultaneously provide for the release of inhibitions and satiate the need for release.[12] In the liturgical experience the communicants are likewise made aware of the fellowship of error but simultaneously freed to welcome that fellowship as they vow to amend their lives. The Puritan's traditional opposition to the theater, May Day, and Communion may expose his consistently literalminded attitude toward each of these "feignings."[13] While he despises human aberration, his Catholic and Anglican counterparts channel it through rituals that celebrate its acknowledgment and encourage its purging. While he abhors the graven gargoyles, his Anglican and Catholic contemporaries find ethical and spiritual pleasure in the distortions they expose. Of course, the state of social or comic grace that results from May Day or comedy is psychological, not mystical. Its mediators are charitable and absurd men and women, neither ministers nor angels. But sometimes the comic analogy is very close to the surface. In *Much Ado* a friar through his gracious wisdom sets in motion the chain of actions that leads to humility, repentance, forgiveness, faith and love, and Leonato prescribes penance to an erring Claudio. Such examples, combined with the feast of folly Shakespearean comedy customarily serves up for us, suggest that its unique tendency to embrace folly and skepticism and translate them into humility and faith is not unlike the mediation of grace we associate with both preaching and the liturgy.

The most obvious liturgical expression of this state of grace occurs in the General Confession of the Anglican Communion service. Because Shakespeare's comic, romantic state of grace is so consistently analogous to that spiritual state described here and known by most Elizabethans, I have not bothered to detail its occurrence in each of the plays. Here, however, to quote the confession in full might provide a useful summary of the extensive parallels. As we recall, the service occurred at least every fortnight, probably far more frequently in most parishes; attendance was required of each communicant at least thrice a year.

Almighty God, father of oure Lorde Jesus Christe, maker of all thynges, Judge of all menne, we acknowledge and bewayle our manifolde synnes and wyckednesse, whiche we from tyme to tyme moste grevously have committed, by thoughte woorde and deede,

8

against thy divine Majestie, provokynge mooste justlye thy wrathe
and indignation againste us: we do earnestly repente, and bee hartely sorye for these oure misdoinges, the remembraunce of them is
grevous unto us: the burthen of theim is intollerable: have mercy
upon us, have mercye upon us, mooste mercyfull father, for thy
sonne oure Lorde Jesus Christes sake, forgeve us all that is paste,
and graunte that we may ever hereafter serve and please the, in
newenes of lyfe, to the honour and glorye of thy name throughe
Jesus Christ our Lorde. Amen.[14]

The acknowledgment and repentance of error, the prayer for forgiveness, and the resolution to amend one's life are the basic constituents
of this liturgical document and of repentance as it is set forth in the
prescribed homily.[15] Faith in the grace of God, transmitted through
the liturgical vehicle, makes the acknowledgment joyful and the
amendment possible. With the help of human mediators, a similar
grace is administered to the flawed community of Shakespearean
comedy.

## ii. Faith and Folly in St. Paul and Erasmus

But if the Anglican liturgy would have been the probable vehicle of
this paradoxical comic and Christian attitude toward faith and folly
for Shakespeare and his contemporaries, the individual writers with
whom the paradox would have been most immediately associated are
St. Paul and Erasmus. In fact, most of the important doctrinal allusions
in Shakespeare's romantic comedies will refer to St. Paul, or to controversies arising out of his Epistles. Shakespeare's frequent and
knowledgeable allusions to both writers might become less surprising
when we understand their prominence in Renaissance England and the
unusual relevance of their comments on faith and folly to Shakespeare's unique comic vision.

That Shakespeare often alludes to St. Paul to accentuate the Christian analogies to his comic themes seems inevitable, even if sometimes
unconscious, for wherever we look at Renaissance theology, St. Paul's
name and his doctrine emerge as the central facts of organized Christianity. Although most English commentators stop short of idolatry,[16]

9

they are universally in awe of the man and his teachings. First, he was revered as the foremost interpreter of Christianity by its new interpreters. Read William Tyndale, New Testament translator and Protestant martyr, echoing his master Luther: "This epistle [Romans] is the principle and most excellent part of the New Testament and most pure evangelion, that is to say . . . gospel, and also a light and a way unto the whole scripture. . . . No man verily can read it too oft, or study it too well." [17] We would hardly consider that echo of "I am the Way and the Trueth and the Life" [18] an accident on the part of such a scholar as Tyndale. John Colet, humanist interpreter of St. Paul, echoes the same respect when he refers to "the divine mind of St. Paul." [19] But one of John Donne's sermons most vividly assures us of the immense reputation St. Paul possessed as virtually the Logos, the Word of God: "Now the holy-Ghost was in all the Authors, of all the books of the Bible, but in St. *Paul*'s Epistles, there is, sayes *Irenaeus, Impetus Spiritus Sancti,* the vehemence, the force of the holy-Ghost." [20] Coupled with this unrestrained praise of the biblical commentators is the phenomenon of homiletic and liturgical allusion. St. Paul is almost invariably the Anglican homiletic authority. "As St. Paul saith," is the greatest commonplace of the homilies, and the greatest compliment. Invoked by name during each communion service for his "comfortable wordes," [21] he is the voice of organized Christianity, the "elect instrument of God"; [22] his texts are repeatedly cited in sermons about Christian ethics or Christian epistemology. [23] Shakespeare would have found it difficult to avoid using the letters of St. Paul for immediately recognizable and universally acceptable Christian texts and doctrines. His audience would just as certainly have inherited the scholars' awe and respect. The author of the Epistles and a large proportion of the *Book of Common Prayer,* the namesake for churches and places throughout England, and the persona of organized Christianity is Shakespeare's most obvious choice.

One aspect of St. Paul's teaching makes it particularly understandable that Shakespeare's romantic comedies should refer to Pauline passages when enriching their celebrations of faith and folly with biblical allusions. An analysis of the Bible's use of *folly* and related words like *fool, foolishness, fools, fool's,* and *foolishly* reveals a significant pattern. St. Paul frequently, and almost exclusively, exploits the Christian (and comic) paradox that acknowledged folly signals the blessing of humility, a paradox introduced by Christ both in the Beatitudes and when he says, "Whosoever shall not receive the kingdom of God as a little child, shall in no wise enter therein" (Luke 18:17). In over one hundred and fifty occurrences of *folly* and related words in the Old Testament, and eleven more in the New, none employs them paradoxically or positively. As William Empson and *The Interpreters' Bible* both observe, the Old Testament meaning of *folly*, like that of satiric comedy, is always contemptuous. As the opposite of wisdom, which is good, folly is a quality much to be avoided.[24]

Now St. Paul does not completely abandon these negative associations. But he frequently views folly with a positive or a paradoxical eye. On the one hand, it is a state not unbecoming to those who preach Christ and try to follow his teachings of humility. Further, it is the opposite of that intellectual pride, sensuality, and practical worldliness that make it so difficult for a rich man to enter into the kingdom of heaven. The most elaborate of Paul's developments of this paradox comes in the first chapter of his first letter to the Corinthians, whose repeated failing seems to have been intellectual and spiritual arrogance. To them St. Paul preaches of the wisdom of folly and the foolishness of wisdom:

> For the preaching of the crosse is to them that perish, foolishnesse: but unto us which are saved, it is the power of God. For it is written, I will destroy the wisedome of the wise, and will cast away the understanding of the prudent. . . . For after that in the wisedome of God, the world through their wisedome knew not God, it pleased God through foolishnesse of preaching, to save them that beleeve. For the Jewes require a signe, and the Greekes seeke after wisedome. But we preach Christ crucified, unto the Jewes a stumbling blocke, and unto the Greekes, foolishnesse: But unto them which are called, both Jewes and Greekes, Christ, the power of God, and the wisedome of God. For the foolishnesse of God is wiser then men: and the weakenesse of God is stronger then men. Brethren, yee see your calling, how that not many wise men after the flesh, not many mightie, not many noble *are called*. But God hath chosen the foolish things of the world, to confound the wise: and God hath chosen the weake

things of the worlde, to confound the things which are mighty.

(Bishops' Bible, verses 18–27)

This paradox occurs often in St. Paul's letters, but especially in First Corinthians (2:14; 3:18–20; 4:10; 13:1–13). It explains why a Christian must be born again, and also why he so seldom can be reborn. For all of his worldly experience—all the attractions of the world, the flesh, and the devil—teach him the folly of Christ crucified. His reason cannot grasp the paradox of Christ's victory in defeat. Not many wise, or mighty, or noble men can be called to this preaching. They must give over the pride of this world, the pride of the mind and the pride of the senses to receive such a lesson, and such pride dies hard. They would be fools to recant such values, and so they must become fools before they can become Christians. No wonder so few can find in such foolish preaching "the power of God."

The Geneva glosses are particularly rich at this point, and they shed additional light on St. Paul's paradox of the wisdom of folly. Paul would not convert with "the wisdome of wordes," or "rhetoricke, or arte oratorie," lest "men shulde attribute that unto eloquence, w^e onely belonged to the power of God." What is wrong with the wise, the scribe, the disputer, "he that is so subtil in discussing questions?" "Herein Paul reproacheth even the best learned, as thogh not one of them colde perceive by his owne wisdome this mysterie of Christ reveiled in the Gospel."[25] We will see an interesting manifestation of this commonplace in the words of Theseus in *A Midsummer Night's Dream*.

But intellectual arrogance is not the only target here. For St. Paul is also addressing those men who cannot admit their own imperfect actions: "He speaketh in the person of the wicked, who contrarie to their conscience rather attribute these things to God, then acknowledge their owne follie & weakenes." "Thus he calleth man in contempte & to beate down his arrogancie."[26] In our consideration of Shakespeare's romantic comedies, these two flaws will be again and again the stumbling blocks to comic happiness. Characters will repeatedly lack the humility to acknowledge truths which transcend their reason or their deserving or to admit follies which undermine their arrogant self-images. Their benevolent edifications gently but surely lead them to this dual wisdom of intellectual and ethical folly. When they have achieved that wisdom, then they can rejoice in a profound festivity. Its profundity has many dimensions, of course; one is its persistent analogy to this Pauline teaching of the humble wisdom of folly and faith.

Some of us might be more comfortable at the outset knowing that these Pauline commonplaces would also have been made available to Shakespeare's contemporaries through the much more "modern" and "fashionable" vehicle of Erasmus's *The Praise of Folie*. First translated into English by Sir Thomas Chaloner in 1549, this widely known work saw two more English editions in the sixteenth century. It had also seen thirty-seven Latin editions at the time of Chaloner's translation.[27] So there is little question of its currency in Renaissance England and Renaissance Europe. Its comic framework and its popular, even secular nature make Erasmus's work another likely vehicle through which these paradoxical Pauline attitudes towards faith and folly might have made their way into Shakespeare's comic vision.

As a biblical scholar, Erasmus was fully aware of the Pauline basis of his own paradoxical praise of folly. In fact, Folie discusses that influence overtly as she begins the peroration of her unusual sermon:

But now at last I lepe backe againe to sainct Paule, and GLADLY (saieth he) . . . *beare with unwise men,* (speakyng it by him selfe): also in an other place, *receive you me, as unwise that I am:* and further, *I speake not this precisely as upon gods precepte, but rather in mine owne unwisedome.* Than againe, *we* (saith he) *are become fooles for Christes sake:* Dooe you here now how great praises of Foly this so great an autour alleageth, yea, and that more is, he plainely enjoygneth Folie unto us, for a thyng moste necessarie, and right importyng to salvacion? *For who so semeth* (saieth he) *to be wise amonges you, let him become a foole, to the ende he be wise in deede.*                              (Pp. 115–16)

As Erasmus then has Folie ask, "woulde ye any more evident prouffes than this" that St. Paul is a strong precedent for this unique comic-Christian vision?

Erasmus agrees with St. Paul that the paradox of saving folly has theological as well as comic meaning. For becoming a fool signifies a humility that is manifest in all of Christ's teaching and examples (pp. 117–18), and that must be present in each man before he can receive the blessing of redemption:

> Now all these textes that I have alleaged, doe thei not plainly testi-fie, *that mortall men beyng fooles, are godly also?* and that Christ hym selfe mindyng the relefe and redempcion of mankyndes folie, although he was the ineffable wisedome of the father, became yet a maner foole, wheras takyng mans nature upon hym, he was founde bothe in fourme and habite lyke unto other men. Evin as Paule saieth, *he was made sinne also, to cure and heale the synnes of the worlde:* to which sinnes yet it pleased him to ministre none other medecines, than the *Folie of the crosse,* by the handes of the APOSTLES, beyng grosse and unskilled men. (P. 118)

It is essential that we notice the voice of Erasmus, a respected Renais-sance theologian and intellectual, identifying the concepts of universal folly and universal sin. For this is the identification which will permit the natural transition of this doctrine from theology to comedy. This analogy culminates in the discussion of forgiveness: "Perchaunce it shoulde not be the feblest argument, to saie that fooles finde so muche grace and favour afore god, as to Folie onely is gevin perdone and forgevenesse of trespasses . . . [to] who so ever dooe axe at god for-gevenesse of theyr sinnes" (p. 119).

But in the Epistles of St. Paul, as in *The Praise of Folie,* this ac-knowledgment of folly is only half of the comic-Christian equation. For Christian faith also demands another kind of humility, one that "plucketh and retyreth the mind of man from visible and corporall thynges, to those that are invisible and ghostly" (p. 121). Erasmus, like St. Paul, thus sees a paradoxical relationship between madness and the ecstasy of religious faith. But Erasmus carries this paradox one step further than St. Paul can, and again it is an important step for our understanding of these patterns in Shakespearean comedy. All true believers are, according to Folie, in a manner mad. But so are all true lovers. With respect to the folly of both their selflessness and their faith the two are "nere sybbe" (p. 122). In fact, the greatest folly, the finest madness of all, is the analogous madness of romantic love and religious faith:

PLATO . . . wrote, *that the passion and extreme rage of fervent lovers was to be desired and embrased, as a thing above all others most blisfull:* because that a vehement lover liveth not now in hym selfe, but rather in that that he loveth. . . . The depelier such love is impressed, . . . so muche the greatter, and the blisfuller is the rage also. Whiche so beyng that soules yet pinned within these bodily foldes maie smacke a little of suche a felicitee, consider ye than what a life the sainctes soules leade in heaven? wherunto . . . the sprite selfe shalbe mervailously ravisshed and soked up by the farre more stronge and attractive power of the hieghest sprite of all, whiche is God.                                                          (Pp. 126–27)

This strongly Platonic passage links the foolishness of religious and romantic love on the highest level. For the ultimate love-attraction is to God, and God's love is also the highest promise of the Christian faith. St. Paul states the inexpressible wonder of this promise in I Cor. 2:9, "Evin the very gwerdone that the PROPHETE promyseth, Saiyng, *was never mans eie sawe, nor eare heard, nor thought of hert yet compassed, what, and how great felicitee god hath prepared unto suche as dooe love him"* (pp. 127–28). Only a romantic or a religious fool could believe such a promise as this.

St. Paul and Erasmus share, then, the essential outlines of both of these comic-Christian perspectives on faith and folly. There are inconceivable blessings of love and faith for those who can admit with humility the profound folly of their limited knowledge; there is abundant grace and forgiveness for those who can acknowledge with humility the profound folly of their imperfect behavior. These paradoxes were obviously "in the air" in Renaissance England. Their dimensions, still largely inseparable, were both secular and religious by the time Shakespeare was writing his romantic comedies. Shakespeare seems to have assimilated them into the vision of his romantic comedies. It is certainly no accident that Shakespeare's Bottom follows Erasmus's Folie in alluding so directly to St. Paul's most famous description of the folly of faithfulness in *A Midsummer Night's Dream;* or that Feste, who echoes in his epilogue an equally famous Pauline passage about folly as childishness, is so active an agent of humility and maturation in *Twelfth Night.*

Scholars have isolated and discussed these paradoxical Erasmian

attitudes towards faith and folly, but they have been slow in understanding their important relationship to the vision of Shakespeare's
romantic comedies, or their connections to his frequent and informed
Pauline allusions. Barbara Swain's excellent study *Fools and Folly*, for
example, understands the Christian dimensions of Erasmus's celebration of folly. But she never applies them to Shakespearean comedy:
"the mystic glorification of unreason did not produce any notable
pieces of English writing in terms of folly."[28] Other scholars have
noticed connections between Shakespeare and Erasmus, but they have
done very little with either their prominence in the romantic comedies
or their important Christian overtones. Kenneth Muir, for example,
notices a few figures and names Shakespeare might have derived from
Erasmus, but only treats them in a brief note. Walter Kaiser and Roy
Battenhouse have contributed to our understanding of Erasmus and
Shakespeare, but both of them have focused almost entirely on the
considerable figure of Falstaff. William Empson's " 'Fool' in *Lear*"
discusses the Erasmian context, but only in its application to this one
tragedy.[29]

Only Thelma N. Greenfield, William E. Willeford, and Emrys
Jones have begun to develop the relationships between Erasmus, St.
Paul, and the vision of Shakespeare's romantic comedies. Greenfield
notices a number of general parallels in spirit between *A Midsummer
Night's Dream* and *The Praise of Folie,* and finds that "both show us
the fool who glimpses paradise and both utilize the same Biblical
passage to indicate his response."[30] But by focusing almost exclusively
on Bottom's dream, she misses most of the intriguing verbal and
thematic parallels between the lovers and Theseus and Erasmus and
St. Paul. She also draws no conclusions about the other comedies. Because the scope of Willeford's *The Fool and His Sceptre* is so comprehensive, it can only touch Shakespeare's romantic comedies lightly.
Willeford knows that the lovers in *Twelfth Night,* as well as Bottom
and the lovers in *A Midsummer Night's Dream,* are steeped in an
important Erasmian context.[31] But he mentions only the most obvious
connections without considering their rich presence in the other plays.
Similarly, Jones knows that "among the Elizabethans Shakespeare
responded more deeply than anyone to the Erasmian paradoxes of the

16

wisdom of folly and the folly of wisdom."[32] But like Willeford he can only point out the influence and move on. Willeford's work, like Kaiser's *Praisers of Folly,* is an indispensable precursor to mine, and provides excellent intellectual background sensitively applied to many literary works. But no one has studied with any comprehensiveness the workings of Pauline and Erasmian paradoxes concerning faith and folly in Shakespeare's romantic comedies. That is what I propose to do in this work.

Because of the misunderstandings that studies of Christian patterns in Shakespeare sometimes seem to provoke, let me reiterate at this point the limits of my thesis. I have no interest in showing that Shakespeare was a teacher of Christian doctrine or a disciple of St. Paul or Erasmus. I have no interest in establishing Shakespeare's own personal observances or beliefs, or even in speculating about such mat-ters (*in Love's Labor's Lost* he is characteristically ambiguous in this regard, thereby creating some interesting comic effects). Rather, I will consistently maintain that Shakespeare's Pauline and Erasmian allu-sions and commonplaces would have invited his audience to under-stand the comic action in a context at once both rich and familiar to them—their Christian context. The Christian doctrine, the Pauline and Erasmian allusions, elucidates the comic action—not the other way around. Like any creative artist, Shakespeare is using inherited truths to articulate new ones. In arousing these associations, Shake-speare is reflecting the most widely disseminated Renaissance sources of applied Christian doctrine and value: the homilies, the liturgy, the foremost commentators, and the Bible itself. As we have seen, St. Paul's vision is as prominent in these works as it is in Shakespeare's romantic comedies.[33]

## iii. Faith and Folly in Shakespeare's Comic Epilogues

As we have considered the liturgical, the Pauline and the Erasmian heritage of the uniquely Christian qualities of Shakespeare's treat-ments of romantic faith and comic folly, we have come again and again to an awareness that the concluding festivity of Shakespearean comedy often evidences intriguing parallels with the festival of Christian communion. Both celebrate the profound joy, the freedom of humility, that can accompany the constructive, often ritualized acknowledgment of universal and personal error. In the comic as well as the liturgical form the acknowledgment of error admits a character to the concluding festival of folly, forgiveness, faith, and love. Two of the romantic comedies, *Love's Labor's Lost* and *Much Ado about Nothing,* embody in their comic structures the ideology and even the form of repentance and communion—acknowledgment, lamentation, amendment, and rejoicing. All of them end with marriage, hence communion.[34] In four of them, *Love's Labor's Lost, A Midsummer Night's Dream, As You Like It,* and *Twelfth Night,* Shakespeare uses the comic epilogue to invite his audience not only to understand this analogy but also to participate in it. Through the epilogues the audience is asked to affirm ritually and publicly, with the celebrating characters, the follies they have so strenuously discovered. Thus this unique modification of his comic legacy is the one that can lead us most directly to see the importance and the interrelationship of Shakespeare's comic themes of faith and folly.

The comedies interested in the blessed madness of love's truth consistently enrich their thematic interest with allusions and analogies to religious faith and religious rituals. Several Pauline and Erasmian allusions in *A Midsummer Night's Dream* explicitly connect the transcendental visions of the true lovers and true believers, most obviously Bottom's words and the lovers' upon awakening from their dream. *Much Ado about Nothing* dramatizes the conversion of three skeptics into faithful lovers. Like these two plays, *As You Like It* and *Twelfth Night* contain important liturgical, Pauline, and Erasmian allusions. They also have several characters who must learn to dismiss their reason, distrust their senses, and accept a comic joy they can neither engineer nor understand. *As You Like It, Much Ado about Nothing,* and *A Midsummer Night's Dream* are also concerned with the rituals of lovers and of art, and convert those rituals into comic games which can lead, like religious rituals, to expressions and experiences of faith in the transcendental. Two of these plays end with an epilogue which asks the audience to affirm their faith in a transcendent but fragile artistic reality along with the players.

The comedies interested in the fortunate folly of love's conduct will similarly find frequent doctrinal enrichment in close analogies and specific allusions to such familiar Christian patterns as acknowledged universal imperfection, repentance, celebrated and shared folly, and humiliating edification. Feste's epilogue in *Twelfth Night* contains the best-known of these direct Pauline allusions. But *Love's Labor's Lost* alludes at least seven times to a very controversial Pauline passage concerning universal folly, or to issues related to it. *Much Ado about Nothing,* which fits both groups quite comfortably, has Benedick articulate several Erasmian or Pauline paradoxes concerning the blessings of folly, and contains the foolish watch that so effectively confounds the would-be wise all around them. As before, epilogues in two of these plays encourage the audience's participation in and acknowledgment of shared error and common forgiveness.

Of the six mature romantic comedies only two, *Much Ado about Nothing* and *The Merchant of Venice,* lack this festive epilogue. The probable reasons are instructively dissimilar. As we shall see in chapter five, *Much Ado about Nothing* celebrates the achievement of humility, the acknowledgment of imperfection, and the miracles of faith and forgiveness. So directly and self-consciously is this theme developed that no such elusive epilogue seems needed to celebrate the truth of the play or to invite us to participate in it. In complete contrast, *The Merchant of Venice* (discussed in chapter seven) uniquely ends with a celebration which disregards human imperfection. None of the Belmontians seems even vaguely aware of their similarities with Shylock. Therefore they neither forgive him nor appreciate the magnitude of their fortunate, indeed providential, deliverance from the Law that would punish their own naiveté. Belmont thus becomes the only escapist's world in Shakespeare's romantic vision. As a consequence it is a world we are neither invited into nor care to enter.

Each of these four comedies which contain festive epilogues is also interested to some degree in the nature of art as an expression of transcendental wisdom, and in the relationships between the foolish conventions of art and those of the human personality. As a result each of their epilogues links together the faith and folly of the dramatic characters with the inevitable absurdities of the dramatic form. Artistic self-realization is similar to personal becoming. The inadequate assumptions underlying artistic forms and conventions find counterparts in the foolishly conventional behavior of man and woman in love. The efficacy of wit, imagination, conventions, and role-playing are legitimate psychological and aesthetic issues. Shakespeare's comic form can therefore seek its own ideal of comprehensiveness while his comic characters and audience are seeking theirs. The roles will finally coalesce in *As You Like It* and *Twelfth Night*. In his *Anatomy of Criticism* Northrop Frye describes the festive invitation in Roman comedy as an explicit invitation to eat and rejoice with the players.[35] Shakespeare adapts this device to a final consolidation of theme and a final education of audience. Communion in Shakespearean comedy transcends the literal feast to become a sharing of psychological, aesthetic, and perhaps even religious insight.

The earliest invitation to festive communion occurs in *Love's Labor's Lost*. The predominantly flippant play ends on a pensive and artistically self-conscious note. The death of the Princess' father helps initiate a final scrutiny of the efficacy of wit in the lords and in comedy, which delays the expected festivity for a year. Maturing is a sobering experience, and the concluding lyrics enhance this awareness while they contrast with the farcical actions which preceded them.[36] Their imagery achieves a comprehensive and paradoxical union of sorrow and success, urging that comedy can encompass such a broad perspective. Intermixed with the clean, fresh, delightful colors of spring's rebirth (stanza 1) and its resumed songs and pursuits (stanza 2) is the jeering note of the cuckoo, which suggests infidelity as well as fulfillment. In fact, the exuberance of spring, the restored energy and the invitations of nature, are as responsible for human folly as they are for human fulfillment. The lords must apply the same principle to their excessive wit, conventionality, and self-love. Each is inherent in man and in art. But each can also be used excessively to prohibit self-realization. The winter lyric displays the same ambivalence. Its stanza recognizes the harshness of winter, its painful labor, cold, and sickness:

"When blood is nipped, and ways be foul" (v.ii.905).[37] But like spring, the harsh context of winter creates its own paradoxical consolations, its merry notes, its warm fires, and its roasted crabs hissing in the bowl. Just as awareness of human weakness is inseparable from Christian communion, so festive, comic communion is empty without a concurrent awareness of human imperfection. Life is more than pain and responsibility, of course, more than the song of the cuckoo and the cleaning of greasy pots. But it is also more than empty festival and frivolity. "The words of Mercury are harsh after the songs of Apollo" (v.ii.919–20). But both perspectives are necessary if we, or the comic form, are to achieve the paradox of responsible, cognizant festivity.

The epilogue of *A Midsummer Night's Dream* is far more complex in its invitation to festive communion. The whole play asks us to suspend our rational and imaginative prejudices as we try to reconcile the realities of both points of view.[38] For three acts we participate in the imaginative, intangible, symbolic world of the fairies with some acceptance of their reality. Even Bottom flirts with transcendental wisdom when he paraphrases Paul upon awakening from his dream (IV. i.203–11). But daylight has almost destroyed their existence, in a classic confrontation of reason and varieties of faith. When Puck reappears in reasonable Athens he thus reestablishes for us that haunting verse rhythm and imagery of the other, supra-rational world; his world, that of the imagination, becomes as real once again as Athens, in Athens: "Now the hungry lion roars, / And the wolf behowls the moon" (v.i.360–61). Puck's epilogue is a perfect, final, inconclusive assessment of his own degree of reality. He tells us that we may accept him as a vision, a dream, a product of our own slumber, if we must, although dreams are variously real:

> If we shadows have offended,
> Think but this, and all is mended—
> That you have but slumb'red here
> While these visions did appear.
> (v.i.412–15)

And then audaciously, brilliantly paralleling the failure of the rustics' performance, but with totally different effect, Puck breaks the distance between actor and audience. He promises to enter the audience, to shake their hands, and to become friends: "Give me your hands, if we be friends, / And Robin shall restore amends." [39] Far from destroying the stage illusion, as happened in Bottom's show, this action solidifies it. For Puck is urging the audience to accept and balance rational and imaginative belief. He is showing them in a final appeal for their faith that he is indeed real and of their world too. And on this splendid ambiguity the stage is emptied. When Puck finally unites the worlds of Athens, fairy, and audience, the obstructions of an inadequately integrated personality or society have been symbolically overthrown. Such an integration seems possible only at transitional moments like dawn (IV.i.93), midnight (V.i.352), or the ending of the play. But at least it can occur then, although the leaving of the theater, like the leaving of a church, plunges us into daylight that is often too brilliant for the retention of such a fragile substance as understanding or atonement.

The third invitation to festive communion is offered by Rosalind in *As You Like It*, and it employs methods similar to Puck's. Once again it reflects upon the nature of art, the audience's perception of the play's meaning, and the relevancy of that meaning to their own experience. Throughout the play Shakespeare has studied role-playing and conventional behavior as universal psychological phenomena.[40] Inadequately understood, either can obstruct self-knowledge and human fulfillment. But rightly used, both can become the means to defining the most comprehensive personality available to an individual, and to expressing the inexpressible. After the dénouement, characters are returning to their most natural roles, though they are still, and always will remain, role-players to some extent. But in Rosalind's final role as epilogue and conjurer, there occurs that final, shocking reminder that she is not a woman at all but a boy actor. The false role that Rosalind assumed throughout most of the play was actually the more natural for the actor himself. This revelation encourages our quiet understanding that while the play was no more than an assumption of roles by actors, still the play's truth, like all transcendent knowledge, was as valid while the illusion lasted and even after it was shattered, as *scientia* could ever be. As in *Love's Labor's Lost* and *A Midsummer Night's Dream*, frankly admitting the stage's realistic limits and then merging play world and audience world in such a whimsical manner obviates the desire either to identify the two or to choose between them. Christian communion achieves a similar momentary union of transcendental and temporal. Rosalind, the conjurer, so comprehensive that she can exist in both worlds, has awakened the audience from the dream world they were momentarily living in and from the roles they had to assume to participate in that dream. Real life, also a play upon a stage, has returned with its good and bad beards, complexions, breaths, and its own inevitable pretenses. In its magical blending of literal truth and literal falsehood, Rosalind's epilogue reasserts the precarious balance between feigning and honesty that has characterized so much of *As You Like It*. The conventions a person must use and the role he must play if he is to express the inexpressible, in love, in art, or in worship, may need to be most false that they can finally be most true. Such a paradox is central to the vision of *As You Like It*.

Feste's concluding lyric in *Twelfth Night* fittingly perfects the comic epilogue as an invitation to festive communion. It summarizes the play's major issues; it places those issues in a context which is far more serious or aware than our normal expectations of comedy; and it exposes once more the play as play to remind us again of our general and particular relationships to drama.[41] Finally it answers the question of the efficacy of wit, or comedy, raised but not answered in *Love's Labor's Lost*. For the sadness and the seriousness of Feste's epilogue heighten the value of comedy by assuring us that festive communion is consistent not with comic naiveté but with a mature, sophisticated awareness that man suffers as he attempts to become mature, and that edification is not always successful. To accept the imperfection of man and yet to proclaim festivity both in spite of and because of that imperfection is the genius of Shakespeare's maturest festive comedy.

Feste has exposed repeatedly the inadequate self-knowledge in Illyria,[42] especially the narcissism of Olivia and Orsino, suggesting that too many delusions about self and environment signal, if not tragedy, at least an incomplete, unfulfilled humanity. The play equates this ignorance with the literal exclusion of the fool, or the parallel refusal to admit that foolishness is universal. Feste the fool is excluded from Olivia's and Orsino's households until they become sufficiently hum-

bled to see their own foibles, to laugh at them, and to accept graciously
the failings of their peers. Malvolio, in contrast, never opens his gates
to the fools; thus he never attains that broader perception of the fool
as something more than a thief of reputation and self-esteem, as something inherent in himself and in all men.

The whole play also deals with the Pauline topos of maturing in
faith (or love), reaching man's estate, and putting away childish
things. A "foolish thing" can be a child's prank or an affectation which
is innocent only until adulthood. It also suggests the essentially innocent gulling of Malvolio, which his antifestive reaction, his refusal to
be educated into humility, makes appear so sinister. Too often the
first maturity, psychological, artistic, or religious, means antifestivity
or total seriousness, an inadequate perspective. Additionally, the ob-
scenity suggested by the boy's playing with his "foolish thing" [43] suggests the responsibilities of mature love. Malvolio's playing with that
"foolish thing" must emblematize his extreme self-love. But the
clown's phallic humor also reminds us of Orsino's and Olivia's need
to accept love physically as well as spiritually. To Orsino, at first, love
is but a hollow bauble, lovers only toys. Feste mentions that his sister
has been dallied with to expose Orsino's childish attitude, his dallying
with words (III.i.14–20). Olivia's falling in love with another woman
illustrates her own reluctance to accept the complete physical and emo-
tional responsibility of love.

The third and fourth stanzas suggest that honesty in life as well as
art demands the acceptance of its pains along with its pleasures, an acceptance that requires the shucking of the false self (oversimplified
conventions and genres), the inadequate role, or the exaggerated phal-
lus. Swaggering or any affectation, anything that is not natural or honest, will "never thrive" because in a mature, realistic relationship it
will become exposed. Viola's hilarious duel, with Toby's references to
her naked sword, suggests this. We also recall Orsino's ignorance both
of the physicality and of the complexity of love and lovers. Exposure
of affectations is inevitable because "the rain it raineth every day," because life has constant affliction and man inevitable imperfections
which must be borne and shared. No more than art can life be a con-

stant make-believe or a naive festival. Even Toby rejects that path. We have Feste to remind us of the eternal human problems—age, drunkenness, isolation, ineducability. The refusal to include these realities in a vision of life, be it artistic, psychological, or religious, is a sickness, if also a jest.

The refrain and the last stanza provide the necessary corrective to this rather sombre comic epilogue. The world is an old place, and none of these problems are either new or astonishing. Those who ignore either the physical or the moral realities, or who try to rationalize them away, are not living honestly. But likewise, to overemphasize the somber perspective is just as inadequate. For most foibles are not symptomatic of sickness, but of the natural human condition of imperfection. Life is also pleasant; it must celebrate festively the equally possible human improvement through education and maturation and providence. This modified, gentler perspective is strongly urged in the last lines: "But that's all one, our play is done, / And we'll strive to please you every day" (v.i.396–97). The play and its epilogue were both moving and significant, but it was just a play, another toy, another action in the continuum of actions. Only the audience must return to the wind and the rain of London. The characters can remain forever in Illyria, that bright comic utopia where only an occasional Malvolio dampens its spirits.

By calling the play a play [44] as he does in *As You Like It*, *A Midsummer Night's Dream*, and *Love's Labor's Lost*, Shakespeare again has urged that life be considered in its relationship to the stage. They are not the same, to be sure. But life also has cyclical actions, all of which eventually pass; it also has conventional behavior and role-playing, comic and tragic perspectives; it occasions the need to perceive and express the inexpressible and imperceivable. With the correct perspective, life's player can accept his foolish, flawed existence with festive equanimity, as Feste does here, and as all of the play's participants finally do, with the unfortunate exception of Malvolio. Even Malvolio, as the only unfulfilled character among many festive ones in Illyria, should not appear more significant than he actually is. We all know that "the rain it raineth every day." That is one of the

25

reasons Shakespeare's comedies are so refreshing. They help those of us outside Illyria comprehend the rain without becoming drenched by it.

Students of general relationships between Christianity and comedy are persistently drawn to many of Feste's awarenesses. Of the first, Nelvin Vos suggests that comic man must learn that it is the acceptance of "the irreconcilables of the real and the ideal, the finite and the infinite, which indicates that his stance is one of faith." [45] Harvey Cox states the second in a spirit very similar to Feste's:

> Both for Christianity and for the comic sensibility nothing in life should be taken too seriously. The world is important but not ultimately so. Like the clown, the man of faith can snicker at the pretence of the prince because he knows the prince is but a man who will return one day to the dust. But more than that, the man of faith can even chuckle at his own snickering. He can see the prince and himself in a perspective that cuts both down to size but also opens to both new worlds of possibility.[46]

This blend of finitude and infinitude, impossibility and potentiality, humility and hope, is the "whole truth" Nathan Scott ascribes to the comic vision.[47] One feels that Feste's articulation of this delicate mixture in his epilogue would be as comfortable within the visions of Dante or Cervantes as it is central to Shakespearean comedy.

Feste's epilogue presents this perspective more comprehensively than Armado's men, Puck, or even Rosalind can. For his view comprehends not only the ideal blending of the potentialities of each viewer and of the art form, but also an occasional failure either to blend or to reconcile. His comic vision is therefore as inclusive as the tragic one. The emphasis differs, of course. In the festive world of *Twelfth Night* the perspective, in order to become adequately inclusive, must be modified toward a greater awareness of imperfection, just as Christian man must accept his imperfection as a basic premise of his communion with God. In the tragic world of *Lear* (III.ii.74–77) Feste's lyric becomes equally relevant by reminding us and Lear that suffering is both as transient and as inscrutable as the wind and the rain. Otherwise the perspective could become too grim, the suffering intolerable, and the act of tragic communion seemingly futile. Flawed man must also accept his potentiality to become perfect for this communion to occur.[48] That the community of suffering as well as the community of festivity can find Feste's lyric relevant convinces us of the efficacy of Shakespeare's festive, comic epilogues. Each of them encourages us to participate in a joyous communion that accepts with faith, like the Christian communion, the folly of all of life, as it is, without personal or cosmic delusions. When Shakespeare's comic vision has achieved that flexibility, it too has found its maturest, fittest role.

# CHAPTER II

# "Love" versus "Charity"
# Folly in *Love's Labor's Lost*

THE PREFACE documents the intense pressure for uniform religious doctrine and procedure during the last three decades of the sixteenth century in England. But it also mentions its inevitable corollary, the intense nonconformity of the period of Reformation and Counter-Reformation. The *Short Title Catalogue* is crammed with confutations and defenses that illustrate, along with the many polemical marginal notes, appendixes, indexes, and prefaces the frenzied vitality of English doctrinal controversy during this same period. This chapter will investigate through *Love's Labor's Lost* the possibility that Shakespeare weaves strands of these highly visible disputes into the most basic fabric of his romantic comedies.

*Love's Labor's Lost* contains an unusual amount of doctrinal controversy, all of it stemming from two crucial Pauline passages. The play alludes at least seven times to central issues of the Catholic-Protestant debate concerning the proper translation of *agape* as "love" or "charity." Such frequent verbal allusions to this pivotal controversy[1] strongly suggest that Shakespeare understood its affinities to the actions and themes of this comedy, and that he wanted his audience to share those affinities. The affinities are overt, they are pervasive, and they are self-conscious. Central actions like the pact of celibacy, the formation of the small congregation with Armado as priest, the garden confessions, the explosions of foolish languages and disguises, the Pageant of the Nine Worthies, and finally the administration of penance and the deferred promise of festive joy seem incompletely understood without some knowledge of the basic doctrinal issues the controversy evokes. Such important disputes as justification by faith or works, penance versus repentance, and the usefulness of sacrament or priest can be shown to stem from the controversy concerning *agape,* and to relate rather extensively to our understanding of *Love's Labor's*

*Lost.* They also provide more valuable background to our investigation of the pervasive theme of faith and folly in Shakespeare's romantic comedies.

Yet with this wealth of doctrinal controversy, we can never isolate a character, action, or theme with consistent, unambiguous, sectarian affinities. Threads of the debate are everywhere. But the tact and ingenuity of their weaving are among the most remarkable qualities of the play. For they achieve a syncretic comic vision that knits together the sectarian differences with a humour, a forgiveness, and a love of folly that approaches *agape,* the subject of the controversy, more closely than any of the controversialists do. David Bevington has elsewhere noticed the unusual delicacy of Shakespeare's skill in this area.[2] Characters or issues may lean toward a Catholic or a Protestant perspective, but they inevitably swing back toward the center. Shakespeare thus seems to avoid the potentially uncomic fragmentation of sectarianism by avoiding commitment on the one hand and by making the polarity itself comic on the other. In fact, a dextrous shifting from one point of view to another becomes an important part of the doctrinal humor of *Love's Labor's Lost.*

His subsequent romantic comedies will be more selective in their use of such controversial materials, and less overt in their incorporation of doctrinal analogies and allusions. Only *The Merchant of Venice,* with its similar incorporation of debates over the nature and efficacy of communion, will approach this play's intense use of a pertinent controversy. But the later comedies will continue to develop a central thematic pattern that almost certainly receives its shape and discovers its doctrinal dimensions from its first investigation in *Love's Labor's Lost.* That pattern requires that the lords recognize and acknowledge their own folly—their lust and self-love in this case—before any of them can achieve humility, forgiveness, or festive joy. The lords only begin to learn the lesson during the play. But Shakespeare never forgets it.

Such a close relationship to the vision of the later romantic comedies suggests that *Love's Labor's Lost* is much more than the occasional, allegorical piece critics have long considered it. Of course, such ghosts as Henry of Navarre, Gabriel Harvey and Thomas Nashe,

Raleigh, Chapman and the School of Night, Essex and Southhampton, John Eliot and the Earl of Northumberland, and the many originals for the pedantic Holofernes do haunt the scenes of the play and are still fascinating to pursue. But to be persuaded with Bullough that because of them the play is merely "an intellectual fantasy," or even with David that it is a "battle in a private war between court factions" is simply not fair.[3] For the play's informed use of this doctrinal controversy will demonstrate it to be a seminal work in the development of Shakespeare's comic-Christian vision, one which could have been understood and enjoyed in the public theater without an inordinate amount of "inside" information.

## i. The Controversy

Richmond Noble alerts us to the primary allusion to relevant doctrinal controversy in *Love's Labor's Lost,* and explains its pronounced visibility in the sixteenth century. Of Berowne's famous equivocation,

> For charity itself fulfills the law,
> And who can sever love from charity?
>
> (IV.iii.359–60)

"there can be no doubt as to either the identity or the source." It alludes to St. Paul's Epistle to the Romans, 13:10, in the unique and controversial Bishops' version: "Thou shalt love thy neighbour as thy selfe. Charitie worketh no ill to his neighbour, therefore the fulfilling of the lawe is charity." The Bishops' Bible is recognizable because alone among Protestant Bibles it prefers the Catholic "charitie" to the reformers' "love" in this pivotal passage.[4] By that choice it involved itself in some of the most significant doctrinal issues separating Catholics and Protestants in the Reformation.[5] The two classic sixteenth-century manifestations of the controversy occur first between William Tyndale and Thomas More, later between the Calvinist William Fulke and the Catholic Gregory Martin. Once we understand through their exchanges the basic doctrinal issues and their widespread visibility, we will understand how often they reverberate both seriously and trivially through the play, giving it a shape, a focus, and a relationship to the later comedies few have before granted it.

Both Tyndale and More were well aware of the full ramifications of what was ostensibly a translators' squabble. As W. E. Campbell says, "No other discussion [of the English Reformation] was carried on between men of such pre-eminent ability and with so clear an apprehension of the points at issue." [6] Of course, the Word was important per se to Catholic humanists as well as Protestant reformers.[7] But beyond the abstract truth to scripture embodied in the choice of *charity*, *priests*, and *Church* over *love*, *senior*, and *congregation*, lay far deeper issues. The institution of the Catholic Church, the distinctive or interrelated social and mystical concepts of love, salvation by faith or works, the efficacy of sacraments or priesthood as mediators of grace, and finally the mysterious fabric of Christianity itself were some of them.[8] Restated and amplified later in the century by Fulke and Martin, in fact by most controversialists, these issues would have been well known to Shakespeare's contemporaries.

First, More objects to the broad and bawdy connotations of *love*. "For though charity be always love, yet is not, ye wot well, love alway charity." St. Francis, in his innocence, could watch a gentleman kiss a lady's hand and thank God for charity, but "men be nowadays waxen so full of mistrust, that some man would, in faith, ween his wife were nought if he should but find her in bed with a poor frere."[9] More's comic self-assurance is awesome at this point, introducing so sensitive a possibility as pastoral inconsistency in the midst of his defense of *Priest* as well as *charity*. His point, however, is clear. *Charity*, like *priest* and *Church*, has ecclesiastical connotations. Its replacement, *love*, is dangerously secular and general (2:209).

More's extensive reading in Lutheran tracts and his attention to Tyndale's marginal glosses further suggests to him that these three changes, and others, represent a conscious propagation of the Lutheran doctrine of salvation by faith: "For since Luther and his fellows, among other their damnable heresies, have one that all our salvation standeth in faith alone, and toward our salvation nothing force of good works, therefore it seemeth that he laboureth of purpose to minish the reverent mind that men bear to charity" (2:209). Even worse,

More concludes that the formal agency of the Church, mediating grace to erring man, is severely threatened by these assaults on liturgical words like *grace, confession, penance,* and *contrition:* "For he changeth commonly the name *grace* into this word *favour;* whereas every favour is not grace in English for in some favour is there little grace. *Confession* he translateth into *knowledge. Penance* into *repentance. A contrite heart* he changeth into *a troubled heart*" (2:211). His later list of related heresies against Catholic sacraments and mysteries, especially confession, penance, marriage, ordination, and the worship of saints (4:ii), culminates in More's charge that Tyndale was out to "destroy the Mass" (2:212).[10] Of course this is again exaggerated. But More perceives—in the direction of Tyndale's translation, his polemical pamphlets, and of the Reformation itself—a humanizing, an individualizing, and a demythologizing of Christianity, and he senses that those tendencies away from mystery and the supernatural would ultimately damage the Church and the faith. History has not been unkind to his judgment.

Tyndale is disgusted by More's implication of bawdy intention. In fact, his literal and unhumorous response may give too little weight to the perverseness of the human imagination and the delightful incongruity of its whimsy: "The matter itself and the circumstances do declare what love . . . is spoken of."[11] On the other hand, Tyndale staunchly defends both the doctrinal flexibility and the lexical aptness of "love" against More's attack. *Charity* to Tyndale means alms, patience, and mercy, but *agape* means more; it means love of man and woman, love of friend not in adversity, love of God. *Agape,* love, is a more universal, a less condescending, a more generous concept. It is also a more natural English term: "we say not, This man hath a great charity to God; but a great love." "*Agape* is common unto all loves" (p. 21). If this concept can lead to comic confusion, it can also lead to theological wealth.

Recent studies of the interrelationships of *eros* and *agape* have concluded that the Fathers, from Duns to Augustine to Aquinas, were constantly confusing and creatively blending all of the facets and degrees of love into one comprehensive vision.[12] Luther Weigle, a modern Protestant interpreter of the debate, and the respected editor of the

English *Octapla*, stresses this connection as the primary issue in the historical controversy. To move from "God is love" (I John 4:16) to "Charity never faileth" (I Cor. 13:8) is to lose the connection between the two passages, the essential theological link between St. John and St. Paul, between Christian mystical and social doctrine.[13] Somewhere within these same issues may lie the essential but elusive relationships between romantic and religious love, connections that have persisted throughout much of the Christian era. To the pure theologian such connections might appear either embarrassing or trivial. But when even so secular a comic vision as Shakespeare's can evidence so many analogies to the religious tradition, it would seem that the connections need further examination.

Tyndale readily agrees with More that he is defending justification by faith rather than works: "The scripture saith, that as soon as a man repenteth of evil, and believeth in Christ's blood, he obtaineth mercy immediately; because he should love God, and of that love do good works; and that he tarrieth not in sin still, till he have done good works, and then is first forgiven for his works' sake, as the pope beareth his in hand, excluding the virtue of Christ's blood" (pp. 172–73). Love and faith are the necessary precursors of all good works; works are not a cause of grace but an effect (p. 173). This position summarizes the idealism of Tyndale's Lutheranism and predicts a major issue later in the century. Men are capable of perceiving their own errors and of perfecting their own actions. Therefore they do not need the ritualized enactments of these achievements, the sacraments, any more than they need a priest to lead them to understanding and contrition.[14] These awarenesses, especially the last, are central to the debate, and vital to an understanding of *Love's Labor's Lost*.

John Calvin reasserts and sometimes redefines these issues for the later sixteenth century. So do Gregory Martin and William Fulke, the Catholic editor of the Rhemish New Testament and his authorized Anglican confuter. Beyond its growing political implications,[15] their controversy continues, naturally enough, to focus on "the central theological tenet of the Reformation," the issue of justification by faith or works.[16] It continues to scrutinize the biblical passage Berowne alludes to. It reconsiders and expands Tyndale's suggested distinctions between love as cause and effect, or grace and merit. New features include a sharp, conscious severance of love from charity and an insistence that man cannot conquer his "natural depravity" without grace. The immediate topicality of the debate is obvious. Fulke's *Confutation* first appears in 1589, following the Rhemish New Testament earlier in the same decade. Its combined doctrinal centrality and political sensitivity assure us that Shakespeare's contemporaries would have been adequately aware of it. Finally, the debate's two new features, natural depravity and the severance of love and charity, are so directly alluded to in the play as to suggest that Shakespeare expected his audience to grasp and consider the relevancies, and even invited that consideration.

The famous Bishops' translation of Romans to which Berowne alludes receives the closest attention. Its implication that charity fulfills the law is at least superficially devastating to the central Lutheran and Reformed positions that faith, not good works (charity) takes precedence in justification. As a consequence, Fulke and Calvin must sever the concepts of love and charity, must as we do today, and much as Berowne does in excusing himself for his failure: "And when he repeats that the fulfilling of the law is love, understand this, as before, of that part of the law which refers to mankind; for the first table of the law, which contains what we owe to God, is not here referred to at all."[17] Literal good works, charity, can have no relevance to Christ's first commandment, "thou shalt love the Lord thy God." Only the second commandment, "love thy neighbour as thy selfe," could possibly be the subject of St. Paul's evaluation of the relative merits of faith and love.[18] Faith in God takes precedence in salvation because it leads a man to love God, and therefore to do good works (charity) toward his fellow man. This self-conscious separation of doctrinal love into human and divine suggests that Protestant viewers of predominantly secular dramatizations of the "second table," man's love for his fellow man, might quite naturally have understood them in quasi-doctrinal terms, especially if encouraged by other analogies.

The Calvinist doctrine of natural depravity becomes the second assault on the Catholic interpretation of this crucial Pauline passage. Fulke concedes for the sake of argument that if a man loved his neighbor as himself he would fulfill "the Law of the second Table" (p. 258v). However, "Wee never saw the man, nor ever shall, that loved his neighbour as himselfe. Therefore unperfect love doth not perfectly fulfill the law: and it is still impossible to keepe the commandments, in such perfection, as the justice of the law requireth" (p. 258v). That imperfection, of course, man's inevitable folly, is the reason God's grace is amazing to the sixteenth-century Protestant.[19] Only Christ in his righteousness can fulfill the law:[20] "The righteousness and redemption of Christ, is receyved of us, made ours, not by workes, but by fayth."[21] The audacity of the lords to think they could save themselves from "the world's desires" (1.i.10) or their "affects" (1.i.147)! The audacity of Antonio and his friends to believe similarly in *The Merchant of Venice* that he could "stand for sacrifice" and fulfill the law![22] Both assumptions would have run counter to vitally important Protestant positions of the late sixteenth century.

Following Tyndale and Calvin, Fulke must also sever love from charity by distinguishing between cause and effect, between a state of mind and the actions produced by it. Otherwise their doctrine of salvation by faith is threatened by still other troublesome Pauline comments in First Corinthians 13 and in First Timothy 1:5: "But the ende of the commandement, is charitie out of a pure heart, and of a good conscience, and of faith unfained." Gregory Martin's Rhemish gloss naturally uses such Pauline passages to argue the primacy of charity: it "proveth that faith is nothing worth to salvation without workes, and that there may be no true fayth without charitie."[23] Calvin and Fulke confute his logic, as they must, by reducing *charity* to mere actions, effects of faith Tyndale would have said, while elevating *love* to the causative state of mind.[24]

It is at least conceivable that such controversial acrobatics may underlie Shakespeare's perception of the comic potential of this material. In fact, this elusive Protestant distinction is the position we must understand in order to appreciate Shakespeare's irony and Berowne's wit concerning severing love and charity, and the penance that is levied at the end of the play.[25] Under the pressure of doctrinal debate, the Protestant controversialist holds that faith justifies, and that love and then good works spring from that faith. The Catholic, and in fact the moderate Anglican too, e.g., Hooker, maintains with More that because man is naturally selfish, the prescribed prayers, the sacraments, and other such forms are means to grace which God has given him so that he "may become by degrees *supernaturally unselfish.*" [26] The challenge to rituals and to ceremonies which More infers to be part of the debate denies or diminishes this fact of their practical efficacy. They are more than signs or mysteries; they are a necessary psychological and mystical mediation of grace. In *Love's Labor's Lost* we are led through the syncretic magic of Shakespeare's comic vision to agree with the ladies that their lords would never reach that state without their formal administration of penance and their charitable mediation of grace. The lords ask that their repented follies be accepted "on faith." The ladies are both doctrinally and psychologically wise to demand some proof, some "effects"—regeneration and sincere repentance—of their proclaimed "cause." What better proof than the tangible good works which they prescribe?

A final ramification of the debate over charity and love and its satellite issue, salvation by faith or works, is so relevant to the play as to be almost certainly one of the associations Shakespeare exploited. Martin attributes Luther's doctrine of salvation by faith to his decision to renounce his vows of celibacy and to marry a nun. Since the central issue for the lords is their vow of a secular celibacy and then their attempts to evade it, Martin's charge against Luther can also be lodged against the lords: "Luther, who before always had read with the catholic church and with all antiquity . . . these words, 'Labour that BY GOOD WORKS you may make sure your vocation and election;' suddenly, after he had contrary to his profession taken 'a wife' (as he called her), he preached that all other votaries might do the same, and that faith only justified, 'good works' were not necessary to salvation." [27] The charge was a traditional one against Luther and the Reformers. It led Erasmus to the quip that "the Reformation, which had appeared a tragedy, was really a comedy, the end of which was a wedding." [28] Since this vow of the lords also alludes to the heretical assumption that they can labor to save themselves from their natural imperfections; since they consistently confuse the concept of charity with self-love and lust throughout the play; since they behave so uncharitably toward the foolish "worthies," and finally plead with the ladies to bestow grace upon them before they have either achieved the "cause" or demonstrated the "effects" of repentance, it is at least plausible that Shakespeare expected his audience to include even their memory of this attack on Luther's character into the already elaborate context of controversial associations in the play. But again the other side of the syncretic coin also appears. For the world of this romantic comedy, like that of *Measure for Measure*, pressures this intended monasticism so severely that its continent vows finally prove untenable.

Such an elaborate context of doctrinal controversy might have been more readily expected in *Love's Labor's Lost* because the name of the King of Navarre would have immediately suggested to Shakespeare's audience that greatest Protestant hero of the late sixteenth century, Henry of Navarre. The Battles of St. Bartholomew and Ivry in 1589 and 1590 were almost as widely celebrated by Shakespeare's contemporaries as the defeat of the Spanish Armada. As that earlier conflict bequeaths Armado to the play,[29] so Navarre's followers number among them a Marshal de Biron, ambassador to the English, a Longueville, and several possible sources for Dumaine. The setting of the play, called Navarre, was known as a tiny Huguenot kingdom separate from French Catholic domination until 1607. Henry's mother, a D'Albret, was in fact the Protestant queen of the little kingdom, and raised her son in the same faith. But her heroic Protestant son converted to Catholicism in 1593 in order to become King of France the following year. As Bullough says, "He had forsworn himself for power when he turned Catholic, so it would not surprise an English audience to find a fictitious King of Navarre forswearing himself more innocently for love." Add Navarre's notoriously difficult marriage with the Catholic Marguerite de Valois and his family's confrontations with the Catholic King Ferdinand of Spain,[30] his own namesake in the play, and we find a topical context that almost guarantees that Shakespeare's audience would have expected the play to exploit a wide variety of Protestant-Catholic controversies for their romantic and comic potential.

The name Holofernes would also have elicited pointed associations of Catholic-Protestant controversy. It is first the name Rabelais gave to his parody of the antihumanist, Sorbonne-trained Catholic theologian, Gargantua's teacher. But more important, Jesuit controversialists identified Queen Elizabeth with this religious tyrant, and urged that she be similarly executed.[31] With such a rich layering of topical awareness, Shakespeare would have disappointed his audience had he failed to exploit some equally prominent doctrinal debates. He fulfilled their expectations, but delicately, shifting his characters and his comic values so subtly from one set of positions to another that we are neither invited nor required to make sectarian judgments. We respond only to the consistent comic appropriateness of the controversial material.

## ii. The Play

Topical allusions to Navarre, to Queen Elizabeth, and to traditional Catholic-Protestant tensions would have reinforced seven direct allusions to the doctrinal controversy to alert the audience to perceive and enjoy the implications of the controversy in the play. The issue of celibacy, the distinctions between lust, love, and self-love, the need for penance, the question of salvation by merit or grace, works or faith, the distrust or misunderstanding of rituals, the dependence on personal salvation, and the little congregation all seem to derive from facets of the controversy. The liturgical, Pauline, and Erasmian paradox of fortunate folly that we have already discussed also lies close to the heart of the play and the controversy. So does the related doctrinal concept of the edifying, unnaturally selfless, forgiving, and regenerative nature of charity. Doctrinal authorities like Calvin and Luther, as well as Marbeck and the homilies, characteristically distinguish between the natural love of self and the unnatural love of others, selfless and pure, called charity. Marbeck represents their position: "It is naturally given to us all to love ourselves, and [so] there is no neede to give any commaundement concerning this manner of love." A comment by Luther on the idea of charity in Romans could as well describe the lords, and certainly helps explain them: "We abhor . . . humility, . . . [and] love ourselves, . . . are turned in upon ourselves and become ingrown at least in our heart, even when we cannot sense it in our actions."[32] This is how they make their vow, confess their common failure, court the ladies, talk, respond to the pageant, and finally expect an easy forgiveness. They are an almost perfect embodiment of imperfect love.

In complete contrast, the forgiving, wise, patient, and regenerative ladies, helped by the fools, will charitably lead their lords through games, comic rituals, and direct humiliation into a humility which frees them to understand and forgive error in others, to rejoice in their common imperfection, and to try to amend their lives. Ceslaus Spicq leads us to understand that their Communion-like bringing of the lords to grace reflects the charitable edification of the liturgy: "To St. Paul, liturgy, like morality is governed by the necessity of 'edification'; and edification is the work proper to charity."[33] Their mediation of this corrective grace to the lords predicts a pattern which is to become as central to Shakespearean comedy as we have shown it to be in the Christian liturgy. Because of its newness and its consequent self-consciousness in *Love's Labor's Lost* the doctrinal affinities seem most vivid in this play.

The lords have four formal opportunities late in the play to experience this edifying humiliation and thereby to understand and to enact the concept of charity. They include the confessions in the garden, the explosions of inexact language and absurd disguises, and the pageant of unworthiness. The allusions to the controversy punctuate its relevance during these moments. Like Malvolio they never learn the lessons the ritualistic humiliations can teach them. Unlike him, their future edification is promised after the play by a fifth device of grace, the formal and liturgically precedented penance.[34] As we shall see, each of the moments becomes gradually more formal, more conventional, more metaphorical, and even more ritualistic, until the last is framed within an actual Catholic sacrament. Characteristically, Shakespeare's vision remains so syncretic that the use of such Catholic sacraments as confession and penance never assert a "Catholic" position. It is just very funny, and very pertinent.

The lords' most elaborate opportunity to perceive and to celebrate their absurdity occurs during the garden unmasking when each of them formally, almost ritually, confesses his sin against the pact only to be discovered and shamed. Their impulse to confess reminds us of another familiar liturgical difference between Catholic and Protestant. The auditors are unseen, but they are hardly priestlike, except again in their ironic, uncharitable vow of celibacy. Like Luther, they have found it impossible to keep. Scorn, not charity, is the attitude they bring to the confessional; exposure, not edification, is their only goal; and evasion, not contrition, is their final direction of the embarrassment. Berowne's urging that they embrace in human imperfection (IV.iii. 209–14) celebrates not forgiveness, not even amendment, but evasion of responsibility, a grotesquely passive defeatism. He is so elusive, so witty, that he leads his friends to expect grace without amendment of life, as he does again near the end of the play. They use the doctrine of universal folly as a behavioral rationalization, while Christian doctrine and Shakespeare's comic values demand that it be the first step in a strenuous regenerative effort.

Berowne first alludes to the controversy in the opening scene of the play. He glibly predicts their human deficiencies, but either fails to understand or ignores their fullest implications:

> Necessity will make us all forsworn
> Three thousand times within this three years' space:
> For every man with his affects is born,
> Not by might mast'red, but by special grace.
>
> (I.i.146–49)

Both Catholic and Protestant would acknowledge that man lacks the might to fulfill the law by himself. But in no way would that position lead them to abandon their ethical responsibilities as Berowne is here advocating.[35] Conversely, good works naturally derive from the faith and the love of that recipient of God's special grace: "Justification supposes man's cooperation, but it is God's grace that enables him to lend his cooperation; of himself he cannot do anything as he should, because concupiscence or inordinate self-love inevitably vitiate his actions . . . unless healing grace purifies them."[36] This commentary exposes the inadequacy of Berowne's rationalization and predicts the areas in which the lords and Armado will be naturally incapable of fulfilling their naive and uncharitable vow.[37] Only when the ladies mediate grace to them will some evidence of that grace, their good works, begin to appear. Thus elaborately and delicately does the controversy inform moments of the play.

Berowne's most obvious allusion to the controversy concludes their scene of formal exposure and confession. Its interpretation is again so logically and doctrinally inadequate that the informed Christian would have immediately perceived Berowne's absurdity:

> Let us once lose our oaths to find ourselves,
> Or else we lose ourselves to keep our oaths.
> It is religion to be thus forsworn,
> For charity itself fulfils the law
> And who can sever love from charity?
> (IV.iii.356–60)

In this second allusion Berowne unconsciously indicts their depravity by invoking their first principle—themselves—as higher than any other principle, even the oath of a king. Do we find ourselves or lose ourselves? To such selfish men, the answer is self-evident. Thus emerges the ridiculous position that forswearing can be religious, one the Princess later upbraids (v.ii.780–81).[38] Berowne then confuses the distinctions between love and charity by forgetting that the law can only be fulfilled by Christ, after just citing that commonplace in their defense in an earlier scene. The pact they have failed to uphold vividly indicts their similar shared assumption that they can fulfill the law by mastering their own affects.

Perhaps because of this absurdity, Berowne has to try to blur the distinction between love and charity. He confuses their self-love and Armado's, and their mutually flippant pursuit of the ladies, with the wise, selfless, forgiving, and regenerative love of a Viola, a Hero, or the ladies in this play. The lords are themselves severing love from charity as Berowne asks the question, severing human love from divine, and severing the charity of deeds or labors, mere effects (puns, disguises, letters, pageants) from the love which is spiritual and causative. The third and fourth allusions to the controversy, the title pun on the lost labors (works) of love and the Princess' restatement of it in the final scene ("When great things laboring perish in their birth" [v. ii.518]), point out the inadequate forms of their love. Their works are misspent, their labors lost because they do not derive from that causative spirit of selfless love that Calvin and Fulke emphasize when they discuss the Pauline passage in First Corinthians.[39] Shakespeare again walks the syncretic tightrope between the two sides, and again there are no slips.

Longaville makes their divorcement between love and charity even clearer during the same scene when in a fifth allusion to the controversy he upbraids Dumaine, "Thy love is far from charity" (IV.iii. 122). This is true; Dumaine loves himself far too much. Although his wish for fellows in folly has doctrinal affinities, with him it is purely selfish. He simply does not want to bear all of the shame alone. The ritual of humiliation that has just begun will guarantee that he has plenty of fellows in folly, but it will not guarantee their edification and the humility that should follow. The lords will need tangible spiritual medicine to reach that awareness. The irony is that they need a supernatural means to grace, but have assumed instead sufficient personal might. The ladies seem to need no such means at all, but still have them at their disposal. The ladies have a sacrament to administer; the lords need one. The comedy exploits the humor of this situation by making the ladies finally priestlike and the men penitents. But before that happens the lords will be given three more opportunities to become naturally charitable and naturally humble, opportunities culminating in the Pageant of Unworthiness.

The first two moments that could result in their benevolent humiliation, the exposure of inexact language and absurd disguises, fail because the lords lack both the wisdom and the will to engineer their own regeneration. The ladies try to humiliate them for their careless use of language (II.i.90–215) because their language is as symptomatic of their spiritual dilemma as Armado's sexual puns are of his. Both types of linguistic error mirror an inability to love purely. By taking everything the lords say literally or superficially, the ladies and Boyet give the lords the chance to take themselves and their words more seriously. Naturally the ladies distrust the lords' words, because they have not kept their word in the oath. The Princess' comment to Boyet, "It was well done of you to take him at his word" (II.i.215), explains the technique and its need. As Feste later tells us, it is almost as corrupt to dally with words as with maidens (III.i.14–20). The ladies have perhaps one further reason for fearing the lords' dalliance with language. The lords' absurd love of language manifests a self-love that is the ladies' chief rival, as perverse as that might seem. The ladies' continued concern with this rivalry, even in the second scene of Act V, keeps the competition between the lords' love of themselves and of the ladies constantly before us. Berowne's speech (v.ii.395–416) suggests that he has at least begun to speak without too many *"sanses."* Yet a later moment may indicate that he has already forgotten even that simple lesson (v.ii.743–66).

In their courting with the Russian disguises, the last of their formal opportunities before the pageant to learn some humility, the lords seem saved from recognition of their folly by the folly itself. Their stratagem is so silly that they can finally believe that it is their "sport" which is being mocked, not themselves (v.ii.519). This fits nicely into the now-established pattern of their evasion of enlightenment and of blame. Their language, their vow, their sport are all excessively absurd, but somehow the lords have been able to divorce themselves from these foolish manifestations of themselves. That they will do the same thing during the Pageant of the Nine Worthies assures the ladies of their profound need for a sacrament of penance.

The lords could symbolically, almost ritually, recognize, enjoy, and repent their folly when it is enacted for them in the Pageant of the Nine Worthies. Traditionally a pageant that encourages a sense of mutual unworthiness on the part of the audience,[40] this comic version goes the tradition one better. It not only presents the worthies but presents them unworthily, enacting for the lords their own over-parting, first as celibates, then as lovers. By dramatizing the doctrinal principle of universal human unworthiness, the pageant potentially assures the lords that their folly is not unique but common, not monstrous but natural, therefore "worthy" of that undeserved forgiveness the doctrinal controversy is interested in. But once again their response is partial, the lesson lost. Laughing not with but at the absurdity of the pageanteers, their mirrors, the lords experience no humility and they exhibit no charity. If Dumaine senses the ultimate point of this lesson, he chooses to ignore it: "Though my mocks come home by me, I will now be merry" (v.ii.626–27). Consequently they all remain outside of that awareness of the communion of folly that becomes in *Love's Labour's Lost,* and remains in most of the other romantic comedies, the prerequisite to comic festivity.

Details of the pageant support the context of common error and the need humbly to accept it. Costard confuses *big* (v.iii.546) and *great,* a small but apt error. But he can acknowledge the error, and beg forgiveness for it (v.ii.554–55). The lords put Alexander out, and once again Costard pleads for compassion and understanding. His request is an eloquent and pointed invocation of charity. Not surprisingly, it goes finally unheeded:

> There, an't shall please you, a foolish mild man; an honest man, look you, and soon dashed. He is a marvellous good neighbor, faith, and a very good bowler; but for Alisander—alas, you see how 'tis—a little o'erparted. (v.ii.575–78)

His sincere, colloquial humility silences the lords during Moth's part, but Holofernes' Judas is too much for them, and the relentless ridicule continues. In its crescendo against Holofernes, the cutting stichomythia of the attack exposes the compassionless wit of the lords (v.ii.603ff). When Holofernes sputters his last judgment on these proud, witty lords, we see how far they are from festive awareness, from humility and its great product, charity: "This is not generous, not gentle, not humble" (v.ii.621). There it is, explicitly outlined by an Erasmian fool. The lords are failing again as gentlemen, as comic heroes, and as Christian neighbours.

In contrast, the Communion service constantly emphasizes the "good neighbourhood" of humility, love, and faith. The instructions which preface the service clearly direct its ministrant to deny the Communion to any who "have done any wrong to hys neighbours by word or dede," until he has confessed, repented, and "amended his former naughty lyfe" (p. 92). The last six of the ten commandments deal with relationships to others, the last two explicitly with "neighbours." The offering is prefaced by "sentences" emphasizing stewardship and sacrifice. The invitation includes only those "in love, and charite with your neighbors" (p. 100). And the entire service celebrates the mystical neighbourhood of true believers and imperfect men, all partaking of a common meal in common folly. That they "may evermore dwell in him, and he in us," the communicants become "membres incorporate in thy mistical body, whiche is the blessed company of al faithful people" (pp. 103–4); promise to walk "from hence furthe in his holy waies" (p. 100); and hope to "continue in that holy felowship, and do all suche good workes as thou has prepared for us to walke in" (p. 104). In the light of such an emphasis, Costard's gentle reminder about the lords' mistreatment of Nathaniel ("He is a marvelous good neighbour, faith") might point up the lords' "ill neighbourhood." This is even more likely when we learn from Frances Shirley that even such a simple oath as "faith" is seldom random in Shakespeare's hands.[41]

A particularly apt biblical allusion directs our proper reaction to the lords' lack of charity and humility at this crucial moment of the pageant. Rosaline's reaction to the lord's absurd disguises prefaces the poor performance perfectly, from either the Christian or the comic perspective: "I dare not call them fools" (v.ii.372). Her reason: in Matthew 5:22, Christ instructs his followers thus in humility and compassion: "Whosoever shall say, *Thou* foole, shalbe in danger of hell fire." We dare not call them fools, for it exposes a lack of humility, a lack of the sense of common folly, a lack of charity, and finally even a lack of faith. The enormous error of the lords during the performance is placed in sharp focus by Rosaline's simple reminder of this basic Christian teaching.[42]

The lords' abuse of Armado and his fellow fools is all the more effective to us as comic ritual because the lords in abusing him are also abusing themselves, regardless of their intention. They are connected most obviously by their common self-infatuation and its manifestation in their abuse of language. Typical of the comic use of fools, Armado has the severer symptoms, but they all have the disease. Further, Armado's lust for Jaquenetta combines with the lords' self-love and their self-gratifying pursuit of the ladies to compose a fairly complete picture of imperfect, blameworthy forms of love. Two phenomena in the play, the formation of the heretical congregation or sect with Armado as priest in the first scene, and the pervasiveness of sexual puns in their minister's language, combine to assure us that Armado would have been recognized as a mirror both of the lords and of the controversy. This classic but early Shakespearean use of the fool culminates just before the end of the pageant when Jaquenetta becomes "quick by him," the first lover's labor not lost in the play. As proof of the braggart Armado's paternity we hear, "the child brags in her belly already" (v. ii.666). How like this Pompey the Huge. That this consequence of his verbal and physical dallying is a purifying, "woolward" penance (v. ii.700) paves the way at least structurally for the lords' penance and experience of productive love.

The congregation that Armado forms with the lords in Act I, Scene i links their heresies against human nature, their attempt to deny a healthy sensuality,[43] to other issues of the religious controversy about the nature of love and the nature of worship. Not coincidentally, more biblical and liturgical allusions than in any other scene in Shakespearean comedy mark the initiation of their heretical sect. But the ironic echoes of the litany and the controversy ("To hear meekly" and "Not by might mastered but by special grace"),[44] during which the lords praise their own powers of salvation in terms of their own humility, alert us to the larger dramatic irony of their congregation. Thinking both that they can save themselves—"make us heirs of all eternity" (i. i.7)—and that they are analogous to cloistered divines (1.i.24–32), their comic and spiritual hubris fits nicely into the doctrinal controversy. For a similar hubris was thought by More to characterize Luther's belief that an individual could interpret scripture, save himself without the church, or even constitute his own congregation of believers. Aiding Shakespeare's syncretism here is the fact that Luther's position would have seemed as extreme to most Anglicans as it would to Catholics by 1590. The laws requiring church attendance, not to mention Hooker's elaborate defenses of ritual and sacrament in the nineties, illustrate how close the two positions had become by that time.[45] The old issues, while still remembered, would have been less divisive in 1595. The hubris of the lords, and hence its comic and doctrinal pertinence, would thus have seemed threatening to almost no one this late in the century.

In a similar vein, if the lords can choose a priest so flippantly in the first scene, they can also cavalierly dismiss him in the last. More also has some caustic comments on that score that might apply to *Love's Labor's Lost:* "Ye must understand that Luther and his adherents hold this heresy that all holy order is nothing. And that a priest is nothing else but a man chosen among the people to preach. . . . By that choice to that office, he is priest, . . . and no priest again whensoever the people choose" (2:210). Though Tyndale might have agreed with the substance if not the spirit of this biased report a century earlier, no moderate Anglican by 1590 would have taken it very seriously. Such an extreme Lutheran position would have become a well-known footnote to the history of the Reformation by that time. Further, all would have abhorred the lords' reason for dismissing Armado. For they do so to disclaim their similarity with him; they scorn him in the pageant because, unlike us, they cannot perceive that his self-love and his linguistic abuse, but particularly the lust and the sexual puns which manifest these flaws, are his true priesthood to the lords.[46] They can mirror the lords' own imperfect charity to themselves; but the lords will not look closely enough at the image of their own folly to be edified. They want nothing to do with his going "woolward for penance" as was "enjoined him in Rome" (v.ii.700–701). Again, if "Rome" seems a momentary anti-Catholic slur, Armado's hair shirt neatly anticipates the penance the lords will finally have to undergo. The controversy continues to be refracted through the play so tactfully as to threaten almost no one.

The lords deny their communion with the fools, even after the pointed reminders of Costard, Armado, and the Princess. Yet they expect the ladies to accept their professed repentance on faith alone. The King's callous request for her love shows a dearth of compassion for the grieving Princess, who is justly stunned by his insensitivity: "I understand you not. My griefs are double" (v.ii.742). She has simultaneously lost a father and seen a lover prove himself unfeeling of that loss. Because the ladies distrust the lords' mere stated repentance, they must turn the lords' request for forgiveness into a counterdemand: grow up, gain responsibility, charity, and self-knowledge, and prove your love and your amendment of life. In the sixth formal allusion to the controversy the Princess advises, "by these deserts . . . I will be thine" (v.ii.795, 797). More (and Hooker) would have quickly confirmed the ladies' judgment that such flawed and naive men need a formal, holy ritual to guarantee the sincerity and the performance of their repentance (2:209, 212).[47]

This elusive push and pull of Catholic versus Protestant positions has permeated the play, sometimes favoring one side, sometimes the other, but neither too seriously nor too long. We would associate the monastic vow and the shriving and confession of the lords with Catholicism, and they come off absurd. On the other hand, the conclusion presents a rather positive case for Catholic penance versus repentance and for formal, public sacrament versus informal, individual conscience. The men's charity is so naturally and quickly perverted to lust or self-love that it suggests natural depravity. But the ladies exemplify with equal naturalness and ease a greater love that can forgive, edify, and proffer grace. In fact, unlike the lords' early and silly priesthoods, the ladies make excellent priestesses, mediating an efficacious if not an amazing grace. The first labors of the lords are wasted works, because their vow of chastity was both shallow and uncharitable. But at the conclusion new works, literally charitable acts, will be demanded of them as proof of their greater love. And if Armado's hair shirt is an uncomfortable reminder of odd monastic habits, it also anticipates their needed penance. In such a shifting comic situation, narrow sectarian disputes are absorbed into human complexity, probably to the profound relief of the theater audience. Such syncretism, such charitable humor is truly a joyful achievement in any disputatious age. It may well be noteworthy that Shakespeare is never really anti-Catholic in his plays; neither, however, is he anti-Protestant. Even with the Puritans, arch-enemies of dramatists and theatergoers alike, Shakespeare, unlike Jonson, satirizes only tendencies, never religious practices. Malvolio is a classic example of Shakespeare's characteristic delicacy in these controversial matters, a delicacy that would seem to frustrate attempts to ascertain a particular sectarian leaning.

A good example of his light touch occurs when the Princess twits her Forester for being too Catholic in his flattery of her:

> See, see—my beauty will be saved by merit.
> O heresy in fair, fit for these days.
>
> (IV.i.21–22)

This seventh allusion to the controversy is again deliciously noncommittal. If salvation by merit is heresy, it is the heresy of a romantic insult, the implication that her beauty is more the result of her own good handiwork than God's grace. Thus easily does Shakespeare translate a bitter theological dispute[48] into a brilliant if brief psychological moment in comedy.

The final penitential actions likewise require a sense of the doctrinal controversy to be approached with much critical sophistication, but their explicit relationship to the issues of that debate remain elusive. Though later comedies occasionally repeat the motif of penance (*Much Ado* and *Measure for Measure* most obviously), they generally dramatize the beginning of regeneration within the play, thus avoiding both the possibly controversial overtones of sacramental need and the agonizing year-and-a-day delay of festivity. When that regeneration has hardly begun, as with Bertram, the festivity is difficult indeed for us to celebrate.

The penance levied upon the four lords summarizes their gross imperfections. Their acceptance of a year's celibacy devoted to charity signifies their final willingness to amend their lives and overthrow their trivially motivated pact. The King must repent his perjury, but also his selfish insensitivity to the Princess' grief over her father's death, by living for a year in austerity to prove his love. The two lesser sinners, Dumaine and Longaville, are simply asked to mature and become more virtuous. But Berowne, as the proudest, wittiest character, is given the fullest penance, a painful orientation into his own personal limitations. Not only must he spend twelve months visiting the sick, for his "faults and perjury." Perhaps seeing that his beloved Rosaline is dissatisfied with her penance, perceiving at last that he deserves more correction than he has gotten, possibly understanding or beginning to understand that her grace exceeds his desert, he asks for more penance:

> Studies my lady? Mistress, look on me.
> Behold the window of my heart, mine eye,
> What humble suit attends thy answer there.
> Impose some service on me for thy love.
> (v.ii.827–30)

Is he sincere? Is he still the old Berowne, still trying for the most elaborate words and the most impressive quest, still playing the court-ier? The possibilities remain in delicious balance. But loving him more truly than he can yet imagine, Rosaline grants his request tenfold. For his merciless wit, which lacks both charity and wisdom:

> You shall this twelvemonth term from day to day
> Visit the speechless sick, and still converse
> With groaning wretches; and your task shall be
> With all the fierce endeavor of your wit
> To enforce the painèd impotent to smile.
> (v.ii.840–44)

He resists, sensing the impossibility of the task, hence finally sens-ing, really experiencing, his own impotency, his own imperfection: "To move wild laughter in the throat of death? / It cannot be; it is impossible" (v.ii.845–46). That is precisely the point. Berowne's pen-ance is a reversal of the punishment he administers to the fools. He must learn compassion by experiencing his own shortcomings. He must be witty and hear no laughter. Like Duke Theseus, Rosaline makes Berowne aware of the humbling interrelationship between hu-morist and audience, and between man and man:

> A jest's prosperity lies in the ear
> Of him that hears it, never in the tongue
> Of him that makes it.          (v.ii.851–53)

Every performer, writer, wit, teacher who has ever tried a joke has sometime come to this humbling awareness amidst stunning silence. If sickly ears laugh at his scorn, he may continue to reap laughter from the suffering and the infirmity of others.

> But if they will not, throw away that spirit,
> And I shall find you empty of that fault,
> Right joyful of your reformation.
> (v.ii.857–59)

Finally humbled and sobered by this revelation of the dearth of his humility and the imperfection of his charity, Berowne will do pen-ance, "befall what will befall." Only such an experience can teach him the limits of mere wit, the depths of his own folly, and the consequent grace of Rosaline's love.[49] The play will therefore not "end like an old play," for it cannot end festively until he reaches that state of wisdom:

> Our wooing doth not end like an old play;
> Jack hath not Jill. These ladies' courtesy
> Might well have made our sport a comedy.
>
> (v.ii.864–66)

Because these men and women are operating in a Christian context, the stakes of their happiness are greater than the superficial resolution of a comic plot. Similarly, their achievement will supersede romantic love, though it will contain it. "Twelvemonth and a day" is "too long for a play," but it seems adequate penance for men whose spiritual triviality and whose inadequate humility and charity make them undeserving of marriage until that time. Shakespeare will gradually have his comic characters grow through folly into humility and therefore become capable of love during the play. Then their festivity can celebrate through marriage a strenuously achieved joy and wisdom. Here, because wisdom is just beginning, the harsh, quiet words of Mercury, the religious tone of responsible adulthood, close the play with uncharacteristic seriousness. For lyric wisdom we hear a cuckoo's mocking song and feel the deprivations of winter; for lyric joy the summertime that song heralds, and the inviting fire after the winter's chill. Without an awareness of folly, without a sense of deprivation, comic celebration is no more than an empty form, and comic joy no more than shallow laughter. Henceforth in Shakespeare's comedies it will never be that. The song of the cuckoo will be replaced by that of the owl, a merrier note because wisdom is preferable to flaccid joy, because comic understanding of one's own folly and its universality is preferable to the satiric scorn of others, because mature adulthood is more joyous than eternal irresponsibility. The song of Apollo represents the sunny and the reasonable comic mode; the words of Mercury the otherworldly, religious one.[50] Their self-conscious, verbal combination here is an intriguing one when Shakespeare is simultaneously and self-consciously blending a secular, classical dramatic mode with so profound a religious awareness. Their blending will become more and more subtle, until by *Twelfth Night* they will have become almost indistinguishable.

# CHAPTER III

# "Most Rare Vision"
## Faith in *A Midsummer Night's Dream*

IN *Love's Labor's Lost* Shakespeare seems to have discovered through his exploitation of the controversy of "love" versus "charity" a basically Christian attitude toward folly that will influence the rest of his romantic comedies. If a character can be brought to acknowledge the folly of his behavior and to know that folly to be universal, then he can paradoxically rejoice with faith and love in its promised forgiveness. Frequent and overt allusions to prominent biblical and liturgical passages and controversial doctrinal issues demonstrate that Shakespeare was aware of the interplay of various facets of Christian doctrine with this comic perspective on folly, and suggest that he wanted his audience to share such insights with him.

In *A Midsummer Night's Dream* allusions to less controversial but equally prominent passages from St. Paul's Epistles and Erasmus's *The Praise of Folie* further intensify our understanding of the Christian dimensions of Shakespeare's comic vision. In vastly different ways, Bottom, the lovers, and Theseus all invite the audience through these allusions to connect Pauline and Erasmian paradoxes about the divine madness of religious faith to the analogous follies of romantic faith and the imaginative experience. Once again a celebration of human limitation becomes the necessary precursor to comic happiness. But this time the center of that folly is epistemological, focusing as it does on limited knowledge rather than imperfect behavior. In a Renaissance troubled by growing skepticism, it is hardly surprising to find such delicate thematic relationships between romantic and religious faith, or between imaginative and religious belief. Sebastian, Olivia, and Orsino in *Twelfth Night;* Claudio, Benedick, and Beatrice in *Much Ado;* Orlando, Oliver, and Silvius in *As You Like It*—each comes to accept love with faith as a gift of grace transcending his understanding and his merit. Each of their plays uses metaphor and allusion to underline this analogy between romantic and religious faith. In *Love's Labor's Lost* Rosaline's injunction to Berowne clearly fuses spiritual and secular repentance, especially in the play's rich context of doctrinal controversy. In *A Midsummer Night's Dream* a similar use of Pauline and Erasmian allusions brings the doctrinal dimensions of romantic and imaginative faith close to the surface, and allows us to understand its subtler operations in the later plays as well.

## i. Bottom and St. Paul

The most obvious Pauline allusion in the play is also the most important, for it alerts us to the central position St. Paul occupies in its comic vision. The allusion occurs during Bottom's delightful monologue upon awakening from his dream, a moment that has always struck the audience as perfectly balanced between the ridiculous and the sublime:

> I have had a most rare vision. I have had a dream, past the wit of man to say what dream it was. Man is but an ass if he go about to expound this dream. Methought I was—there is no man can tell what. Methought . . . I had—But man is but a patched fool if he will offer to say what methought I had. The eye of man hath not heard, the ear of man hath not seen, man's hand is not able to taste, his tongue to conceive, nor his heart to report what my dream was.
> (IV.i.203–11)

We are right when we ascribe Bottom's reluctance to expound upon his dream to his grotesque vision of himself as an ass. Surely his hands reach for those Midas ears and that long, hairy nose as he speaks. But this unmistakable parody of one of the most familiar passages from St. Paul certainly encourages us to speculate that Bottom's dream at least flirts with profundity as well as asshood, and that his one silence may bespeak a momentary if inexpressible wisdom. In his confused silence Bottom may even be asking Shakespeare's audience to understand the vital interrelationships between the act of faith and the fact of folly in St. Paul's Christian community and in Shakespeare's romantic, comic one.

His echo of St. Paul is more extensive than first appears. The obvious allusion is to First Corinthians 2:9, which reads: "The eye hath not seene, and the eare hath not heard, neither have entred into the heart of man, the things which God hath prepared for them that love him." But as R. P. Rashbrook has pointed out, there is another Pauline allusion in the same passage which encourages us still further to investigate the doctrinal affinities of Bottom's "most rare vision" and his delicious folly.[1] Second Corinthians 12:1–6 reads:

> It is not expedient doubtlesse for me to glorie, I wil come to visions and revelations of the Lord. For I knew a man in Christ, above four-teene yeeres agoe . . . taken up into the thirde heaven: And I knewe the same man (whether in the body, or out of the body, I cannot tell, God knoweth,) How that he was taken up into paradise, and heard unspeakable wordes, which is not lawfull for man to utter. Of such *a man* wil I glory, yet of my selfe will I not glorie, but in mine infirmities. For though I would desire to glory *of them,* I shall not bee a foole, for I will say the trueth, but I now refraine, lest any man should thinke of me above *that* which hee seeth me *to be,* or *that* he heareth of me.

Notice briefly the close verbal and structural parallels between Bottom's monologue and this second passage. Both begin with references to visions. Both start twice to reveal a vision, only to stop out of prudence. In both cases the vision is believed, but the visionary realizes that its expression would render him a fool, while its repression proves his wisdom. Such close similarities to both passages almost demand that we pursue the doctrinal relevancies of Bottom's transcendental experience, however close that pursuit leads us to to our own ass' ears. For though we have been well warned, "Man is but an ass if he go about to expound this dream," yet it tantalizes us to try.

The general biblical context of Bottom's allusions helps us understand both the absurdity and the profundity of Bottom's brush with the transcendental. St. Paul's unique sense of the paradoxical relationship of faith and folly has already been discussed in chapter one. It culminates in eleven verses in the first chapter of First Corinthians (17–27) immediately preceding Bottom's Pauline allusion. The Corinthians were notorious for their intellectual and spiritual arrogance, and St. Paul knew only too well their kinship to his own Pharisaical past. Thus his preaching to them that folly is proper if not inevitable to those who try to preach Christ and follow his teaching of humility is both pointed and poignant. Faith and folly are opposed in this passage to that intellectual pride, sensuality, and worldliness that make it so difficult for the rich man, for any man, to enter into the kingdom of heaven.[2] The Pauline passage is so close in the biblical text and in spirit to the passage Bottom alludes to, and so pertinent in meaning to this and all of the romantic comedies, that some of its verses bear repeating:

> For it is written, I will destroy the wisedome of the wise, and will cast away the understanding of the prudent. Where is the wise? where is the scribe? where is the disputer of this world? Hath not God made the wisedome of this world foolish? For after that in the wisedome of God, the world through their wisedome knew not God, it pleased God through foolishnesse of preaching, to save them that beleeve. . . . God hath chosen the foolish things of the world, to confound the wise: and God hath chosen the weake things of the worlde, to confound the things which are mighty.

Bottom confounds us all with his "most rare vision." As dull and undeserving as he appears, he has nevertheless been loved by a Titania who will certainly never look our way. In his foolishness he may also be closer to ultimate truths than we, or Theseus, can ever be. "That peace which passeth all understanding" is certainly more accessible to a character with little understanding than to those, like the Corinthians or like Theseus, with too much. John Colet, commenting on some of these paradoxes of the wisdom of folly in First Corinthians, notes that St. Paul and his followers saw little connection between human reason and divine revelation: "They deemed it an unworthy thing that human reason should be mixed up with divine revelation." There is not much chance of that with Bottom.

Colet goes on to observe that the recipient and conveyor of this spiritual truth must become transformed; once again Bottom is the perfect ironic vehicle:

> These mysteries of God are in truth of such a kind, that he who denies not himself utterly, he who becomes not a fool that he may be wise, he who ceases not to be a man that he may be God, shall never

feel what God is, nor what are the Divine wisdom and Spirit. A man must needs be wholly moved by the Spirit of God, and born again, and made anew after a spiritual form, that, being wholly spiritual, he may spiritually discern, search out, gather, and receive, the spiritual things of God.[3]

Though he would rather not, thank you, Bottom certainly becomes the fool before touching the transcendental. The parallel is too appropriate and too well known to be entirely coincidental. In fact, Shakespeare will use it once more in *Twelfth Night,* where Feste not only alludes again to the Pauline and Erasmian paradox about foolishness being the greatest wisdom and the greatest preacher,[4] but also becomes transformed into a curate to preach the wisdom of folly to Malvolio. We also perceive in Bottom's strange experience with the fairies—the spiritual, imaginative entities of this play—how he tries to discern, gather, and receive their offerings, albeit literally. Bottom ceases to be a man, is in fact transformed into an ass, but simultaneously into a spirit, and this miraculous transformation allows his brief communion with inexpressible reality (and humiliating folly).

The third appropriateness of Bottom as oracle is his Bottom-ness, his position as the social, imaginative, and spiritual dregs of the play. Even St. Paul was at pains to debase himself before the Corinthians in order that God's word, not his, might be heard. Hear Colet again: "It was not that he [Paul], himself, poor ignorant and feeble man, might be thought the agent, but that the wise and wonder-working God might be thought to have done all things in him."[5] How much more miraculous, then, for Bottom to communicate these wonders! Faith from a Bottom is almost too miraculous, of course; but then that is the comic point—the inconceivable, stunning contents of such foolish vessels of truth. Shakespeare has similar fun with the wisdom of Dogberry and Verges in *Much Ado.*

Harvey Cox and Nelvin Vos suggest yet another way Bottom functions as an Erasmian fool: he prompts all of us to admit that we too are bottoms as well as heads, bodies if also souls, flesh if spirit, absurd if dignified. To them the Bottom-like characters in all comedy both affirm and make ludicrous "the incongruous involvement of the finite and the infinite." They stand as evidence that "the grossly human and the grandly sublime" are "wonderfully and repugnantly mixed" within us.[6] It takes a healthy blend of wisdom and humility for us to embrace and celebrate such a comic message as this. St. Paul's First Letter to the Corinthians, and of course Erasmus's later articulation of the same paradox in his *The Praise of Folie,* would have been among its most prominent conveyors to Shakespeare's contemporaries until Bottom in *A Midsummer Night's Dream.*

So Bottom confounds our imaginations with his dream. He has been loved by a fairy queen, and we must look on amazed and not a little envious. Moreover, since he has lost none of his "mortal grossness," he embodies simultaneously our lowest potentiality, our utter folly, our asshood, our comically fallen state. If we can acknowledge both sides of that most rare vision, what we cannot have and what we must have—Titania and ass' ears—we will have taken a large step towards attaining *sapientia,* what St. Paul or Erasmus called supernatural foolishness. Bottom's reluctant discovery of the "mystery" of man's fallen nature[7] finds a higher and more positive comic counterpart in the lover's acceptance of the inexpressible, irrational wonder of love and the audience's celebration of the madness of its own imagination. The lunatic, the lover, and the poet are, after all, types of the religious mystic. All of them walk on the edge of absurdity. Harvey Cox reminds us of a particularly apt example of this precarious position. One of the earliest representations of Christ in Christian art is of "a crucified human figure with the head of an ass." With Cox we might agree that perhaps "those catacomb Christians had a deeper sense of the comic absurdity of their position than we think."[8] In a similar spirit, using the very bottom of humanity, Shakespeare has elevated the issue of his comedy to the most sublime sphere. His audience, probably the best theologically trained audience in the history of Christendom, would have heard the Pauline allusion, and most of them would have grasped its crucial implications. Even Bottom knew most of the words.

But as William Willeford has suggested, though Bottom sets these religious associations in motion, he cannot really profit by them; he cannot even articulate them: "We would like to know Bottom's dream; we would like to have it for ourselves. . . . At the borders of consciousness the fool has seen and heard the transcendent value that,

according to St. Paul and Erasmus, is only available to fools. And yet
he has not the means to make it intelligible to us. . . . He bears the
value of a transcendent perfection and is the living reminder among
us of its inaccessibility."[9] In his tantalizing and frustrating monologue, Bottom thus alerts us to the possibilities and the impossibilities
of our own knowing, the limits of human reason and human behavior
evoked by all profound fools of Christian or comic persuasion. Hamlet is constantly frustrated by similar epistemological limitations. In
fact, he sometimes plays the fool and the madman in his frustration.
But Shakespeare's comic vision demands the acceptance of these intellectual limits and their celebration, just as it demands the celebration
of inevitable and universal behavioral folly once it has been acknowledged. For Shakespeare's tragic characters this lesson is often too hard
to learn. For his comic characters its wisdom is a major prerequisite
to joyous festivity.

## ii. The Lovers and Erasmus

The attitudes of Theseus and the lovers towards reason and unreason,
faith and love, are as important to understand as Bottom's dream if we
are to grasp the full dimensions of the Pauline and Erasmian allusions
operating in this play and in Shakespeare's comic vision. Theseus's
comments about lunatics, poets, lovers, and orators in Act V fit comfortably into the Pauline context of Bottom's dream. And the lovers'
common, strenuous progress into an acceptance of love's transcendence
of the senses and the reason bears close analogic ties to the same biblical context. Theseus may also allude to St. Paul in some of his most important speeches. The lovers echo important words from *The Praise of
Folie* as they grope towards an understanding of their wondrous experience in the forest. Through all of these prominent connections
Shakespeare seems to be inviting the audience to understand their own
imaginative faith and folly and the blessed madness of poets and lovers, through their analogies to the familiar Christian understanding of
the wonders of divine love and the mysteries of religious faith. Like
the attitudes toward universal folly discussed in the previous chapter,

this system of analogies is dramatically fitting without ever being narrowly dogmatic or allegorical. Far from using drama to teach doctrine, Shakespeare, with the ingenuity we expect of him, is using doctrine which his contemporaries would have known very well to elucidate a new and unusual, even an esoteric, comic interest in the imaginative process. To the degree that the process of imagination is analogous to the process of belief—to that degree his audience might better understand and participate in the comic, romantic action he is portraying for them.

Striking parallels can be shown to exist between the lovers' awakening from their dreams and passages about the analogous experiences of romantic and religious love in Erasmus's *The Praise of Folie*.[10] Even the language describing the two experiences is sometimes similar. It is essential, then, that we continue our discussion of Shakespeare's first, self-conscious linking of these particular comic and Christian motifs by glancing at their counterparts in Thomas Chaloner's widely available English translation of Erasmus's work. To some readers, its great currency among the intellectuals of Shakespeare's day, its unique comic-Christian vision, and its relative secularity in contrast to the Pauline Epistles make it seem a more likely influence upon Shakespeare's comic vision. We mentioned in the introduction that the Pauline linking of faith and folly was reiterated in Erasmus's work. St. Paul is inevitably Erasmus's best precedent for folly's praise. And so Stultitia, Erasmus's voice of folly, cites this biblical precedent again and again in the best manner of the Schoolmen as she focuses the peroration of her sermon in praise of folly on the natural affinities between folly and faith. Since Erasmus also links romantic and religious madness as closely analogous blessings, it is crucial that we perceive and understand Shakespeare's use of Erasmus in depicting the lovers of *A Midsummer Night's Dream*.

Folie begins her 350-line peroration linking folly and faith with a historical survey of the tradition of such an association: "CHRISTIAN RELIGION seemeth to have a certaine sybship with simplicitee, and devoute foolisshenesse, in nothyng agreyng with worldly wysedome. . . . The apostles were judged by the wicked Ethnickes *to be drunkardes,* . . . [and] . . . *Paule likewise was holden for madde*" (pp. 120–21).

But if these early Christians seemed mad to the worldly, they were also inherently mad, "ravyng" with a "godly foolisshenesse" which amounts almost to a death to this world: "Whereupon Plato defineth *Philosophie to bee a meditacion or remembraunce of death,* in as muche as it plucketh and retyreth the mind of man from visible and corporall thyngs, to those that are invisible and ghostly" (p. 121). In the pages which follow, Folie discusses through this perspective of freedom from the senses and the reason the paradoxical relationship between madness and religious ecstasy, agreeing with Plato that they are "nere sybbe" (p. 122).

But the greatest folly and the finest madness of all is the madness of romantic and religious love. And here, in Erasmus's clear connection between the romantic and the religious spheres, do we find the precedent for and sense the implications of similar connections in Shakespearean comedy:

> PLATO . . . wrote, *that the passion and extreme rage of fervent louers was to be desired and embrased, as a thing above all others most blisfull:* because that a vehement lover liveth not now in hym selfe, but rather in that that he loveth. . . . The depelier suche love is impressed, . . . so muche the greatter, and the blisfuller is the rage also. Whiche so beyng that soules yet pinned within these bodily foldes maie smacke a little of suche a felicitee, consider ye than what a life the sainctes soules leade in heaven? wherunto . . . the sprite selfe shalbe mervailously ravisshed and soked up by the farre more stronge and attractive power of the hieghest sprite of all, whiche is God.
> (Pp. 126–27)

This is basic Neoplatonic doctrine, of course. We are hearing yet another statement of the commonplace of the ladder of love. But Erasmus's blending of the comic, the romantic, and the Christian contexts reminds us forcefully of its adaptability to Shakespearean comedy. For if this attraction to the "hieghest sprite of all, whiche is God," is the ultimate goal of romantic love, it is also the greatest promise of the Christian faith, "evin the very gwerdone that the PROPHETE promyseth, Saiyng, *was never mans eie sawe, nor eare heard, nor thought of hert yet compassed, what, and how great felicitee god hath prepared unto such as dooe love him"* (pp. 127–28). Erasmus's *The Praise of Folie,* like Shakespeare's *A Midsummer Night's Dream,* alludes to St. Paul's most famous passage in First Corinthians as the definitive statement of this ultimate promise, this ultimate reward of faith and love.

What follows this allusion in *The Praise of Folie* is a description of those that "have suche grace." It is so pertinent to the experiences and the words of Bottom and the lovers in *A Midsummer Night's Dream* as to deserve our most careful attention:

> They are subjecte to a certaine passion muche lyke unto madnesse or witravyng, when ravisshed so in the sprite, or beyng in a traunce, thei doo speake certaine thynges not hangyng one with an other, nor after any earthly facion, but rather dooe put foorth a voyce they wote neuer what, muche lesse to be understode of others: and sodeinely without any apparent cause why, dooe chaunge the state of theyr countenaunces. For now shall ye see theim . . . wepe, now thei laugh, now they sighe, for briefe, it is certaine that they are wholy distraught and rapte out of theim selves.                      (P. 128)

The lovers in *A Midsummer Night's Dream* do not speak in tongues, to be sure. They do appear and often feel mad to themselves and others during their forest experience, speak disconnectedly to one another, change and change and change again under the strange influence of Puck's liquor, but "without any apparent cause why." Theseus even links their "seething brains" and "shaping fantasies" with those of lunatics and poets, and finds their testimony "more strange than true." He cannot understand them, at least not with "cool reason." Still, he might know that their experience is analogous to the prophet's as he glances "from heaven to earth, from earth to heaven" at "the forms of things unknown," but not necessarily nonexistent. Hippolyta is more literally believing, and finds in their strange narrative "something of great constancy," albeit beyond the veil. We are deliciously left in Act V with this suspended judgment, though we know that the lovers were "wholly distraught and rapte out of theim selves" in the woods.

The next part of Folie's description of this ultimate experience of faith and folly is even more pointedly suggestive of Bottom and the lovers in the forest, almost at times anticipating the very words they use: "In sort that whan a little after thei come againe to their former wittes, thei denie plainly thei wote where thei became, or whether thei were than in theyr bodies, or out of theyr bodies, waking or slepying:

remembring also as little, either what they heard, saw, saied, or did than, savyng as it were through a cloude, or by a dreame" (p. 128). Listen again to the lovers as they try to describe the wondrous experience they have just undergone. Lysander "shall reply amazedly":

> Half sleep, half waking; but as yet, I swear,
> I cannot truly say how I came here.
> (IV.i.146–48)

Demetrius similarly testifies,

> But, my good lord, I wot not by what power
> (But by some power it is) my love to Hermia,
> Melted as the snow, seems to me now
> As the remembrance of an idle gaud
> Which in my childhood I did dote upon.
> (IV.i.163–67)

These are almost the very words Folie uses to describe the analogous experience of the foolishness of faith. In fact, Demetrius says just after these words,

> And all the faith, the virtue of my heart,
> The object and the pleasure of mine eye,
> Is only Helena.    (IV.i.168–70)

He has rediscovered the true faith of love. And the language of his discovery is strongly evocative of its Erasmian source.

Many of their succeeding comments evidence a similar relationship to Folie's description of such transcendental experiences, even as they gradually find its ephemeral shapes leaving their minds. Demetrius, for example, finds that

> These things seem small and indistinguishable,
> Like far-off mountains turnèd into clouds.
> (IV.i.186–87)

Then he asks yet again,

> Are you sure
> That we are awake? It seems to me
> That yet we sleep, we dream.  (IV.i.191–94)

But the dream is over, and so is their experience with transcendental foolishness. It was a midsummer night's dream for them, a midsummer madness, during which they wore, briefly, ass-heads of their own. But how richly analogous was their experience, through St. Paul's prism or Erasmus's, to the divine folly of faith.

Such Erasmian responses to their dream in the forest suggest that the four lovers in *A Midsummer Night's Dream* must free their minds from the evidence of their senses and the rules of their reason in order to discover the transcendent truth of love's madness. In fact, their experience in the play (like that of the audience) is a carefully developed liberation from their misconceptions that love (or transcendental knowledge) has secure rational and sensual foundations, or that it can somehow be earned or deserved. A look at their disabusement from these misconceptions will reveal that once the lovers can dismiss their reason and their senses, once they can accept love on faith as an undeserved blessing, their confusion will come to an end in blessed confusion. We have already seen that their joyous if puzzled discovery of this liberating paradox echoes Erasmian passages about the liberation of religious faith. Just as surely as Bottom's dream it leads the audience to a deeper appreciation of the wisdom and the folly of their own imaginative experience.

The lovers come to their final accord through an almost anarchic process of finding all of their assumptions concerning love's reason and its desert reversed in the forest. Oberon's potion, Puck's (Love's and the Imagination's?) unpredictability, their own misconceptions, and the mysterious, dreamlike, almost subconscious forest environment combine to reorder their realities. The process deserves some detailing because many of us have taken the lovers' pasteboard qualities for granted for so long that we cannot see them otherwise.

Demetrius obviously assumes that love is a matter of legal right and personal desert. He thinks he has earned Hermia's hand by winning her father's voice:

> Relent, sweet Hermia; and, Lysander, yield
> Thy crazèd title to my certain right.
> (I.i.91–92)

The law of Athens seems to support his assumption. But because of the "certain" rationality of his position, Demetrius does not appreciate or deserve that "crazed" love which is really his, namely, Helena's. Consequently, he can be justly called "spotted and inconstant" as the play begins (1.i.110). Demetrius will come painfully to understand this evaluation of himself when he learns from Hermia that love has to be freely given. Then he can better cherish the one love he is so fortunate as to possess.

Helena is equally certain of love's logic and deserving at the beginning of the play, when it is most illogical. Her certainty will cause a humiliation as intense as Olivia's in *Twelfth Night*. Helena assumes that Demetrius must love Hermia for tangible reasons. Evidence to the contrary notwithstanding (1.i.227), she must be more fair, her eyes lovelier, her tongue "more tunable" (1.i.181–93 *passim*). Evidence of love's paradoxes and Demetrius's irrationality also surround her. He dotes on Hermia's frown, curses, and hatred; he scorns her own smiles, prayers, and love (1.i.194–99). Ignoring this evidence, Helena still concludes that love is explainable and deserved. Her misconceptions culminate in her final soliloquy of Scene i. Calling love blind, irrational, and childlike, she seems finally to have penetrated its paradoxical essence:

> Love looks not with the eyes, but with the mind,
> And therefore is winged Cupid painted blind.
> Nor hath Love's mind of any judgment taste;
> Wings, and no eyes, figure unheedy haste.
> And therefore is Love said to be a child,
> Because in choice he is so oft beguiled.
> (1.i.234–39)

But Helena cannot embrace these paradoxes; they offend her as mutations of her sense of ideal love. Consequently she immediately contradicts her thesis by resolving to do Demetrius a good favor, thereby "winning" his love. Her resolution is even irrational in its scope— she plans to further her cause by reuniting her lover with her rival. Surely this is but the latest in this early series of revelations of the transcendent illogic of love. That illogic is part of the mystery which she and her fellows will finally accept with wonder and without question.

The experiences of Hermia and Lysander are somewhat simpler because they begin and end in love. Nevertheless, like Demetrius and Helena, both must learn in the forest that they do not deserve and might not retain each others' love, because love is neither predictable nor logical. Their gamelike, dreamlike experience teaches them to cherish the love to which they are restored by illustrating how equally they "deserve" scorn and loneliness. From their insipid, predictable, immature sense of suffering (I.i.128–55) they come in the forest to sense the paradoxical and violent wellsprings of their passion, and then to transcend them. With that new understanding and a healthy fear of rejection, the fact of love becomes an unexpected and unexplainable gift—a transcendental blessing.

Oberon's potion functions as agent and symbol of love's irrationality and undeserving, just as the forest becomes both setting and symbol of the progress of their minds (and ours) into transcendental awareness. When Lysander is given the potion by mistake and awakens to love Helena and forsake Hermia, he is bewitched, but only in a context which confirms the complexity of love. Confusion is love's dramatic medium; mistaken identity its psychological reality. The potion creates sounder persons who will return to amity strengthened by their "most rare visions." Lysander learns at least how absurdly he can behave, how capable all men are of fickleness. Hermia realizes that she can be both unloved and alone; she was not born to happiness. Helena learns that she can be loved, though it is hard for her to accept it readily. Demetrius grasps the miracle of a single act of love. In mysterious yet discernible ways the lovers are directed—figuratively by the fairies and their potions, literally by their own imagination and ours—to understand love's irrationality, its disdain of desert, and its transcendence of reason and the senses. The curses, the disorder, and the threatened violence of Act III, Scene ii is likewise a necessary prelude to the wondrous amity which follows. Only when they have perceived love's unpredictable madness can they accept and appreciate its transcendent sanity.

Paradoxically, the lovers seem most intensely "real" when they are farthest removed from the "normal" reality of Athens and daylight.

Although their violence is like a game, it also contains the passion that love requires, its energy and its complexity. In the last forest moment all of the creative and destructive potentiality of love 'seems briefly poured forth. Of course, no one can continue to live with the intensity they experience in the forest, or within its suspension of normal human behavior. Order and reason must return to audience as well as lovers and with such normality must come diminished, dim visions, stereotypes of character and action, crude playlets. The lovers call for light and sleep in a fashion that suggests this need for order. But for a moment there was a greater order in the forest—lightless, intense, and transcendental—just before dawn.[11]

When the lovers awaken from their dream, we notice immediately that a transcendent humility of faith has supplanted those earlier assumptions of their deserving and of love's reasonableness. The lovers do not and cannot understand this grace, but they do believe in it, no longer in themselves. Demetrius, the most dramatically transformed, speaks their mutual wonder best, and compares it to faith·

> I wot not by what power
> (But by some power it is) my love to Hermia,
> Melted as the snow, seems to me now
> As the remembrance of an idle gaud
> Which in my childhood I did dote upon;
> And all the faith, the virtue of my heart,
> The object and the pleasure of mine eye,
> Is only Helena.        (IV.i.163–70)

In First Corinthians St. Paul compares spiritual growth in faith to maturing into adulthood: "When I was a childe, I spake as a childe, I understoode as a childe, I imagined as a childe: but assoone as I was a man, I put away childishnesse" (or "chyldesh things"—Geneva).[12] The young lovers have awakened into adulthood; they have been reborn into the faith of love. In fact, their final state of mind contains that wondrous combination of humility, joy, charity, and faith that Dante ascribes to Beatrice in his *Vita Nuova:*

I say that when she appeared from any direction, then, in the hope of her wondrous salutation, there was no enemy left to me; rather, there smote into me a flame of charity, which made me forgive every person who had ever injured me; and if at that moment anybody had put a question to me about anything whatsoever, my answer would have been simply "Love," with a countenance clothed in humility.[13]

Theseus notices the wondrous change that has overcome the lovers in the woods in strikingly similar terms:

> How comes this gentle concord in the world
> That hatred is so far from jealousy
> To sleep by hate and fear no enmity?
> (IV.i.142–44)

How indeed but by the grace of love and faith?

This rebirth, this awakening, is decisively not the lovers' own doing. That is why their final amity is so amazing; that is also why Henry Bullinger's description of religious grace can bear such a resemblance to these romantic experiences in *A Midsummer Night's Dream:*

> The Grace of God, is Gods favour and gentleness, yea the very good-nesse and mercy of God, whereby without any desertes, for no re-spect of our worthiness or recompense of his owne goodnes and mercye, he doth love and embrace with a fatherly minde, miserable & wretched sinners, receyveth them into grace, clenzeth them from their sinnes, and adopteth or choseth them unto sonnes and heires.[14]

Each lover suffered from grievous misconceptions about love's ra-tionality and order, and about his own deserving and worthiness. Then, reduced to a miserable and wretched state and a final awareness of that wretchedness, he was wondrously purified and restored. In the wonder of the gift—undeserved, undecipherable, and unexpected—lies the grace. Shakespeare's audience might well have recognized and enjoyed the similarity, since it is frequently exploited in the romance tradition.

This grace, this faith, is what allows the lovers finally to dismiss their senses. Their experience seems to have taught them a new hu-mility, a healthy sense of folly which urges that there are things that are true that can neither be seen nor understood. Fulke's "A Comfort-able Sermon on Faith" glosses this relationship of faith and humility for us: "Yea, we may plainly perceive that true faith is alway joyned with great humility."[15] There is a great joy in their resultant liberation, which comes through in their refrain:

> DEMETRIUS. These things seem small and indistinguishable,
> Like far-off mountains turnèd into clouds.
> HERMIA. Methinks I see these things with parted eye,
> When everything seems double.
> HELENA. So methinks;
> And I have found Demetrius like a jewel,
> Mine own, and not mine own.
> DEMETRIUS. Are you sure
> That we are awake? It seems to me
> That yet we sleep, we dream. (IV.i.186–93)

Sleep and awakening, vision and insight, momentarily join for the lovers in the forest, and that mysterious joining frees them briefly from the restraints of their senses and reason. Their resultant acceptance of the miracle of concord, personal and social, is a manifestation of that faith in love and rejoicing in a shared, liberating folly which consistently marks Shakespeare's festive conclusion and becomes a prerequisite for it.

The audience of *A Midsummer Night's Dream* seems to share the lovers' gradual edification into this "graceful," joyous folly of romantic faith. We share it in part because we have seen what they have dreamed and know it to be "real." But such sure knowledge would not constitute a common experience at all. For an analogous imaginative faith would require that we also embrace what we cannot understand, the implausible, irrational, inexpressible, and inconceivable wonders of their forest escapade. And so we are also given a Bottom, who with us flirts with the transcendental, even touches it, but remains the same old "bully Bottom" he always was. His blend of sublimity and absurdity is also ours, and we had better not forget it as we go about to expound his dream, or the lovers'. His folly can take us to the very limits of knowledge, if only our own. And so we are also given the fairies, to see and to hear and yet never to believe in simply or completely. When we meet them they are both real and unreal. Puck's vivid language and Oberon's vivid images score our imaginations, especially the delicious matter-of-fact about the "mermaid on a dolphin's back" and "a place where the wild thyme grows." But even as we are ravished by their truth, we are also reminded of their untruth, of their unsure existence in the popular imagination as soured milk and overturned gossips' bowls. We hear of changelings and we see the preposterous feud between Oberon and Titania and we question the hyperbolic, macrocosmic results of that quarrelling even as we are immersed in the beauty of its descriptions and the unity of its worldview.

To our minds, the play can in fact be as interrogative in its mood as *Hamlet*. Are these nighttime creatures two inches tall, or six feet? Are they really only metaphors of good luck and bad, blessings and curses, or causes? Is their potion to be literally believed, or is it rather a "mere symbol" of love's irrationality and changeability and our own? Is it instead sometimes literal, sometimes symbolic, like the fairies themselves, or something even more complex? And then, is this "literal" more or less real than "symbolic" anyway? Is a patent romantic convention like love at first sight any more, or less, believable because it is a convention, or because it is delightfully parodied by Titania and Lysander? Isn't it also something very real if also inexplicable to the lovers in the forest, and very desirable, if also preposterous, to the audience? And what of the forest? Is it a real place, a dramatic setting, a symbolic state, or all of these at once? Are the lovers believable enough for us in their foolish wisdom, or later in their wise folly, or too conventional for belief? And if the latter, does our unbelief paradoxically help us respond less conventionally and therefore more "truly" to their illusion? These are a few of our "far off mountains turned into clouds" in *A Midsummer Night's Dream,* our precarious balance between "wakyng and slepyng," between looking "through a cloude or by a dreame." When Shakespeare manipulates our minds and emotions with Hermia's recounting of her dream (or Bottom's); Lysander's love at first sight (or Titania's); Oberon's fury (or Helena's, Demetrius's, Lysander's, Egeus's), are we not deliciously like Erasmus's faithful: "now shall ye see theim wepe, now thei laugh, now thei sighe, for briefe, it is certaine that they are wholly distraught and rapte out of their selves" (p. 218). This rapture is our imaginative ass' head; but it can also be the concord of our discord, if we can celebrate such folly with the humility of imaginative faith.

And so we are asked as audience to exercise a faith much more complex than that of the lovers. For we are required to believe and not to believe at once if this vision is really to work, never to lose either our faith or our skepticism toward the play. Bottom's "Pyramus" is such a fine culmination of all this precisely because his play is so patently unbelievable. Every time its illusion fails, it also succeeds, by reminding us of the successful illusion that contains "Pyramus," and of our nearly absolute belief in it. And we also believe in this vivid character, Bottom, whose foolish wisdom has got them, and us, in this fine mess. Then the fairies end the play, and we are asked one last time to believe in Puck and his band, to bless with them the married lovers, and thus to display again the great folly of our imaginative faith. This rigorous imaginative experience is constantly enriched by the Pauline context of Bottom's folly and the Erasmian context of the lovers' faith. We are inevitably like them all in our own imaginations.

Erasmus has Folie make one more comment near the end of her sermon that helps us complete our sense of relationships between these comic and Christian themes, and distinguish between them, too. It will appear much more pertinent to Sebastian's experience in the fourth act of *Twelfth Night* than it does to the lovers or the audience here. But there is some appropriateness in each case. Folie concludes of these fools: "This thei know certainely, that whiles their mindes so roved and wandred, thei were most happie and blisfull, so that they lament and wepe at theyr retourne unto theyre former senses, as who saieth, nothyng were leefer unto theim than continually to rave and be deteigned with suche a spece of madnesse. And this is but a certaine smacke or thinne taste of theyr blisse to come" (p. 128). Sebastian welcomes his analogous madness: "If it be thus to dream, still let me sleep!" (*Twelfth Night*, IV.i.59). The audience too is loath to leave the imaginative madness of good theater for the glaring sanity of the world outside. But these Athenian lovers were most unhappy in their wandering, and they are glad to be awake again. The unreason of love or faith is too threatening for most human sensibilities, and they do not knowingly carry it back to Athens with them. Still, when they awake from their dream they are all "new in amity." And though they willingly follow Theseus back to Athens, they also want to prolong their forest experience a little longer: "And by the way let us recount our dreams" (IV.i.198). These lovers are not equipped to remain such fools for very long. Nor would most of us want them to celebrate such profound folly indefinitely. That way madness lies, or perfect faith. That Shakespeare has invited us to glimpse this much of the wisdom of their folly, or Bottom's, or our own through his Erasmian and Pauline allusions is surely significance enough. Theseus and Hippolyta, with Pyramus and Puck, seal these impressions for us in the final act.

## iii. Theseus and Hippolyta, Pyramus and Puck

Chapter 2 of St. Paul's First Epistle to the Corinthians contains far more than the famous "Eye hath not seene" passage Bottom alludes to. Its preface articulates St. Paul's intense distrust of Greek intellect, and his disinclination to be impressed by glibness or "tongues." St. Paul's purpose is to indict and advise those who cannot accept transcendental wisdom (like Bottom's dream, the lover's experience in a magical forest, or the existence of the fairies). He begins by humbly minimizing his personal importance and expressing his distrust of tongues:

> And I brethren, when I came to you, came not in gloriousnesse of words, or of wisedome, shewing unto you the testimony of God. For I esteemed not to know any thing among you, save Jesus Christ, and him crucified. And I was among you in weakenesse, and in feare, and in much trembling. And my wordes and my preaching was not with entising words of mans wisedome, but in shewing of the spirit, and of power: That your faith should not stand in the wisedome of men, but in the power of God.

At this point St. Paul begins the "Eye hath not seene" passage, stressing with one of his vivid natural metaphors his distrust of *scientia,* the knowledge and power of this world. *Sapientia* is the timeless "hidden wisedome" which Bottom foolishly evokes when he alludes to this

Pauline context. His allusion makes us more sensitive to the charming if lighter parallels between Theseus and Hippolyta, Pyramus and Puck, and these Pauline and Erasmian commonplaces about faith and folly.

Colet is especially helpful in alerting us to such connections because his gloss uses Renaissance terminology and evokes the Renaissance conflict between reason and faith, a conflict which finds its oblique but important way into *A Midsummer Night's Dream, Much Ado about Nothing,* and *As You Like It:*

> By no human resources, by no faculty of reason even in its highest vigour, by no spirit of the world, by no supports of human learning and eloquence, accumulate them in what manner and to what extent he pleases, is man enabled to soar to the designs and acts of God, placed as they are far above all human reason, in His own absolute reason and will. These things are known to the Divine Spirit alone, and to those who are inspired by the same spirit, to the intent that they may in this life see by faith, and *through a glass, darkly,* until they are ready to see *face to face.*[16]

Somewhat like Christ repudiating Satan's proffered learning in *Paradise Regained,* the scholar Colet is eloquent in his catalogue of the learning which must be transcended in order to achieve faith. He reminds us again of Bottom, who had no such hindrances to his vision. He reminds us as well of Theseus and Hippolyta's complex and puzzling discussions of the imagination, and of the lover's acceptance of an experience which was "above all human reason." He also alerts us to the traditional associations between First Corinthians 2:9, "The eye hath not seene," and First Corinthians 13:12, "wee see in a glasse, euen in a darke speaking," part of the great Pauline chapter on *agape* and faith.[17]

Aware now of some of the possible connections between these Pauline and Erasmian passages and the play, let us look at Theseus in Act V. His articulate distrust of some products of the imagination is part of his more general distrust of the sophisticated, of the worldly, the "tongues" of this life. Theseus, in choosing the rustics' performance, perceives with us and for us that learning and eloquence are not necessarily the greatest wisdom. He similarly distrusts the fabulous tale of the lovers, with good reason. But Theseus is no simple advocate of reason against love or imagination in *A Midsummer Night's Dream*. Pauline echoes in Act V make this quite clear.

The most distinctive echo concerns Theseus's and St. Paul's mutual distrust of tongues. Their reasons are as similar as their articulation of them. Theseus states:

> Where I have come, great clerks have purposèd
> To greet me with premeditated welcomes;
> Where I have seen them shiver and look pale,
> Make periods in the midst of sentences,
> Throttle their practiced accent in their fears,
> And, in conclusion, dumbly have broke off,
> Not paying me a welcome. Trust me, sweet,
> Out of this silence yet I picked a welcome,
> And in the modesty of fearful duty
> I read as much as from the rattling tongue
> Of saucy and audacious eloquence.
> Love, therefore, and tongue-tied simplicity
> In least speak most, to my capacity.
>
> (v.i.93–105)

Theseus exhibits worldly wisdom here, of course. But he is also articulating a basic Pauline truth about love, as he says, and about faith: the imperceptible is often also the inexpressible. The most eloquent language, without love, is nothing; love, like faith, best expresses itself in simplicity, even in silence. Listen to St. Paul concerning the language of love and faith, from First Corinthians 13, the same passage just used by Colet to gloss First Corinthians 2:9: "Though I speake with the tongues of men, and of Angels, and have not charitie, I am *as* sounding brasse, or *as* a tinckling Cymbal: And though I have prophecie, and understand all secrets, and all knowledge: yea, if I have all faith, so that I can remoove mountaines, and have not charitie, I am nothing."

Alexander Nowell in his widely disseminated Anglican catechism further articulates the traditional Pauline and Christian distrust of "saucy and audacious eloquence": "God doth . . . abhor and detest their prayers that feignedly and unadvisedly utter with their tongue that which they conceive not with their heart and thought."[18] Shakespeare often exploits this Christian commonplace, nowhere more notably than in the words with which Claudius concludes his futile attempts to pray in *Hamlet:* "My words fly up, my thoughts remain below: / Words without thoughts never to heaven go" (iii.iii.97–98). With doctrinal commentators, the catechism, the homilies, and St. Paul himself articulating it to Shakespeare's contemporaries, the identification is neither unnatural nor unlikely.

Theseus has a far more cogent Pauline comment to make about prophets or frenzied poets. In fact, our Pauline awareness reveals that Theseus's famous speech about the lunatic, the lover, and the poet, hitherto often considered antagonistic to poets, lovers, and dreamers, is neither absolutely uncharitable nor unimaginative. It is rather directly supported by St. Paul's humble distrust of vain show and empty eloquence, and his realization of man's limited powers of perception. Theseus, then, may be reaffirming Bottom's Pauline awareness: "The eye hath not seene, and the eare hath not heard, neither have entred into the heart of man, the things which God hath prepared for them that love him" (I. Cor. 2:9).

What Theseus says is this:

> The lunatic, the lover, and the poet
> Are of imagination all compact.
> One sees more devils than vast hell can hold:
> That is the madman. The lover, all as frantic,
> Sees Helen's beauty in a brow of Egypt.
> The poet's eye, in a fine frenzy rolling,
> Doth glance from heaven to earth, from earth to heaven;
> And as imagination bodies forth
> The forms of things unknown, the poet's pen
> Turns them to shapes, and gives to airy nothing
> A local habitation and a name.    (v.i.7–17)

Far from dismissing true imagination, this speech confirms the ability to believe in the imperceivable, but laughs at futile attempts to perceive, categorize, or express it. Man can understand only so much; he must take the rest on faith. With St. Paul, Theseus smiles charitably at the poet, the prophet, or the lover who tries too hard to shape the shapeless. Like Bottom, he knows that man can become an ass if he goes about expounding all dreams. His speech is thus an affirmation of faith in the imagination, freeing the mind as it does from temporal evidence and its own limited wisdom.

Poor Bottom, for all his flirtation with these Erasmian and Pauline commonplaces, remains unedified, however. His play of Pyramus is thus a fitting final celebration of the differences between his mind, if mind it can be called, and that of the lovers. His play's literal-minded stumbling over punctuation marks, figurative language, properties, lighting effects, and almost every other convention of poetry and the stage suggests his entrapment by the literal world, the world of the senses and the reason that the others have momentarily escaped. The horned moon, the chinked wall, the "bloody, blameful blade," are all part of this final, literal foolishness, the bondage of the finite mind. But as in *Love's Labor's Lost* the hilarity of this fond pageant lies partly in our acknowledgment of kinship with it. "Lord, what fools these mortals be" is thus Puck's vital statement of a comic truth we must all embrace to experience the fullest joy at the end of *A Midsummer Night's Dream*. Only then can we celebrate with the lovers our mutual liberation from excessive reasonableness and our entry into imaginative faith.

Typically, Theseus is charitable but not enthusiastic toward their performance: "The best in this kind are but shadows, and the worst no worse, if imagination amend them." At the end he thanks them nobly for their noble efforts. But Hippolyta, as she was toward the lovers' analogous story of their great folly, is moved again by the performance to a moment of aesthetic faith despite her better judgment: "Beshrew my heart but I pity the man" (v.i.283). Only the actress can tell us whether she pities Bottom or Pyramus or both for this fleeting moment, but each possibility is present in the line. Theseus and Hippolyta represent in their responses to the lovers and the players an interesting blend of charity and imagination, forgiveness and faith. He charitably forgives vain attempts to express the inexpressible, for to him all such attempts are, like drama, but shadows of truth. The world of ideas must always transcend them. That he is but another of these shadows undercuts his certainty with some irony. *Shadows* can also mean "spirits" (Epil.; *OED* 7), or "symbols" (*OED* 6c). But we have seen that

Theseus's position here is not necessarily one of absolute skepticism; he merely questions the possibilities of expressing the transcendental. Hippolyta simply believes. She believes the tale of the lovers. And, "beshrew her heart," she even believes, momentarily, in the illusion of the rude mechanicals. St. Paul says at the end of First Corinthians 13, "Nowe abideth faith, hope, and charitie, these three, but the greatest of these is charitie." It is fitting that Theseus, the ranking lord in the play, should exhibit such charity towards the players, the lovers, and even the fairies at the play's conclusion. But Hippolyta, as ranking lady, is not so much laggard in her faith.[19] Their union is a happy note on which the play could end. Still, the fairies must have their last ephemeral words to remind us of their world, still just tantalizingly beyond our own, though our hands can almost join at certain magical moments.

And so we return at last from Theseus's court to Oberon's. Here the fairies, intangible, nighttime creatures, flit about the stage as the final symbols of that elusive truth Bottom, Theseus, Hippolyta, and the lovers all flirt with during the play. Theirs is no truth for the wise or the prudent. St. Paul warns, "for it is written, I will destroy the wisedome of the wise, and will cast away the understanding of the prudent" (I Cor. 1:19). "God hath chosen the foolish things of the world, to confound the wise" (I Cor. 1:27). Most of the characters in the final scene of *A Midsummer Night's Dream* know in their own ways that they are among the foolish things of this world. The fairies symbolize the fleeting shadows of their imaginations and our own, the truths seen through a glass darkly. Puck's intensely human if paradoxical attempt to communicate with us during his epilogue reveals how important it is that the audience also sense, however dimly, its close kinship to all of these foolish shadows, and celebrate that kinship as well. For only then can the play's festive communion in faith and folly be a completely successful celebration of transcendental, theatrical, and human unity. We must give Puck our hands, our hearts, and our belief for the festive experience to be complete. Without such an expression of our epistemological folly, we cannot truly affirm our imaginative faith.

# CHAPTER IV

# "Man Is a Giddy Thing": Repentance and Faith in *Much Ado about Nothing*

THE FIRST CHAPTER stresses the importance of humility in the teachings of St. Paul and the comic vision of Erasmus. The man of faith, like the comic hero, must acknowledge his folly to achieve true festivity. He must know and admit that his behavior and his perceptions are imperfect. Only then can he embrace a comic or a Christian doctrine that teaches him to celebrate his fallen state, because it is universal, because it is forgiven, and because that forgiveness leads to inconceivable joy. The Anglican liturgy is richly characterized by the same paradoxical awareness. So, quite explicitly, are the two romantic comedies we have already considered.

*Love's Labor's Lost* and *A Midsummer Night's Dream* are both conscious enough of their relationship to this doctrine to have alluded to some of its most familiar or controversial Pauline and Erasmian expressions. Further, both require of their characters a humble acknowledgment of imperfect behavior or imperfect understanding as an important prerequisite to their festive joy. But in *Love's Labor's Lost* the regeneration that should result from this acknowledged folly is not dramatized in the play. Amendment of life, comic penance, the proper result of the ladies' benevolent humiliation, is only promised in a year and a day. Similarly, in *A Midsummer Night's Dream* the moments of epistemological humility only occur for Bottom and the lovers as fleetingly as dawn or midnight. The process of regeneration is dramatized through the humiliating role-reversals in the forest. And the lovers' amity throughout the final act attests to its continued efficacy. But though we are made aware of the doctrinal dimensions of their changed perspectives at the end of Act IV, the fact that the lovers' humility is seldom demonstrated in Act V, and Bottom's not at all, makes it somewhat more ephemeral than we might like. Much like the promised regeneration of the lords in *Love's Labor's Lost*, we are

77

asked in *A Midsummer Night's Dream* to take a continued humility largely on faith. The audience of both plays seems to have learned more of the folly of wisdom and the wisdom of folly than the characters.

These two plays, then, discover and begin to exploit this paradoxical comic attitude toward faith and folly. They also alert their audiences through allusions to its most important Christian dimensions. But they do not dramatize the achievement of this attitude of humility and faith nearly so much as they dramatize the need for that achievement. The later romantic comedies contain fewer explicit allusions to those Erasmian and Pauline paradoxes, though allusions still appear. However, they increasingly direct their action to the achievement of a humbling edification of the flawed characters. Increasingly, acknowledgment of folly and amendment of life become their comic heart and soul. *Twelfth Night,* the culmination of this process, insists upon varieties of this regeneration as the prerequisite of its comic festivity, and contains characters like Feste and Viola who remind us of its Pauline and Erasmian heritage. *The Merchant of Venice* also has intriguing allusions to Pauline commonplaces and doctrinal controversies. However, its enduring ambiguities stem in large measure from a lack of humility on the part of its self-consciously Christian comic celebrants. In both of these plays, though in opposite ways, edifying humiliation remains central to comic structure and comic vision.

The relative lack of such allusions in *Much Ado about Nothing* and *As You Like It* suggests quite accurately that the delightfully realistic humiliations and regenerations of their complex characters and actions are pushing the explicit doctrinal parallels into the background. Because Pauline and Erasmian influences are becoming more skeletal than skinlike, infusing structure and metaphoric undertone rather than comic surface, the balance will shift in this chapter and the next between doctrine and drama. Freed from the need to reestablish Christian patterns whose explicit place in Shakespeare's comic vision we have already demonstrated and analyzed, we will be able to give their relationships to the fascinating surfaces and subsurfaces of these four later comedies the closer attention they demand. That closer look will reveal that the final attitudes of the major characters towards the inescapable imperfections of their behavior and their knowledge, their folly and their faith, still determines the dimensions of their final happiness and defines the quality of their concluding festivity. Those attitudes will have occurred through a delightful but strenuous regenerative humiliation that has now become central to Shakespeare's comic action. If the allusions to Erasmus and St. Paul diminish in these later plays, their thematic and structural pertinence does not.

*Much Ado about Nothing* is especially interesting from this perspective because it contains two pairs of lovers who stand at opposite poles of psychological and thematic interest. Hero and Claudio are pasteboard characters whose heavily stylized psychologies will never compete for our attention in the play. But thematically they are worth our scrutiny, for they practically embody the process of regenerative humiliation that is going on so much more attractively in Benedick and Beatrice. Claudio is little more than a *humanum genus* figure from the old morality plays.[1] He is erring man, grotesquely flawed in his faith in Hero as well as in the charity with which that lack of faith is finally expressed in the church; he is imperfect even in his enactment of penance for those errors. If we expect too much psychological realism from him, Claudio will surely offend us. Hero, if virtually invisible as a character beside the psychological brilliance of Beatrice, is nevertheless also quite important in her thematic representation of that principle of forgiveness that stands behind Shakespeare's comic attitude toward acknowledged folly. For most of the play Claudio lacks faith and charity, and he lacks as well the knowledge of his folly, yet Hero implicitly accepts his imperfect penance, believes in his eventual repentance, and forgives him everything. However, in spite of watching Claudio enact the most formal penance in the comedies, one conceived by a priest and administered by a priestlike father, the audience has trouble following Hero's most charitable example of forgiveness. Therein lies one of the most enduring interpretive problems in Shakespeare.[2]

The problem is accentuated by the rich psychology of Benedick and Beatrice, and the equally rich enactment of their regenerations into romantic faith and the acceptance of folly. Like Claudio, but of course much less abstractly, they both must be led from the bondage of pride and skepticism to the freedom of humility and faith. Like Claudio, they will learn to distrust their excessive pride in their senses and their reason, and to admit their own imperfection instead of being obsessed with the possibility (should we say certainty?) of imperfection in a mate. These benevolent lessons in faith and humility will make of them the almost perfect match they have always been for each other, appearances notwithstanding. The thrusts and parries of their merry war will continue to edify them both for ever after. Like them, we are glad that this is so. For Benedick and Beatrice are characters the audience loves quickly and deeply, characters they never forget.

Let us start then with Claudio's errors of folly and faithlessness, his abstract and troubling penance, and Hero's equally troubling forgiveness of him. Through their stylized actions, whose doctrinal contexts at least will become quite clear, we will be able to see the subtler doctrinal dimensions of the much more satisfying regenerative experiences of Benedick and Beatrice. Even if we cannot rejoice in Claudio's final forgiveness and his final joy, we might at least come to understand, as Robert Hunter and others have urged, why it has to occur and what it means.[3] Our background in the Pauline and Erasmian paradoxes of faith and folly will enhance our understanding of each of these actions. It can also direct our responses to the play's festive conclusion, whose joy need be no more paradoxical than the doctrine of celebrated universal folly that lies so close behind it. If the manifestations of these paradoxes in the Benedick-Beatrice plot are subtler than before, they will probably also be more interesting.

## i. Hero and Claudio

Claudio's grotesque and ingrained folly will need little documentation, since it is the stumbling block of almost every critic of the play's festivity. He lacks all faith, not only in Hero but also in his friend Don Pedro. He believes naively and obstinately in the evidence of his senses and his reason. He is an uncharitable cad in the church. Also a formalist, he follows far too precisely the format prescribed regarding "impediments" in the marriage ceremony. And his own acknowledgment of his folly, which is almost too charitable a word for it, is very slow in coming. But gradually, guided by what amounts almost to a liturgical ceremony of penance, he does "acknowledge and bewaile his manifold sinnes and wyckedness," and promise to lead a "new and better life, in faith." This highly stylized penance leaves many in the audience (none in the play) unconvinced. But Hero accepts and forgives this flawed man, and in her extraordinary action she redeems him for the comic festivity. Their characterizations are so flat, and their mutual enactments of now-familiar comic motifs of faith and folly so abstract, that they touch the larger play with unresolved ambiguities. However, since they also help to point out important thematic interests of the entire play, especially as they occur in the much more interesting relationship of Benedick and Beatrice, we need to look briefly at the doctrinal and liturgical dimensions of these two virtually allegorical characters.

We might suspect the sincerity of Claudio's affections as soon as he speaks of them in the first scene. True, after Benedick leaves the language turns to poetry. But his first question of Don Pedro has a strangely metallic ring: "Hath Leonato any son, my lord?" (I.i.262). His friend knows his drift immediately: "No child but Hero; she's his only heir." Shortly thereafter Claudio seems too fond of his appearance as a lover: "But lest my liking might too sudden seem, / I would have salved it with a longer treatise" (I.i.282–83). But far worse is to come. Two words of Don Pedro's infidelity spoken to him by the villains Don John and Borachio convince Claudio of its truth; and so immediately and without further investigation he loses faith in his good friend: "Friendship is constant in all other things / Save in the office and affairs of love" (II.i.157–58). Claudio learns of this specific error soon enough, but not of the profounder folly within him that would allow such unwarranted mistrust. And so Don John will work upon him again. When he does, the deception is far more convincing, as is witnessed by its success on Don Pedro as well as Claudio. Kirby Neill suggests that Claudio is less culpable than his predecessors in Shakespeare's analogues because he is less mercenary, less carnal, and taken in by a very effective deception.[4] But Claudio's offense

81

transcends his foolish belief in what he can see, his trust in his senses over his nonexistent intuition. It lies also in the brutal formalism with which he exposes Hero's purported infidelity just before the wedding. Humiliating Hero and appearing to kill her by this uncharitable public action, Claudio has overstepped the bounds of ethical folly prescribed by comic conventions. Perhaps this is why his regeneration for these crimes against romantic faith and these blindnesses to his own comic folly—these severe errors of pride—must be couched within an equally formal framework, one like that for repentance prescribed by the Christian church. Even more than the lords of *Love's Labor's Lost,* Claudio needs a formal means to grace, and an amazing forgiveness. But though Shakespeare provides them both, we are still not sure how to take them.

In fact, the highly stylized presentation of Claudio's repentance and forgiveness has itself been a major stumbling block to critics, who find it excessively formal, hence contrived. There is, however, good reason for that formality, and considerable likelihood that Shakespeare's audience would have appreciated it more than we do today. Claudio's most stunning error is his formalistic, uncharitable abuse of the wedding ritual, the Solemnization of Matrimony he and Hero are about to celebrate in Act IV. At the beginning of that ritual the minister admonishes the congregation, "if any man can shewe any just cause, why thei may not lawfully be joined together let hym now speake, or els hereafter for ever holde his peace" (p. 122). He likewise charges the couple "that if either of you doe knowe any impedyment, why ye may not be lawfully joyned together in Matrimony, that ye confesse it" (p. 123). Among the best known words in the Prayer Book, these admonitions are followed even today by an unquiet hush in the church, so sombre are their implications at so festive a time. Claudio says the thing everyone dreads hearing at this moment, and, technically speaking, he is correct in breaking the ritual. But spiritually he is at fault, not only in mistaking the facts ("Blessed are they that have not seen, but also believe"), but also in insisting on public disclosure and public vindication. For he does not have "just cause." This uncharitable, faithless interruption of one sacrament would seem, then, to require another sacrament, penance, if Claudio is to be restored to comic grace.

Claudio almost certainly enacts something like the Aquinian pattern of penance to which Hunter and Lewalski compare his late experiences with Leonato.[5] A related form of repentance more familiar to the Renaissance playgoer might have been the liturgical pattern prescribed in the Homilie of Repentance and derived from the communion service of the *Book of Common Prayer*.[6] That homily asserts "foure parts of repentance": "contrition of the heart," "an unfained confession and acknowledging of our sinnes," "faith," and "an amendment of life, or a new life." As we shall see, contrition, confession, faith in forgiveness, and the visible amendment of life all occur separately and sequentially in Act V. Their formality as well as their liturgical basis will help us to perceive their much subtler equivalents in the Benedick-Beatrice plot, even if they don't redeem Claudio in our eyes.

The homily introduces its subject with the keen excitement of prophecy: "Now there bee foure parts of repentance, which being set together, may bee likened to an easie and short ladder, whereby we may climbe from the bottomlesse pit of perdition, that wee cast our selves into by our dayly offences and greevous sinnes, up into the castle or towre of eternall and endlesse salvation." We immediately notice the assumption of universal, daily sin, a liturgical commonplace we have discussed before. The first step in repentance is "contrition of the heart": "For we must be earnestly sorry for our sinnes, and unfeignedly lament and bewayle that wee have by them so greevously offended our most bounteous and mercifull GOD, who so tenderly loved us."[7] In order for contrition to occur, there must be events, "which most lively doe paint out before our eyes our naturall uncleannesse, and the enormitie of our sinfull life."

Dogberry and Borachio "point out" that uncleanness for Claudio. First, Dogberry's expounding of the offenses of the deceivers is prefaced by a liturgical reminiscence of the Litany's catalogue of the "sins of the world." In the Litany, or General Supplication for forgiveness, the priest petitions God: "Remember not, Lorde our offences, nor the offences of our forefathers." Then, to the familiar response "Good Lorde, delyver us," he catalogues most of the offenses of erring mankind: "From all evil and mischief; from synne, from the craftes and assaultes of the Devil . . . from all blyndnes of herte, from pride, vayne glorye, and hypocrisy; from envy, hatred and malice, and all uncharitablenes . . . from hardnes of harte . . . frome all the deceiptes of the worlde, . . . *Good Lorde, delyver us*" (pp. 54–55). Though Dogberry's catalogue comically sticks on false report like a broken record, it sounds a similar note:

> CLAUDIO. Hearken after their offense, my lord.
> PEDRO. Officers, what offense have these men done?
> DOGBERRY. Marry, sir, they have committed false report; moreover, they have spoken untruths; secondarily, they are slanders; sixth and lastly, they have belied a lady; thirdly, they have verified unjust things; and to conclude, they are lying knaves.[8]

Borachio establishes the more serious atmosphere of confession when he outlines his complicity in Claudio's guilt. He is contrite, and he confesses publicly and completely:

> I have deceived even your very eyes. What your wisdoms could not discover, these shallow fools have brought to light. . . . My villainy they have upon record, which I had rather seal with my death than repeat over to my shame. The lady is dead upon mine and my master's false accusation; and briefly, I desire nothing but the reward of a villain. (v.i.220–31)

Borachio's painful reciting of his crime reminds the lords of their arrogant belief in their own senses over their intuition. By confessing his own sin, Borachio is the agent of their contrition. After he finishes, Don Pedro and Claudio "unfeignedly lament" their offences against Hero. The first step in repentance is fulfilled: both men are utterly contrite:

> PEDRO. Runs not this speech like iron through your blood?
> CLAUDIO. I have drunk poison whiles he uttered it.
>
> . . . . . . . . . . . . . . . .
>
> Sweet Hero, now thy image doth appear
> In the rare semblance that I loved it first.
> (v.i. 232–34, 238–39)

As the homily predicts, the second stage of their regeneration will be confession:

The second is, an unfained confession and acknowledging of our sinnes unto GOD, whom by them we have so grievously offended, that if he should deale with us according to his justice, we doe deserve a thousand helles, if there could bee so many. Yet if wee will with a sorrowfull and contrite heart make an unfained confession of them unto GOD, hee will freely and frankely forgive them, and so put all our wickednesse out of remembrance before the sight of his Majestie, that they shall no more bee thought upon.[9]

By using Hero's father, Leonato, as their father confessor, Shakespeare secularizes the analogy and makes it more comfortably comical. Hero's father, like Hero herself, is only analogous to the real priest (Friar Francis) Shakespeare could have used, or to the Father of all mercies the Protestant would confess to. But his listening to their confession, his administration of penance, and his eventual forgiveness of them initiates the sequence of sacramental analogies which conclude the play and help to explain its festivity. Similar priestlike functions are performed by the lords and ladies of *Love's Labor's Lost*. Because of Claudio's remaining imperfection, Leonato's forgiveness of Claudio, like Hero's, is a mark of personal grace and an action which establishes this comic world as one pervaded by a forgiveness that is undeserved but almost universal.

Upon Leonato's chiding, both Claudio and Pedro acknowledge their sin and ask for penance:

> CLAUDIO. I know not how to pray your patience;
>            Yet I must speak. Choose your revenge yourself;
>            Impose me to what penance your invention
>            Can lay upon my sin. Yet sinned I not
>            But in mistaking.
> PEDRO.                    By my soul, nor I!
>            And yet, to satisfy this good old man,
>            I would bend under any heavy weight
>            That he'll enjoin me to.        (v.i.258–65)

This moment is their most imperfect during the sacramental sequence. Claudio only grudgingly admits his sin, minimizing it and confessing it defensively. His sin is far greater than mere mistaking. Having failed to forgive, he has legally deprived himself of God's forgiveness. His comic confusion of "revenge" and "penance" illustrates his precarious position. We feel uneasy, then, even though the two men confess their sin and agree to a public penance. They do, however, gamely submit themselves to the dispensation of their creditor; to their good fortune, he can forgive better than they can repent. "The third part of repentance, is faith, whereby wee doe apprehend and take hold upon the promises of GOD, touching the free pardon and forgivenesse of our sinnes. . . . For what should avayle and profite us to bee sorrie for our sinnes, to lament and . . . confess . . . our offences, . . . unlesse we doe stedfastly beleeve, and bee fully perswaded, that GOD . . . will forgive us all our sinnes." [10] Predictably, the Anglican homily here supplements the Catholic, Aquinian formula which Hunter proposes—contrition, confession, and repentance—with "a lively faith in him whom he had denyed." This distinction is central to the Catholic-Protestant controversy over salvation by faith or works. That Claudio is most dramatically repentant in this area of faith suggests how sensitive Shakespeare might have been to the Pauline and Erasmian undertones of his action.

Claudio, like Beatrice and Benedick, has placed too much trust throughout his experience upon the senses.[11] He believes what he sees, and in so doing he is frequently deceived, like Othello, when confronted either by sensible deceptions or by transcendental truth, the intuition of love or purity. Don John exploits this failing twice. Because Claudio twice denies the person he should trust, his penance is finally a crucial test of his faith in love. He must accept blindfolded the mercy of his victim's father and of love itself. After his public confession Claudio joyfully agrees to this ultimate test of his faith:

> O noble sir!
> Your over-kindness doth wring tears from me.
> I do embrace your offer; and dispose
> For henceforth of poor Claudio.
>
> (v.i.279–82)

The old, faithless Claudio is dead; the rebirth to come should remind us of a basic Christian paradox: you must be born again. Such a familiar articulation of this Augustinian and Pauline commonplace[12] suggests how directly the conversion of Claudio would have seemed to parallel doctrinal understandings. It also introduces the fourth step in repentance.

In acting out his faith Claudio begins to fulfill the last requirement, amendment of life. Let us look finally at its homiletic formulation and then see how accurately it describes Claudio: "The fourth is, an amendment of life, or a new life, in bringing foorth fruits worthy of repentance. For they that doe truely repent, must bee cleane altered and changed, they must become new creatures, they must be no more the same that they were before."[13] "A true and sound repentance . . . may bee knowen and declared by good fruits." Claudio first demonstrates his amended life at Hero's grave. There, Don Pedro and Claudio, accompanied by their fellow men, undergo a very formal public confession and penance:

> Done to death by slanderous tongues
> Was the Hero that here lies. (v.iii.3–4)

Their ritual reenacts all of the phases of Claudio's repentance and forgiveness, from acknowledgement and confession to the begging for pardon. Such heavy stylization may be Shakespeare's way of suggesting the restoration of a broken ritual order:

> Pardon, goddess of the night
> Those that slew thy virgin knight.
> (v.iii.12–13)

The slant rhymes, stiff syntax, and uneven meter of the tortured, amateurish verse can suggest in their labored earnestness a new faith. "Tongues," "wrongs," "tomb," "dumb"; then "woe," "go," "moan," and "groan" can impress upon us their sincere contrition—"heavily, heavily"—but earnestly as well.

After the observance is done, Claudio hopefully and faithfully awaits his unknown fate:

> And Hymen now with luckier issue speeds
> Than this for whom we rend'red up this woe.
> (v.iii.32–33)

Still remembering his sin of distrust, still evidently regretting it, Claudio places himself completely in the providence of love. No man can become perfectly faithful or perfectly charitable. But Claudio seems to have followed the prescribed process of repentance fairly well.

We learn that Claudio's forgiveness has begun when Leonato, the father, tells us immediately after the scene of penance that he has forgiven him (v.iv.2). Once Claudio takes the hand of the masked bride and declares, "before this holy friar / I am your husband, if you like of me" (v.iv.58–59), he has performed the last act of faith that will be asked of him. At least partially amended in faith and in charity, and freely admitting his folly, he is as worthy of love and even of Hero as he can become; she unmasks and becomes his.

But partly because her extraordinary forgiveness contrasts so sharply to the uncharitable renunciation which occasions it, clusters of ambiguity still surround both his penance and her forgiveness. As well as Claudio has fulfilled the injunctions levied by Leonato, and demonstrated his "new life" or "new faith," his conversion still leaves the audience dissatisfied with his sincerity and incapable of forgiving him. The formality and suddenness of the repentance, the heavy stylization of his characterization as well as his penance, partially explain this inability to forgive and love him. Even though some of his actions, like the Calvinist or humourous convention of sudden conversion, have ample doctrinal and dramatic precedent, on the stage they also seem stock, unbelievable dramatic conventions. Other reservations abound. Claudio's confusion of revenge and penance (v.i.259–60) suggests a misapprehension of human and divine forgiveness and helps to explain his own unforgiving vengeance in church. His easy acceptance of another bride may be both too soon and too materialistic. His shifting of the blame to Don John occurs ambiguously close to his experience of personal repentance. Finally, his verse may be tortured simply because it is insincere. There are obviously more than enough reasons here for Hero to distrust his penance and withhold her forgiveness. Paradoxically, many of them may stem from Claudio's flat characterization. We seem to be asking a stock figure to be something more than he is, and Claudio cannot oblige us. Shakespeare invites such a problem, of course, because of the complexity of other characters in this very play. But that does not relieve most of us of our discomfort.

Unlike us, however, Hero either accepts these signs of his repentance or she forgives him in spite of their imperfections. Once again we cannot be sure because as a character she is even less complex than her Claudio. Her exceptional forgiveness, no less than Claudio's enactment of penance, is therefore another action we have difficulty understanding or celebrating. But if we accept them for what they are, the most abstract actions of the most stylized characters in these mature romantic comedies, the interpretive difficulties diminish. For Hero and Claudio seem to embody in allegorical fashion the same comic-Christian patterns we have already found to be so central to Shakespeare's comic vision. Their marriage, however unsatisfying it might be on the psychological level, makes good sense allegorically. It represents the blending in all men of the ideal and the real; more especially it represents the yoking together of the promise of forgiveness with erring man, who needs that promise. That the ritual of marriage is also a symbol of the unity of Christ and erring man is surely not an accidental association here.[14] For marriage, like communion, also celebrates both of those unions. Lewalski, in fact, has mentioned her sense of analogies, at this moment of profound forgiveness, between Hero and Christ.[15] The connection is intriguing.

But Hero, as her name suggests, is a static character, ideal but also almost invisible. She performs her extraordinary acts of faith and forgiveness silently and unobtrusively. We are not privy to her misgivings, if indeed she has any. For she remains almost purely an abstraction to the end. In the final scene Benedick and Beatrice wittily celebrate the couples' unions; Hero and Claudio almost evaporate in the warmth of such realism. Indeed, both Hero and Claudio must be understated verbally and psychologically or the whole comedy, including the subtler relationship of Benedick and Beatrice, would become uncomfortably doctrinal, and lose as well the richness of its ambiguous colorings. We understand Hero's allegorical significance well enough. That is precisely why we have so much trouble accepting it psychologically.

George and George suggest in doctrinal terms that seem especially appropriate to this moment and to others in Shakespearean comedy (like Orlando's extraordinary forgiveness of Oliver in the Forest of Arden) how special Hero's acts are, and how natural it is that they make us uncomfortable: "Men typically are enemies to other men; not to be an enemy in turn—to follow the ethics of universal love and to love one's enemies—this is the exceptional achievement of that exceptional individual, the true Christian, the brand plucked from the burning by the hand of God" (p. 77). Claudio is Hero's enemy, as we often remain his. It attests to Hero's election, her "Protestant sainthood" as George and George describe a perfection like hers (pp. 98–114), that Hero can so manifest the grace of God by loving and forgiving her enemy as neither we nor Claudio could. Like Antonio in *The Merchant of Venice,* who may be Hero's ironic counterpart, the Protestant saint is a precariously isolated individual, balanced as he or she is between the conflicting idealism and realism of man's mixed nature, and also between the conflicting Christian ideals of righteousness and humility. Unlike Antonio, Hero maintains her balance, but only at the cost of her virtual invisibility in the play. Like Antonio, therefore, she remains strangely isolated from everyone else, though she willingly participates in the final festivity and actually has a hand in causing it to occur. Such creative ambiguity obviously transcends simple allegory. But if we fail to perceive any of Hero's or Claudio's abstract, doctrinal dimensions, we cannot fully appreciate the festivity of *Much Ado about Nothing.*

## ii. Benedick and Beatrice

Benedick and Beatrice, in contrast, stand before us throughout the play in great psychological complexity. As a result, we can enjoy their antics and their witplay on many levels before we begin to consider their possible relationships to Shakespeare's comic themes of faith and folly. Paradoxically, the abstract depiction of Claudio and Hero, fool and forgiver, faithless and faithful lover, can lead us to understand the connections between doctrine and drama in the depiction of Benedick and Beatrice. Neither Benedick nor Beatrice is as flawed as Claudio; neither is as good as Hero. But their relationships to both of them demand our attention. Like Claudio, both of them have follies they must admit and try to amend. Both of them are also far too sure of their own senses and reason to know truth from falsehood. Like Hero, both of them will have to embrace imperfections in their mates, with humor and with love, if they are ever to thrive in marriage. The old comic equation Shakespeare seems to have discovered in *Love's Labor's Lost* and enriched in *A Midsummer Night's Dream* thus finds two added dimensions here. First, folly becomes both faithlessness and the self-love which occasions it. Second, humility and faith in love involve knowing that imperfection may be thine as well as mine, and loving another both in spite of that knowledge and because of it. Such loving is romantic madness at its finest and most mature.

Both of these changes represent important progressions in Shakespeare's comic vision. The cuckold's horn becomes a paradoxical badge of faith as well as a mark of folly. And while the theme of romantic faith continues to touch the epistemological concerns of the noting-nothing pun, it also becomes with Benedick and Beatrice a vitally important metaphor that defines their love relationship.[16] Like faith, penance becomes another such metaphor, in their words as well as their actions. It is thus no accident that their faithlessness and their folly as lovers, and their ultimate repentance too, are frequently described in religious imagery. That imagery, like their rich characterization, is still not far removed from the Pauline and Erasmian context from which it first emerged in Shakespeare's comic vision. Of course, the religion of love was something of a literary cliché in Shakespeare's time. But with his fresh awareness of its Pauline and Erasmian roots, Shakespeare seems to have given it new life.

One of the best indications of the importance of these thematic patterns in the play is the care with which they have been woven into its structure. We can discuss the regenerative humiliations of Benedick and Beatrice simultaneously because they are so prominent and so contrivedly juxtaposed in the play, not only against the Hero-Claudio action but also against themselves. Their mutual faithlessness or skepticism is articulated in closely parallel early speeches and scenes, and dramatized throughout their merry war. Beneath their scornful façade, again expressed by both characters in parallel speeches, is something suspiciously like love, despite their disclaimers. The benevolent deception directed against both of them thus strikes right at the root of their faithlessness and their fear of folly. It, too, occurs in scenes that are mirror-images of one another. And the good-natured jesting that marks the success of the plots is also highlighted by parallel structure. That Beatrice and Benedick remain unique and believable characters in spite of this symmetry is a remarkable achievement of the play. Each of these moments is worth a closer look through our Pauline and Erasmian perspective. We will simply have to make that perspective more flexible to accommodate their subtler portrayal.

At the very beginning of the play Beatrice places the themes of faithlessness and folly before us by anatomizing Benedick. The Messenger describes him as returning from the wars with all honor: "A lord to a lord, a man to a man; stuffed with all honourable virtues" (1.i.49–50). But Beatrice will see only his folly: "It is so indeed. He is no less than a stuffed man; but for the stuffing—well, we are all mortal" (1.i.51–52). If he is stuffed in Beatrice's eyes with folly, he is also faithless:

> BEATRICE. Who is his companion now? He hath every month a new sworn brother.
> MESSENGER. Is't possible?
> BEATRICE. Very easily possible. He wears his faith but as the fashion of his hat; it ever changes with the next block.   (1.i.63–67)

There is some truth to her caustic observations, but her own considerable faithlessness and folly also shine through them. Benedick needs to be cured of these related diseases; so does she.

The skepticism or faithlessness of Benedick and Beatrice is portrayed by Shakespeare in the lightest comic terms. It is almost a game, a "merry war"; and it will likewise be cured through play. Benedick is, however, seriously flawed in his romantic faith. He is afraid to trust any woman in fact, because he is obsessed with womanly unfaithfulness, with becoming a cuckold:

> That a woman conceived me, I thank her; that she brought me up,
> I likewise give her most humble thanks; but that I will have a rechate

winded in my forehead, or hang my bugle in an invisible baldrick, all women shall pardon me. Because I will not do them the wrong to mistrust any, I will do myself the right to trust none; and the fine is (for the which I may go the finer), I will live a bachelor.

(I.i.212–19)

It is Benedick, of course, who is without faith. Obsessed by his own goodness, and afraid of what he cannot control, he refuses to commit himself to life, to maturity, or to love.

Beatrice similarly fears men, for their unfaithfulness and also for their physicality. She is repulsed by beards, yet simultaneously aware that to get a man she must have his beard:

> BEATRICE. Lord, I could not endure a husband with a beard on his face. I had rather lie in the woollen!
> LEONATO. You may light on a husband that hath no beard.
> BEATRICE. What should I do with him? dress him in my apparel and make him my waiting gentlewoman? He that hath a beard is more than a youth, and he that hath no beard is less than a man; and he that is more than a youth is not for me, and he that is less than a man, I am not for him. Therefore I will even take sixpence in earnest of the berrord and lead his apes into hell. (II.i.26–35)

Beatrice, much better than Benedick, perceives her dilemma. Afraid to trust a member of the opposite sex, and thus in a sense afraid to trust herself to him, she, like Benedick, cannot muster the faith to love. Like Hamlet, and like Antonio, she is deeply aware of the imperfection of man, but unable to place her awareness within a consoling comic or Christian perspective. She would never marry "till God made men of some other metal than earth. Would it not grieve a woman to be overmastered with a piece of valiant dust? to make an account of her life to a clod of wayward marl?" (II.i.51–54). It might indeed grieve Beatrice, but if she or Benedick is to marry at all, there is no alternative. For from the Erasmian or Pauline perspective that Shakespearean comedy shares, we are all fools.

Beatrice ironically expresses this corrective truth at the end of the same speech, but she still does not understand it: "No, uncle, I'll none. Adam's sons are my bretheren, and truly I hold it a sin to match in my kindred" (II.i.54–56). Later in the same scene Beatrice unwittingly repeats the same paradox. She would not have Benedick put her

93

down, "lest I should prove the mother of fools." But she must be the mother of fools if she is to have human children. There is no other kind. That kinship with Adam, with universal imperfection, must become cause for forgiveness, trust, and love if comic festivity is to occur in *Much Ado*. The lesson of humility is thus intensified from *Love's Labor's Lost*, where the lords had to learn only of their own folly. Here, like Viola and Olivia in their relationship with the changeable Orsino and Sebastian-Cesario in *Twelfth Night*, and like Orlando and Rosalind in *As You Like It*, Benedick and Beatrice must learn to expect and embrace imperfection in one another while they learn to accept their own folly. In fact, in *Much Ado* one lesson clearly depends upon the other. That interdependency is enhanced by the irony that its prideful and faithless learners Benedick and Beatrice are destined for one another.

The frequent imagery of faith and repentance during the same parallel scenes is further evidence of the pertinence of Erasmian and Pauline paradoxes about faith and folly to the relationship of Benedick and Beatrice. In the first scene, Benedick cannot abide the lavish praise of Hero by Claudio and Don Pedro. Therefore he replies to their Petrarchan conventions: "That I neither feel how she should be loved, nor know how she should be worthy, is the opinion that fire cannot melt out of me. I will die in it at the stake" (1.i.205–7). Don Pedro continues this religious imagery when he thereupon remarks on the strange pride of Benedick's faithlessness: "Thou wast ever an obstinate heretick in the despite of beauty." This leads Benedick to his just-quoted comments about universal cuckoldry. Then he vows his eternal faithlessness in love:

> Prove that ever I lose more blood with love than I will get again with drinking, pick out mine eyes with a ballad-maker's pen and hang me up at the door of a brothel house for the sign of blind Cupid. (1.i.222–25)

Don Pedro again describes this posture in the ironic imagery of faith: "Well, if ever thou dost fall from this faith, thou wilt prove a notable argument." But Benedick thinks such a conversion highly unlikely:

"If I do, hang me in a bottle like a cat and shoot at me; and he that hits me, let him be clapped on the shoulder and called Adam." As we have just seen, Beatrice also refers ironically to Adam when she is revealing her obsession with infidelity and imperfection. The association is as inevitable as it is pertinent to their mutually fallen state. But for the moment, Benedick will not yet repent his faithlessness or admit his folly. To him, marriage should be signified with horns in the forehead and the inscription "Here you may see Benedick the married man" (I.i.237–38). "The horn, the horn." Benedick abhors such humiliation. Its possibility is one of the reasons marriage is such an act of faith. Benedick replies, "In faith" twice during the scene (at ll. 152 and 175), but he evidences none at all.

In the closely parallel scene at the beginning of the second act, Beatrice illustrates her kinship with this skeptical attitude in another cluster of amusing religious images, this time images of repentance and salvation. As with Benedick, the images mark both the foolish pride and the lack of faith that stand between her and married happiness. The horns she fears suggest cuckoldry, but also too much (or too little) sexuality, like the beard joke earlier: "I shall lessen God's sending that way; for it is said, 'God sends a curst cow short horns,' but to a cow too curst he sends none" (II.i.19–21). Her bondage is still obvious; she would lessen God's sending, when she must instead lesson herself to accept whatever he sends, even as Claudio finally does. But Beatrice prays instead for no husband, for none will be good enough for her: "For the which blessing [no husband] I am at him upon my knees every morning and evening" (II.i.24–26). There follows the business about the beard; in Claudio's parallel scene it was the horns. Her heaven is a paradise of bachelors and maids, for neither of them can have committed the adultery that both she and Benedick seem to consider inevitable in their common faithlessness.

To Leonato's question, "Well, then, go you into hell?" she therefore replies,

No; but to the gate, and there will the devil meet me like an old cuckold with horns on his head, and say, "Get you to heaven, Beatrice, get you to heaven. Here's no place for you maids." So deliver

95

I up my apes, and away to Saint Peter. For the heavens, he shows me
where the bachelors sit, and there live we as merry as the day is long.
(II.i.37–43)

Like Benedick, she swears "Yes, faith," but she has none at all. As she
advises Hero,

> Wooing, wedding, and repenting is as a Scotch jig, a measure, and
> a cinque-pace: the first suit is hot and hasty like a Scotch jig (and full
> as fantastical); the wedding, mannerly modest, as a measure, full of
> state and ancientry; and then comes Repentance and with his bad legs
> falls into the cinque-pace faster and faster, till he sink into his
> grave. (II.i.63–69)

This may be shrewd apprehension, as Leonato suggests; it is also bad
faith. Shakespeare's subsequent dramatic use of repentance, not only
as the formula for Claudio's stilted regeneration but also as the metaphor for the spirited and complex regeneration of Benedick and
Beatrice is thus a significant comic achievement. Theirs becomes a faith
that is the opposite of this skepticism; but it retains a healthy, caustic
awareness of human imperfection that they will never lose.

If they must learn to accept and celebrate the folly of the horns, the
inevitable imperfection they can expect in their mates, Benedick and
Beatrice must also learn the more characteristic comic lesson of their
own folly. In fact, a touch of humility will make the other lesson
easier. They will both be edified in this direction by the charitable deceptions of Act III. Their merry war serves a similar purpose for both
of them throughout the whole play, especially for Benedick. The exchange which comes closest to edifying him early in the play comes
during the masked dance, an occasion for similar humiliation in *Love's
Labor's Lost*. Since their witty skirmishes have been so often discussed, let us look at just this one moment.

Even though Beatrice and Benedick would seem equally to deserve
their comic epithets of Lady Disdain and Signior Mountanto for their
faithlessness and pride, Benedick is the one who suffers (and learns)
the most through their exchanges. Beatrice is much quicker than he is,
very adept at the humiliating jibe. One of her best moments comes
when Benedick unwisely asks if she knows a certain Benedick. She
gladly obliges him with a stinging anatomy of his folly:

> Why, he is the Prince's jester, a very dull fool. Only his gift is in de-
> vising impossible slanders. None but libertines delight in him; and
> the commendation is not in his wit, but in his villainy. . . . I am sure
> he is in the fleet. I would he had boarded me.        (II.i.122–28)

This hard lesson is accompanied by an obvious challenge to reply.
Benedick, intimidated by her wit and his own folly, fearfully refuses
her challenge and later exits rather than bear more blows. He also begins to think about what she has said:

> That my Lady Beatrice should know me, and not know me! The
> Prince's fool! Ha! it may be I go under that title because I am
> merry. Yea, but so I am apt to do myself wrong.        (II.i.183–86)

Later in the same scene he publicly shares her criticism with Don
Pedro, who cagily neither confirms nor denies her observations:

> She told me, not thinking I had been myself, that I was the Prince's
> jester, that I was duller than a great thaw; huddling jest upon jest
> with such impossible conveyance upon me that I stood like a man at
> a mark, with a whole army shooting at me. She speaks poniards, and
> every word stabs.                          (II.i.218–23)

They stab so painfully that he could almost mend under her humiliation. Yet in both cases Benedick finally attributes his wounds to her
scorn and not to his folly:

> I am not so reputed. It is the base (though bitter) disposition of
> Beatrice that puts the world into her person and so gives me out.
>                                            (II.i.186–88)

Through this clever evasion of the humiliating truth of her witty
words Benedick perpetuates both his unwarranted pride and his faithlessness in the other sex.

But Beatrice has frightened him away with her wit. Surely that must
have given him an intimation of his own folly. Benedick says something else as he smarts from her wounds that makes us wonder if his
heretic's "faith" is not crumbling along with his pride: "I would not
marry her though she were endowed with all that Adam had left him
before he transgressed" (II.i.225–27). Here is Adam again, that repeated eponym of universal imperfection. And "my Lady Beatrice"
instead of "my Lady Disdain"? Who asked him to marry her? What

has already entered his giddy brain? We will have to wonder for only another scene or so. There is some suggestion, incidentally, that Beatrice may also have come off halting from this fray. For her later comment in the scene suggests that she fears that the very wit in which she takes such pride may have chased away her favorite target forever: "Thus goes every one to the world but I, and I am sunburnt. I may sit in a corner and cry 'Heigh-ho for a husband!' " (II.i.285–87). Beatrice seems to have precious little desire to remain single. Her momentary lapse from her role as Lady Disdain prompts Don Pedro to promise, "Lady Beatrice, I will get you one." He does so quite nicely, but only after the game he stages (with the help of the ladies and the gentlemen) finally convinces Benedick and Beatrice to throw over their faithlessness, distrust the evidence of their senses, and embrace their inevitable folly with profound joy.

There have of course been earlier indications that behind their façades of wit and hard-heartedness lies something suspiciously like love. To be sure, Benedick proclaims in his first exchange with Beatrice that though he is loved of all ladies he loves none. And she replies "I am of your humour for that. I had rather hear my dog bark at a crow than a man swear he loves me" (I.i.116–18). But in anatomizing Hero for Claudio, Benedick also has these words of praise for Beatrice:

> There's her cousin, an she were not possessed with a fury, exceeds her as much in beauty as the first of May doth the last of December.
>
> (I.i.169–71)

And Beatrice, speaking of the hypothesized union of Don John and Benedick, betrays similar inclinations:

> With a good leg and a good foot, uncle, and money enough in his purse, such a man would win any woman in the world—if 'a could get her good will.          (II.i.13–15)

They would still remake their mates; but the new image would not be too different from the old. We even hear Beatrice admit to Don Pedro that she has loved Benedick once, and thought that he loved her too. Of his heart she says,

> Indeed, my lord, he lent it me awhile, and I gave him use for it—a

> double heart for his single one. Marry, once before he won it of me
> with false dice; therefore your grace may well say I have lost it.
>
> (ii.i.249–52)

We hear no more of this. Still, this false dicing, imagined or no, underlies her lack of faith in Benedick. She cannot forgive him what is past. Like Demetrius with Helena in *A Midsummer Night's Dream,* Benedick seems almost completely unaware of this episode. But he is as afraid of her scorn as she is of his faithlessness. Clearly, then, their mutual disdain is a defense mechanism that is keeping them from noting with faith their mutual love, and accepting with humility their mutual folly. Benedick says at one point, "I can see yet without spectacles" (i.i.168). Beatrice's parallel comment is "I have a good eye, uncle; I can see a church by daylight" (ii.i.71–72). But both of them are believing the appearance of scorn instead of the reality of love. They are skeptics trusting in outer rather than inner truth. In their mutual lack of faith in things not seen, in their excessive trust in daylight and eyesight, they are mutually unaware of their mutual love.

The pageant or game that converts both of them strikes right at their ethical and epistemological pride. On the one hand, Don Pedro and Hero convince their "victims" that looks are deceiving, that they are both really worshipped while they appear to be scorned. Once this first seed of faith is sown, the lovers see with new eyes, and believe, momentarily at least, in things hoped for, not seen. This is not religious faith, to be sure. But the religious-romantic analogy enriches the comic action just as it has before. It continues to be highlighted with appropriate religious metaphors. Simultaneously, the pageant corrects their pride just enough for them to recognize their own follies and thus accept more generously the possibility of imperfections in others, after the manner of Olivia in *Twelfth Night.* Two dedicated romantic skeptics are thus finally, miraculously, converted into true believers in love.

Benedick frames his experience with two soliloquies which vividly illustrate the dimensions of the change he has undergone. Before the play he is to see, he wonders how

> one man, seeing how much another man is a fool when he dedicates
> his behaviors to love, will, after he hath laughed at such shallow fol-

lies in others, become the argument of his own scorn by falling in
love.                                                                 (II.iii.7–11)

How can a proud young man embrace a known folly and rejoice in it?
On the other hand, how, either, can a confirmed skeptic suddenly become transformed by faith?

> May I be so converted and see with these eyes? I cannot tell; I think
> not. I will not be sworn but love may transform me to an oyster; but
> I'll take my oath on it, till he have made an oyster of me he shall
> never make me such a fool.                          (II.iii.20–24)

Remember what John Colet said about man's acceptance of mysteries
transcending his reason and his senses, and about the miraculous trans-
formations that accompany such religious faith: "These mysteries of
God are in truth of such a kind, that he who denies not himself
utterly, he who becomes not a fool that he may be wise, . . . shall
never feel . . . what are the Divine wisdom and spirit. A man must
needs be . . . born again, . . . that . . . he may spiritually discern,
search out, gather, and receive, the spiritual things of God."[17] Bottom
becomes an ass; Benedick may become an oyster. But as both are transformed they touch upon the comic and Christian mysteries of faith and
folly. Benedick, no fool as he is about to embrace his folly, knows
enough about this experience to talk about it in precisely such terms.
Will I become such a fool? Will I be so transformed and converted
to this new faith? Stranger things have happened before. Inside the
barnacled shell of folly may lie the twin pearls of humility and faith.

Nothing else will change, however, until he rids himself of that
fear of imperfection in others that he shares with Beatrice:

> One woman is fair, . . . another is wise, . . . another virtuous, . . .
> but till all graces be in one woman, one woman shall not come in my
> grace. Rich she shall be, . . . wise, . . . virtuous, . . . fair, . . .
> mild, . . . noble, . . . of good discourse, an excellent musician, and
> her hair shall be of what color it please God.          (II.iii.24–32)

As the scene starts, Benedick has glimmers of the wisdom of folly, but
he also has a long way to go to achieve it.

By the end of the scene, having learned what his eyes could not see
of himself or of Beatrice, his conversion is completed. He has heard

his follies recited by his friends, and he has profited by them. He is too scornful; she is wise "in everything but in loving Benedick." He will torment her with it, for he "hath a contemptible spirit." This dose of edifying humiliation is sugared over with some muted praise: "He hath indeed a good outward happiness"; "He doth indeed show some sparks that are like wit." Yet even those moments are mixed with his folly: "In the managing of quarrels you may say he is wise, for either he avoids them with great discretion, or undertakes them with a most Christianlike fear." This jab at the folly of his recent ignominious retreat from Beatrice's assault surely strikes home.

At the same time, his doubt is replaced by faith; he has seen only the outward Beatrice: "most wonderful that she should so dote on Signior Benedick, whom she hath in all outward behaviors seemed ever to abhor." "She loves him with an enraged affection, it is past the infinite of thought" (II.iii. 92–94, 98–99). A lovely touch is Benedick's belief during this gulling in yet more evidence of the senses: "knavery cannot, sure, hide himself in such reverence"; or "Then down upon her knees she falls, weeps, sobs, beats her heart, tears her hair, prays, curses—'O sweet Benedick! God give me patience!' " (II. iii. 116–17, 138–40). This preposterous report of her miraculous transformation is all the evidence he requires.

And so Benedick is doubly transformed. His soliloquy at the end of the scene shows him acknowledging his follies and accepting his love with a new faith. In fact, the "new creature," "clean altered and changed," is nowhere more evident than when Benedick sees in Beatrice's scorn sure marks of love. Like a literary critic twisting a verse until it fits his thesis, Benedick says of her words to him:

> Ha! "Against my will I am sent to bid you come in to dinner." There's a double meaning in that. "I took no more pains for those thanks than you took pains to thank me." That's as much as to say, "Any pains that I take for you is as easy as thanks." If I do not take pity of her, I am a villain; if I do not love her, I am a Jew. I will go get her picture. (II.iii.236–41)

Double meaning, indeed! His faith is just as adamant as his skepticism once was. Heresy—sheer unbelief—is forsworn. Folly is embraced with humility and faith:

I hear how I am censured. They say I will bear myself proudly if I perceive the love come from her. . . . I must not seem proud. Happy are they that hear their detractions and can put them to mending. They say the lady is fair—'tis a truth, I can bear them witness; and virtuous—'tis so, I cannot reprove it; and wise, but for loving me— by my troth, it is no addition to her wit, nor no great argument of her folly, for I will be horribly in love with her. I may chance have some odd quirks and remnants of wit broken on me because I have railed so long against marriage. . . . No, the world must be peopled. When I said I would die a bachelor, I did not think I should live till I were married. (II.iii.206–23)

The freedom and the joy of these strange paradoxes is profound and immediate. There will be more humiliation for Benedick; he is human after all. There will also be great joy. The familiar proverb suggests the Pauline and Erasmian dimensions of this experience: "Happy are they that hear their detractions and can put them to mending." Beatrice is now in his eyes the sum of all beauty, virtue, wisdom. "By this day, she's a fair lady! I do spy some marks·of love in her" (II.iii.223– 25). So now, with considerable irony, she functions for him as her namesake did for Dante. At last Benedick is an inspired lover. But he is not one who can speak by the book, and he never will be. That he and Beatrice will both have the good sense to see how foolish such a style makes them sound, and the humility to celebrate that folly at the end of the play, suggests how completely they are changed.

The tactics of Beatrice's conversion are similar; the scene is in verse and quite compressed. Once again, the scorn of her misconstrued encounter with Benedick after his conversion is juxtaposed against the faith of her new vision at the end of the scene. In between she comes to acknowledge her faults and to accept, with faith, Benedick's love. She hears Hero criticize her pride and disdain:

> Nature never framed a woman's heart
> Of prouder stuff than that of Beatrice.
> Disdain and scorn ride sparkling in her eyes,
> Misprizing what they look on; and her wit
> Values itself so highly that to her
> All matter else seems weak. She cannot love,
> Nor take no shape nor project of affection,
> She is so self-endeared. (III.i.49–56)

Worse, she would laugh anyone to scorn who tried to correct her. Beatrice overhears the recitation of her self-love, her foolish blindness to her own follies and the virtues of others; like Benedick the detractions put her to mending. She also hears Benedick praised and his amazing love proclaimed. We should notice that there is no counter-praise intermixed with this blame, a suggestion, perhaps, of the degree of her self-love and the strength of her ego as contrasted to Benedick's. But the result is the same. Like Benedick, Beatrice is also made new, born again. She accepts her folly and vows to amend it; and she accepts with faith the miracle of Benedick's love against the evidence of her own senses. Most miraculous of all, she manifests the new Beatrice by speaking all of this in impassioned, rhymed verse, her first verse utterance of the play:

> What fire is in mine ears? Can this be true?
> Stand I condemned for pride and scorn so much?
> Contempt, farewell! and maiden pride, adieu!
> No glory lives behind the back of such.
> And, Benedick, love on; I will requite thee,
> Taming my wild heart to thy loving hand.
> If thou dost love, my kindness shall incite thee
> To bind our loves up in a holy band;
> For others say thou dost deserve, and I
> Believe it better than reportingly.
>                    (III.i.107–16)

Like Benedick, she believes it "better than reportingly." Their testimony confirms and crystallizes a love they both have wanted to believe in but never quite trusted. Freed from their twin follies of pride and faithlessness, given a new understanding of the meaning of universal folly, they have both been born again.[18] The newly barbered and tailored Benedick evidences this rebirth just as surely as the rhymed verse of Beatrice. But the content of their soliloquies made the inner conversion evident before we were vouchsafed such external evidence of it. We celebrate their conversion for the rest of the play.

Benedick bears the anticipated scorn of his converters with a new confidence: "Gallants, I am not as I have been" (III.ii.13). In fact, his countenance is much changed, evidencing the new man, reborn in faith and in folly. He is shaved, perfumed, washed, painted, and the folly of these signs of rebirth is bearable. In fact, the anticipated jibes hardly hurt at all: "Old Signior, walk aside with me. I have studied eight or nine wise words to speak to you, which these hobby-horses must not hear" (III.ii.62–65). Beatrice finds her folly a little tougher to bear. But in the parallel Scene iv of Act III, bear it she does. Beatrice says she has a bad cold: "I am stuffed, cousin; I cannot smell" (III.iv.57). What she has caught is that infection she called "the Benedick" in the first scene, and described as great folly. Margaret chides her lovingly, "Get you some of this distilled *carduus benedictus* and lay it to your heart. It is the only thing for a qualm" (III.iv.66–68). Even better is her bawdy pun on stuffed: "A maid, and stuffed! There's goodly catching of cold" (III.iv.58–59). Beatrice had earlier said of Benedick "he is no less than a stuffed man; but for the stuffing—well, we are all mortal" (I.i.51–52). Later Beatrice seemed apprehensive of the physical aspects of love (II.i.26–54 passim). Now she will be stuffed with his folly, with her good will. When Margaret talks of the strange conversions of lovers, Beatrice must enjoy her words almost as much as the other two ladies. For marriage is in the air:

> You may think perchance that I think you are in love. Nay, by'r lady, I am not such a fool to think what I list; nor I list not to think what I can; nor indeed I cannot think, if I would think my heart out of thinking, that you are in love, or that you will be in love, or that you can be in love. Yet Benedick was such another, and now is he become a man. He swore he would never marry, and yet now in despite of his heart he eats his meat without grudging; and how you may be converted I know not, but methinks you look with your eyes as other women do. (III.iv.72–82)

Her image of conversion, like her references to folly and faith, suggests how nicely this scene and this speech highlight the full comic significance of what Benedick and Beatrice have achieved.

They haltingly express the joy of their love in the strange aftermath of the aborted wedding.

> BENEDICK. I will swear by it [my sword] that you love me, and I will make him eat it that says I love not you.

. . . . . . . . . . . . . . . . . . . . . . . . . . . . . . . . .

> BEATRICE. You have stayed me in a happy hour. I was about to protest I loved you.
> BENEDICK. And do it with all thy heart.
> BEATRICE. I love you with so much of my heart that none is left to protest.
> BENEDICK. Come, bid me do anything for thee.
> BEATRICE. Kill Claudio. (IV.i. 272–73, 279–85)

Kill Claudio? We need no longer fear that Benedick and Beatrice will degenerate into a conventional Petrarchan pair now that they have expressed their love. Their learning must continue to progress. Beatrice must finally forgive Claudio; Benedick must believe in Beatrice's faith in Hero. His first response comes from the old Benedick: "Ha! not for the wide world!" His second is more like the new man accepting his strange quest:

> BENEDICK. Think you in your soul the Count Claudio hath wronged Hero?
> BEATRICE. Yea, as sure as I have a thought or a soul.
> BENEDICK. Enough, I am engaged. I will challenge him. I will kiss your hand, and so I leave you. By this hand, Claudio shall render me a dear account. (IV.i.323–28)

So, evidently, he does, through his formal repentance. At least it finally satisfies Beatrice and Benedick. His faith in Beatrice, like hers in Hero, is brilliantly a part of this celebratory and yet tense scene.[19]

Their faith proven, their folly remains to be celebrated. Benedick tries his hand at poetry. Like Orlando, he is no good at it; unlike him, he knows it immediately and laughs at his folly:

> Marry, I cannot show it in rhyme. I have tried. I can find out no rhyme to "lady" but "baby"—an innocent rhyme; for "scorn," "horn"—a hard rhyme; for "school," "fool"—a babbling rhyme. Very ominous endings! No, I was not born under a rhyming planet, nor I cannot woo in festival terms. (v.ii.33–38)

His good-natured attitude toward horns as well as his own foolishness suggests that though he cannot woo in festival terms, he can woo festively. In fact, when Beatrice enters, we see that their wit-battle has returned as a new mark of their love. As Benedick says, "Thou and I are too wise to woo peaceably" (v.ii.64). Predictably, this occasions

Beatrice's corrective barb, "It appears not in this confession. There's not one wise man among twenty that will praise himself." If Benedick has slipped momentarily back into pride, Beatrice has returned him quickly enough to proper humility with a variation on the Erasmian and Pauline theme about wise fools. Their witty relationship will always keep them from taking themselves too seriously.

And so in the final scene, theirs is the festive burden, though the miraculous forgiveness of Claudio, and Hero's unveiling, preface their witty "festival terms." Their faith and their folly come out once more in the cleverness with which they fence with words as the play comes to an end:

> BENEDICK. Do not you love me?
> BEATRICE.                              Why, no; no more than reason.
> BENEDICK. Why, then your uncle, and the Prince, and Claudio
>         Have been deceived—they swore you did.
> BEATRICE. Do not you love me?
> BENEDICK.                              Troth, no; no more than reason.
> BEATRICE. Why, then my cousin, Margaret, and Ursula
>         Are much deceived; for they did swear you did.
>                                        (v.iv.74–79)

They celebrate their love past all reason, but with irony; they celebrate their exposed folly by referring to the merry game inflicted on them. And then, in another replay of the edifying humiliations of *Love's Labor's Lost,* their halting sonnet attempts are produced as indisputable proof of their faith and their folly. As Benedick joyously proclaims, in a clever parody of Hero's miraculous resurrection,

> A miracle! Here's our own hands against our hearts. Come, I will
> have thee; but, by this light, I take thee for pity.        (v.iv.91–94)

Beatrice's last retort suggests that this merry war will last forever after:

> I would not deny you; but, by this good day, I yield upon great persuasion, and partly to save your life, for I was told you were in a consumption.

Benedick seals her mouth and their vows with a kiss. And then he pronounces a fitting benediction to their mutual happiness. They have just ironically sworn "by this light" and "by this day." But both have been liberated from their bondage to the evidence of their senses and their reason. They are in fact now reciting the main outlines of the foolish deception that taught them the joy of that faith. Benedick's benediction also celebrates their eternal, inevitable, and joyous folly:

> I'll tell thee what, Prince; a college of wit-crackers cannot flout me out of my humor. Dost thou think I care for a satire or an epigram? No. If a man will be beaten with brains, 'a shall wear nothing handsome about him. In brief, since I do purpose to marry, I will think nothing to any purpose that the world can say against it; and therefore never flout at me for what I have said against it; for man is a giddy thing, and this is my conclusion. (v.iv.99–107)

Beatrice must smile in spite of herself at this fine, ironic profession of his love. For if man is a giddy thing, he can also believe and do surprising things. Benedick and Beatrice will never be complacent lovers. But they will be happy ones, in their faith and in their folly, forever and a day. What a lovely combination of psychological realism, the conventions of romance, and Shakespeare's rigorous new comic-Christian equation!

Claudio and Hero are also a part of this final scene, and in fact their stylized presentation has contributed to our understanding of it. But Benedick and Beatrice are almost solely responsible for the joyous tone of the final festivity. In fact, were that festivity determined only by the successful working-out of the Hero-Claudio plot, the play's ending would be much less delightful. However, if our reluctance to celebrate their joy can indict the resolution of the Hero-Claudio plot, it can also dramatize both the difficulty and the mystery of forgiveness. After all, their highly stylized presentation may seem static and contrived against the brilliant psychology of Benedick and Beatrice without necessarily being satirized. Claudio does come to acknowledge his comic folly and faithlessness, and to amend his life, and this is the first comedy in which such change is fully dramatized. Hero's "resurrection" and her implicit forgiveness of Claudio when she accepts his hand in marriage are also considerable comic miracles, with a rich tradition of continental drama behind them.[20] Further, crucially, no one in the play distrusts this penance or this forgiveness. Beatrice, who had ordered Benedick to "kill Claudio," and the wise friar who is about to marry them have both evidently accepted his penance. Leonato too, and Benedick, are satisfied and say so explicitly in the final scene:

> FRIAR. Did I not tell you she was innocent?
> LEONATO. So are the Prince and Claudio, who accused her.
>
> . . . . . . . . . . . . . . . . . . . . .
>
> ANTONIO. Well, I am glad that all things sort so well.
> BENEDICK. And so am I, being else by faith enforced
> To call young Claudio to a reckoning for it.
>
> (v.iv.1–9 passim)

The good-natured jokes about cuckoldry (ll. 40–52) between Benedick and Claudio may testify to their reconciliation on the one hand, and on the other to their newfound willingness to embrace the possible folly of an unfaithful wife, at the very moment of marriage. How happy a change this is from their mutual distrust of women earlier! Both seem to have learned the wisdom of folly.

There is still no question but that Hero and Claudio exist in almost totally abstract terms, while their thematic and psychological counterparts Benedick and Beatrice are undergoing Shakespeare's first successful regeneration of complex comic characters within the time-span of the play. This contrast inevitably works to Hero's and Claudio's disadvantage today in terms of the audience's response. But in the Renaissance the novelty of psychological realism plus the inescapable thematic relationships of the two plots would probably have minimized the problem of response. As Hunter suggests, the audience, trained in the Anglican or Aquinian doctrine of repentance, would have been likely to understand the regeneration of Claudio as richer in allegorical or representative content, and that of Benedick and Beatrice as richer in psychological realism.[21] That psychological response could hardly have ignored the comic-Christian overtones of both plots, however, since they are so insistently similar. Benedick and Beatrice, the meaning of their relationship highlighted by the stylized Claudio, are also skeptics who finally evidence their conversion by significant acts of personal faith. Each of them is delivered from an unrealistic belief in his own senses and reason and in his own incomparable goodness. Their consequent acknowledgment of imperfect eyesight and foolish behavior announces a rebirth into humility which is celebrated in the final act. Before we convince ourselves of the darker side of the Hero-Claudio plot, we should remember its intimate relationships to the parallel plot through the paradoxical Christian themes of faith and folly that are so central to Shakespeare's comic vision. For as Northrop Frye and others have argued, only if we demand of Hero and Claudio a psychological complexity which was never intended for them, and ignore the important dimensions of their thematic complexity, will their final joy seem to be unduly puzzling.

# CHAPTER V

# "Most Faining": Foolish Wits and Wise Fools in *As You Like It*

*As You Like It* is a banquet of the follies of human perception and human behavior. But unlike *Much Ado about Nothing* the emphasis is decisively on the celebration rather than the discovery and acknowledgment of this folly. Partly because of the uniqueness of Arden and its inhabitants, absurd behavior is readily acknowledged throughout the play by the lovers, the shepherds, and the courtiers. Paradoxically, only the fool and the would-be fool in Arden, Touchstone and Jaques, seem to lack this humility. Their naiveté is especially amusing not only because it is their profession to know themselves to be fools, but also because they so frequently allude to Erasmian and Pauline statements of this wisdom. That strange and delightful absence of humility in these Erasmian fools, like its unusual presence among the rest of the characters in Arden, can deepen our understanding of the wisdom of folly in Shakespeare's romantic comedies.

*As You Like It* is also unique in its treatment of epistemological folly. Like *A Midsummer Night's Dream* it persistently involves us in romantic and aesthetic truths which surpass all knowledge. But *A Midsummer Night's Dream* focuses most of its attention on Bottom, the four lovers, Theseus, and the audience as beholders or interpreters of the transcendental. *As You Like It,* on the other hand, deals more with its expressive side, with the attempts of the lover or the artist, Orlando or Rosalind or Shakespeare himself, to convey transcendental truths. Like *A Midsummer Night's Dream,* but with more subtlety, *As You Like It* simplifies and enriches these rather esoteric aesthetic and epistemological themes with their analogies to attempts to convey the insights of religious faith. Religious rituals thus become the metaphoric counterpart in *As You Like It* to the observances and conventions of lovers and artists.

But all such conventions inevitably risk the folly of expressing the inexpressible, a folly familiar to both St. Paul and Erasmus.[1] Shakespeare thus joyously and ingeniously links fool, lover, artist, and priest in *As You Like It* into a common bond. They are all fools, and unless they acknowledge that folly they will never be wise. The foolish wits of Arden never quite grasp this wisdom. But the lovers, like the playwright, seem to know or to learn that their great feignings, the conventions they both must use to say what they so deeply feel, might also be great follies. For what they have to express may transcend both their art and human understanding. In an age that was unusually interested in sectarian controversies concerning the nature and efficacy of religious rituals,[2] such a comic interest in the rituals of lovers and artists could have seemed quite timely.

## i. The Folly of the Fools

In *Twelfth Night,* it can be demonstrated that Feste is a truly wise fool. By "venting" a folly that is virtually universal in Illyria, he leads his victims to acknowledge and rejoice in their own absurdities, and he leads some out of their self-love. Viola praises his folly in precisely these terms at the beginning of Act III: "For folly that he wisely shows, is fit" (III.i.65). Feste's catechism of Olivia (I.v.52–67) early in the play and his late conversation with Orsino (v.i.10–20) reveal Feste's own awareness of this role of proving others to be fools, playing their enemy but being their friend. As he says, we are all patched men, some "patched with virtue," some "patched with sin." If we cannot mend ourselves, we must "let the botcher mend" us (I.v.40–44). His work with Toby, Andrew, and Malvolio is a similar if sillier tailoring. Through all of this wisdom, however, Feste never loses sight of his own patched clothes or of the folly that they represent. He always knows that he is a fool. And in that knowledge he is, like Viola in her foolish disguise, most healthy and most wise.

Touchstone and Jaques have quite another role to play in *As You Like It.* Both of them seem superficially aware of the same Pauline and Erasmian commonplaces that Feste and Viola know so well. But though one is clearly an amateur fool and the other both a natural and a professional, neither can consistently admit that he is foolish. Jaques seems completely unaware that the motley coat he desires signifies first and foremost his certain knowledge that he is a fool. Touchstone, though more often aware of his patches, is just as likely to praise the wisdom of his own folly. Their lack of the wisdom of humility is almost always silly rather than sinister. Only Jaques occasionally tries our patience, along with that of Duke Senior and Rosalind, in his not-so-blissful ignorance. But we remain fond of both fools in the forest; we do not blame them too much for their folly.

In fact, their delightful naiveté about their own folly actually highlights the unusual degree of humility elsewhere in Arden.[3] Outcasts all, all seem aware of a common folly, personal and social if not cosmic as well. Duke Senior articulates this philosophy in his "sweet are the uses of adversity" speech, but in fact his attitude runs throughout the forest in courtiers and shepherds as well as lovers. With few exceptions, its inhabitants know their folly or readily learn of it, and they rejoice in the lesson. In one of his rare glimpses of this truth, Touchstone announces a lesson that most of the lovers in Arden would readily agree to: "We that are true lovers run into strange capers; but as all is mortal in nature, so is all nature in love mortal in folly" (II.iv.49–51). Orlando is delighted to be a fool in love: " 'Tis a fault I will not change for your best virtue" (III.ii.270–71). Rosalind, in the same scene and also madly in love, can proclaim as Ganymede:

> Love is merely a madness, and, I tell you, deserves as well a dark house and a whip as madmen do; and the reason why they are not so punished and cured is that the lunacy is so ordinary that the whippers are in love too. (III.ii.376–80)

Look at Oliver and Celia, or Orlando and Rosalind, or even Silvius and Phebe to see how variously this madness is exhibited and finally also embraced. The fools in Arden are those who would make fun of this strange love. The lovers are merely mad, and they know it and love it.

As a result of the unusually widespread humility and self-knowledge in Arden, the fools are consistently rendered foolish by trying to expose a folly that is already acknowledged, or a simplicity that is equally aware of itself. Touchstone glories in confounding the foolish rather than the wise. And while we enjoy his silliness with, say, the shepherd, we know at the same time that Corin is not damned for bringing his sheep together or for his lack of courtly manners. The shepherd's words of simple duty, absolute self-knowledge, and humility render the fool's role useless and elicit our admiration. In fact, he is wiser than the fool who is trying to demonstrate his folly:

> Sir, I am a true laborer; I earn that I eat, get that I wear, owe no man hate, envy no man's happiness, glad of other men's good, content with my harm; and the greatest of my pride is to see my ewes graze and my lambs suck. (III.ii.69–73)

William near the end of the play is similarly impervious to Touchstone's assault. He may be dumbfounded but he is not frightened by either the false learning or the silly blustering of Touchstone's challenge:

> To wit, I kill thee, make thee away, translate thy life into death, thy liberty into bondage. I will deal in poison with thee, or in bastinado, or in steel; I will bandy with thee in faction; I will o'errun thee with policy; I will kill thee a hundred and fifty ways. Therefore tremble and depart. (v.i.51–56)

William leaves, but hardly gasping for fear: "God rest you, merry sir" (v.i.58). For again Touchstone has delightfully proven only himself a fool. These humble innocents are beyond his wit and his wisdom. So is most of the assemblage in Arden.

Touchstone proves his own folly most decisively when he refers naively to Pauline and Erasmian commonplaces about folly and wisdom. The wise fool would use his humility to demonstrate the folly of the proud, the wise, and the powerful, but Touchstone exposes the humility of his quarry by proving his own foolish pride. First he thinks that William is a clown and he, the clown, is a wise man:

> It is meat and drink to me to see a clown; by my troth, we that have good wits have much to answer for. We shall be flouting; we cannot hold. (v.i.10–12)

Then he responds to William's relatively innocent "Ay, sir, I have a pretty wit" with this:

Why, thou say'st well. I do now remember a saying, "The fool doth think he is wise, but the wise man knows himself to be a fool."

(v.i.29–31)

The paradox, of course, is St. Paul's, filtered perhaps through Erasmus's *The Praise of Folie*.[4] But though Touchstone remembers it well, he understands or applies it poorly: "You are not *ipse*, for I am he" (v.i.43). He is proud of his wisdom rather than his folly. When William asks, "Which he, sir?" we know that he has proven Touchstone the fool in his own confounding innocence. The professional fool just doesn't have a chance in Arden.

Neither does the amateur. Jaques is just as adept as Touchstone at proving himself a fool, and just as unaware of the lessons of humility he might be learning. His first scene depicts Jaques as a melancholy fool who has no sense of the absurdity others enjoy in him. Of Amiens' song, he moans as painfully as any lover,

More, I prithee more! I can suck melancholy out of a song as a weasel sucks eggs. More, I prithee more!  (II.v.10–12)

Duke Senior and his brothers in exile love these sullen fits of folly; in fact they encourage them, though without sarcasm or bitterness:

I love to cope him in these sullen fits,
For then he's full of matter.  (II.i.67–68)

But Jaques, like Touchstone, is unaware of his own absurdity. Worse, he is therefore more scornful of that folly which he assumes lies only outside of himself. We see this naiveté throughout the play. But nowhere is it more obvious than in the scene with Amiens.

This is the scene in which Jaques sings his "ducdame" refrain about the universal folly in Arden:

If it do come to pass
That any man turn ass,
Leaving his wealth and ease
A stubborn will to please,
Ducdame, ducdame, ducdame.
Here shall he see gross fools as he.
An if he will come to me. (II.v.44–50)

Throughout the play Jaques evidences this frustrated desire to demonstrate the folly in others. Paradoxically, whenever he tries, he most clearly exposes his own. The Duke will indeed see a gross fool, Jaques, "if he will come to me." In explaining "ducdame," his mysterious invocation of fools, Jaques experiences the same paradoxical proof of his own folly. But again he will not accept it:

> 'Tis a Greek invocation to call fools into a circle. I'll go sleep, if I can; if I cannot, I'll rail against all the first-born of Egypt.
>
> (II.v.52–54)

The conjurer Jaques must be in the center of the circle, and therefore at the center of its folly. The railing Herod is the most obvious exemplar of the folly of pride in all of the mysteries; to our delight, Jaques completely misses the connection.

This blindness to his considerable folly continues throughout the play. With Duke Senior, in his next appearance, Jaques exults over seeing a fool in the forest:

> A fool, a fool! I met a fool i' th' forest,
> A motley fool! a miserable world!
> As I do live by food, I met a fool.
>
> (II.vii.12–14)

We know that Jaques could have seen himself in the fool's edifying glass. Touchstone is aping his melancholy, "deep-contemplative" moralizing "on the time." But characteristically, all Jaques can see is the folly of the fool:

> When I did hear
> The motley fool thus moral on the time,
> My lungs began to crow like chanticleer
> That fools should be so deep contemplative;
> And I did laugh sans intermission
> An hour by his dial. O noble fool,
> A worthy fool! Motley's the only wear.
>
> (II.vii.28–34)

He is already wearing it, of course, already being measured by the fool's dial. But he will not admit it.

As William asks of Touchstone, so Duke Senior asks of Jaques, which fool he refers to. We hear echoes of Feste trying to get Malvolio to acknowledge his share of universal folly in *Twelfth Night:*

"Are you not mad indeed? or do you but counterfeit?" (iv.ii.110–11).
But like Malvolio, albeit with more humor, Jaques remains naive: "O
that I were a fool! / I am ambitious for a motley coat" (ii.vii.42–43).
With "thou shalt have one," the Duke prods to Jaques to acknowledge
the patches that are his birthright. But against all of the Pauline and
Erasmian precepts to which he is at this very moment alluding, Jaques
still assumes his wisdom obvious, and has little sense of his folly:

> Provided that you weed your better judgments
> Of all opinion that grows rank in them
> That I am wise.                    (ii.vii.45–47)

He would be a wise physician to the "foul body of th' infected world"
(ii.vii.60), yet he cannot even diagnose his own sickness. The exas-
perated but still charitable Duke finally assaults his blindness directly.
"Physician, heal thyself," is the thrust of his remonstrance:

> Most mischievous foul sin, in chiding sin.
> For thou thyself hast been a libertine.
>                         (ii.vii.64–65)

Again Jaques evades the Duke's obvious lessoning. By taking the
Duke's thrust as an attack on satire, rather than on his own lack of
humility, he can go on pridefully playing one who "cries out on
pride" (ii.vii.70). His quick wit often allows Jaques to evade edifying humiliation. But this is a comic curse, as it was to Berowne and
Beatrice, not a blessing. For it deprives them all of the greater wisdom
of humility.

The two most familiar examples of the liabilities of his witty pride
occur in exchanges between Jaques and the lovers Rosalind and Orlando. As soon as we see Orlando absurdly tacking up verses all over
the trees in Arden we acknowledge the silliness of his love, but also
its attractiveness. Nowhere is the ambivalence more obvious than in
Rosalind's mixed delight and amusement over his actions. But Jaques,
like Touchstone, can only see the lover's folly, and must try again to
prove it. Instead, he is again the inevitable victim of his proof. For in
his relative humility Orlando is almost fool-proof, as in his witty
pride Jaques is always in absolute jeopardy.

ORLANDO. I will chide no breather in the world but myself,
against whom I know most faults.
JAQUES. The worst fault you have is to be in love.
ORLANDO. 'Tis a fault I will not change for your best virtue. I
am weary of you.
JAQUES. By my troth, I was seeking for a fool when I found
you.
ORLANDO. He is drowned in the brook. Look but in and you
shall see him.
JAQUES. There I shall see mine own figure.
ORLANDO. Which I take to be either a fool or a cipher.

(III.ii.267–77)

Like Malvolio, Jaques will accept neither humbling alternative, even
if he must therefore ignore what everyone else can see. Monsieur
Melancholy is for this reason far more fool than Monsieur Love. For
the latter knows himself to be a fool, and loves it.

With Rosalind, Jaques is again proven a fool for refusing to admit
his folly and its universality. All other melancholies may be foolish—
the scholar's, the musician's, the courtier's—but his is not (IV.i.10–
18). He similarly evades her exposure of the folly of his travels. And
then by sarcastically responding to Orlando's euphoric line of blank
verse ("Good day and happiness, dear Rosalind" [IV.i.27]) he slips
away from further proof. We can assume that Rosalind's parting shots
also fall on deaf ears, for Jaques cannot yet embrace this essential
comic lesson. Even Touchstone wears some humility in his tattered
suit, his foolish antics, and his foul wife Audrey, though he would not
be too well-married. But Jaques still finds the patched suit unbearable.
As a result, he cannot share the experiences of marriage or festivity
which conclude the play. Hymen implies in his final blessing of the
fools and lovers that Touchstone's marriage with Audrey will not last
long. But Jaques, who will hazard neither love nor folly, will therefore lose this chance at festive joy. His departure from the revellers
suggests his inability to celebrate the wisdom of their mutual folly; he
thus remains alien to their paradoxical happiness. Our response to his
departure is not satisfaction, however, but a Jaques-like melancholy of
our own. For we like him still, and we wish him well. After all, he is
our fellow in folly, even if he does not know it yet.

## ii. The Follies of the Play

Uniquely, then, most of the follies that Jaques and Touchstone expose are their own. The few follies they do hit upon in Arden are usually either the unpretentious silliness of innocents and simpletons or the assorted madnesses the lovers have already joyously acknowledged. But the play contains over sixty references to "fool," "folly," "foolish," and related morphemes. Where is the rest of this folly? Oddly, much of it lies outside of Arden, and even outside the world of the play, providing these two fools with some "matter" for their flouting wits in spite of the unusual humility of Arden's inhabitants. The rest lies in the romantic and pastoral fabric of the play itself. Because Shakespeare allows these fools to expose the follies of his dramatic medium and its sources along with their anatomies of general behavioral absurdities, he leads us to understand how the folly of the play and the folly of the players coalesce in *As You Like It*. If the Forest of Arden is an unusually humble place, so is the play itself. For it fosters in Jaques and Touchstone its own worst critics, and smiles like the lovers at the acknowledged follies they persistently try to expose.

Though anatomies of universal follies are among their most familiar moments in the play, few readers have noticed that Jaques and Touchstone are exposing follies that lie for the most part outside of Arden. Touchstone's anatomy of the courtier is in this category (v.iv.42–46), as is his subsequent analysis of the seven "degrees of the lie" (v.iv. 65–97), the "Retort Courteous," the "Quip Modest," the "Lie Direct," and the rest. So is his earlier proof that the knight "that swore by his honor they were good pancakes, and swore by his honor the mustard was naught" was not forsworn (i.ii.59–63). Jaques's anatomy of the seven ages of man (ii.vii.139–66) and his explosion against pride in the same scene also anatomize universal or general follies that lie largely outside of the boundaries of Arden. Both of them are rather successful with this abstract kind of foolery, and Touchstone probably deserves the Duke's praise, "He uses his folly like a stalking horse, and under the presentation of that he shoots his wit" (v.iv.100–101). But while Touchstone and Jaques make us mark the universal pageant of man's general folly, they also emphasize its relative absence in Arden, except among themselves. Jaques's seven ages, like Touchstone's seven degrees of the lie, is a conventional set-piece, a "progress" leading nowhere, a denial of value. So when they try to expose specific and widely acknowledged follies among the lovers, the country-folk, and the exiled court, they expose more of their own absurdity.

But the fools also expose the follies of the play, follies inherent in its pastoral and romantic sources as well as follies unavoidable in the conventions of drama. That Shakespeare gives his fools this latitude suggests that his comic attitude toward folly has grown to include the work itself and its author. As in *A Midsummer Night's Dream* this humility also includes the audience, which is willing to be taken in by these aesthetic follies even after having been made aware of them. We find a similar attitude in *Twelfth Night,* and see its culmination in *The Winter's Tale.* Shakespeare exhibits this aesthetic humility in various ways in *As You Like It,* with implications that are finally epistemological too. In fact, many critics—C. L. Barber, John Russell Brown, T. M. Parrott, and Sylvan Barnet, among others—have noticed the play's fascination with itself as a strangely conventional, pastoral, romantic, and dramatic creature.[5] Because its unusual self-criticism is so widely accepted, we need to review only a few of the most vital moments when the fools, or the play itself, exposes the strange tactics a play sometimes has to use to imitate reality.

We have already mentioned some examples of the fools' exposures of this aesthetic folly. Some of it simultaneously exposes the folly of the lovers. Jaques responds to Orlando's line of verse in the midst of a prose exchange with, "Nay then, God b' wi' you, an you talk in blank verse" (iv.i.28–29). Earlier Touchstone has his own go at Orlando's verse (and Rosalind's charming sentimentality) with parody as well as direct criticism:

> Sweetest nut hath sourest rind,
> Such a nut is Rosalinde.

He that sweetest rose will find
Must find love's prick, and Rosalinde.
(III.ii.104–7)

Admittedly Orlando's verse is not good: "This is the very false gallop of verses. Why do you infect yourself with them?" To Rosalind's response, "Peace, you dull fool! I found them on a tree," he responds, "Truly, the tree yields bad fruit." It does indeed. But both Rosalind and Orlando can smile good-naturedly at the inevitable folly of this conventional expression of their love, even while they are earnestly committing it. The feelings of Orlando are as true as the verse or the courtly pose is false. It takes a bright fool, a Rosalind or a Shakespeare, to know and to cherish this inner truth as she smiles at its outer folly, and to learn how to pick the meat out of the shell.

Touchstone has another go at romance after Silvius describes his love for Phebe in hopelessly conventional terms: "as true a lover / As ever sighed upon a midnight pillow" (II.iv.23–24). Witness Silvius's inexpressible passion:

Or if thou hast not broke from company
Abruptly, as my passion now makes me,
Thou hast not loved. O Phebe, Phebe, Phebe!
(II.iv.37–39)

This too is textbook stuff, hack work, both the cardboard lover and his verse. But they remind Rosalind of a truer love not all that far removed from this highly conventional one:

Alas, poor shepherd! Searching of thy wound,
I have by hard adventure found mine own.
(II.iv.40–41)

Lest we be swept up by her passion, however, Touchstone offers his fool's version of romantic ecstasy. It smacks of love's prick rather than its spirit, and it therefore serves as a vital corrective for the absurdities which true lovers, not to mention their portrayers and viewers, can commit:

I remember, when I was in love . . . the kissing of her batler, and the cows' dugs that her pretty chopt hands had milked; and I remember the wooing of a peascod instead of her, from whom I took two cods, and giving her them again, said with weeping tears, "Wear these for my sake." We that are true lovers run into strange capers; but as all is mortal in nature, so is all nature in love mortal in folly.

(II.iv.42–51)

This little ritual or sacrament of the cods fleetingly suggests the Communion words, "He toke the cuppe, and when he had geven thankes, he gave it to them, saying, . . . drinke it in remembraunce of me" (p. 103). With Touchstone's odd fetishes, it reminds us that the follies of mortal lovers are indeed rich and strange. Such a silly moment corrects a romantic atmosphere that had briefly become too sentimental and too conventional with a healthy dose of comic realism.

The pastoral's tendencies towards philosophising and sentimentality are other conventions both Touchstone and Jaques assault through parody and direct criticism. Touchstone must be mocking Jaques's melancholy philosophizing when he "morals on the time" in front of him. Less consciously, Jaques is Shakespeare's agent of a criticism of similar extremes directed against Duke Senior and his fellow pastoral exiles. To lament the "poor dappled fools" who "should in their own confines . . . have their round haunches gored" (II.i.22–25) is silly stuff all by itself. Jaques's moralizing of this spectacle "into a thousand similes" carries it beyond the brink of absurdity. He stands on the bank, "weeping and commenting / Upon the sobbing deer" (II.i. 64–65). When the first lord describes the weeping of the wounded deer, whose "big round tears / Coursed one another down his innocent nose / In piteous chase" (II.i.38–40) he could as well have been describing Jaques's compassion for the deer as the deer's self-pity. Such extremes are unfortunate characteristics of the pastoral mode. By exaggerating them in Jaques, Shakespeare makes the exiles' folly and that of the genre obvious and funny to all of us.

Similar is Touchstone's confrontation with Corin right after we have heard the first of Orlando's poetical efforts. Its foolish anatomy of the shepherd's life is nonsense on the one hand, but good sense too. Pastorals tend to praise the outdoor life too uncritically. But in truth, whether we are selecting ways of living or dramatic modes, most of our choices are teasingly relative. So is the reality these choices seek to achieve or express:

Truly, shepherd, in respect of itself, it is a good life; but in respect
that it is a shepherd's life, it is naught. In respect that it is solitary,
I like it very well; but in respect that it is private, it is a very vile life.
Now in respect it is in the fields, it pleaseth me well; but in respect
it is not in the court, it is tedious. . . . Hast any philosophy in thee,
shepherd?                                                  (III.ii.13–21)

Literary genres, ways of living, the conventions of artists or lovers'
games, rituals, and disguises—all are partly true and partly false, too
sentimental or not sentimental enough, adequate in this respect, and
inadequate in that. Only a pastoral or a romantic vision that accepts
and celebrates the folly of this relativity has achieved the Pauline and
Erasmian humility that underlies so much of Shakespeare's comic wisdom. Neither Touchstone nor Jaques has this wisdom, at least not
consistently. But during this momentary wit-strike, and while they
parody and criticize the pastoral and romantic conventions of their
play, they at least suggest it to us.

In the scene that follows this one, Touchstone makes the play's
most important statement about the relative truth of its aesthetic conventions. Characteristically, he doesn't understand what he has said.
But if we listen to him we will realize that the folly of the play is
analogous to that of the lovers. The reason is that the conventionality
of art, like that of courtship (or religious ritual), is a great feigning
that can express great truths, so long as it doesn't take itself too seriously. In making this important connection for us, albeit absurdly,
Touchstone leads us, Bottom-like, to sense the epistemological as well
as the aesthetic dimensions of the themes of faith and folly in Shakespeare's romantic comedies.

The scene is well-enough known. Touchstone is trying to explain
to Audrey the concept "poeticall." In this role he is intriguingly like
Bottom blundering into his appropriate paraphrase of St. Paul when
he needs to express the inexpressible. Jaques betrays his continuing
misunderstanding of the paradoxical wisdom of folly when he comments on this vehicle of truth: "O knowledge ill-inhabited, worse than
Jove in a thatched house!" (III.iii.7–8). Audrey then sets Touchstone
up with one of the great straight lines in comedy: "I do not know what
poetical is. Is it honest in deed and word? Is it a true thing?" (III.iii.

14–15). Touchstone replies with unknowing Sidneyan and Platonic sublimity: "No, truly; for the truest poetry is the most faining." We are all familiar with Plato's indictment of poetry as an imitation, "three removes . . . from the truth," which "tends to destroy the rational part."[6] Where Touchstone picked up this piece of Platonic lore is anyone's guess; but that he is about to abuse it is a sure bet.

A logical progression of this warped Platonism is his assumption that only foulness guarantees honesty: "Praised be the gods for thy foulness" he tells Audrey. And later he tells Duke Senior, "Rich honesty dwells like a miser, sir, in a poor house, as your pearl in your foul oyster" (v.iv.57–59). Beauty, like poetry, is most feigning. Touchstone will therefore trust only the opposites of the appearance of truth. The kernel of truth must be distinguished from the chaff and the husk. But the figure of the pearl is much more appropriate to Touchstone in *As You Like It* than that of wheat and chaff, for with it Shakespeare exploits the unexpectedness of imaginative insight, the suddenly perfect, polished shape out of the rough barnacled mass, the pearl out of the mouth of the philosophic oyster Touchstone. Erasmus and St. Paul would have found him a fit spokesman.

For there is wisdom here as well as absurdity. If we look closer at Touchstone's indictment of poetry as "most faining," we will see that his sloppy syntax has caused him to proclaim the value of poetry, its truth rather than its folly. "For the truest poetry is the most faining," is what he acually says. The husk and the chaff are the stuff of the shadow world, the specific moment, *scientia,* accidence. The wheat, the pearl, is the kernel of truth, *sapientia.* The unique capacity of art and of ritual is to capture the primary, the sapiential, in an enduring form. As Sidney says, great poetry does not affirm accident; therefore it never lies. It is not "labouring to tell you what is, or is not, but what should or should not be."[7]

The greatest truth requires as its only adequate vehicle the most elusive and imaginative aesthetic conventions. The truest poetry must therefore always be the most feigning. This is why the great poets must always walk on Ferlinghetti's tightrope across the abyss of folly ("Constantly Risking Absurdity"). In case we are not following the gist of his banter with Audrey, Touchstone then relates this paradox about the reality of artistic conventions to the truth of the feigning conventions of lovers. Again he stumbles upon the wisdom: "and lovers are given to poetry, and what they swear in poetry may be said, as lovers, they do feign" (III.iii.17–18). When Audrey asks him, "Do you wish then that the gods had made me poetical?" he replies incongruously, "I do truly; for thou swear'st to me thou art honest. Now, if thou wert a poet, I might have some hope thou didst feign." His apparent contradiction must go in this direction: if Audrey were poetical, her swearing of honesty would mean lightness, and the shortsighted Touchstone could seduce her on the spot. He would gain then a goat-woman indeed, tarnished physically as well as spiritually, a foul pearl in a foul oyster, the least poetical woman possible. Luckily for him, she is not quite that.

Related types of true if foolish feigning in *As You Like It* are games and similar moments of playing and fantasizing. These frivolities remind us on the surface of childishness and of unsophisticated literary modes. At the same time they can also express and enact complex relationships among characters, and complex epistemological insights. The wrestling, for example, so obviously symbolic as a clash of values and perspectives, is also an image of Orlando's lovelessness and Frederick's loveless society. Grown men should not have to wrestle with such pretty women looking on and wanting to join the fray ("The little strength that I have, I would it were with you" [I.ii. 178]). Running away from home, the courtship game, aimless philosophizing about nature and fortune, playing Robin Hood, carving on trees, saving a brother from a snake or a lion, and then forgiving him and finding him regenerated, love at first sight, oaths, magicians, the rituals and miracles of love—all of these beautifully childish and dreamlike feignings are facets of "inscape" which become almost literal in Arden. The reason is Shakespeare's genius, of course, but also the fact that games and related feignings and follies are natural to the human condition. Literalness is no more natural than figurativeness, nor is work more real than play, or reason than fantasy.[8] Only severely limited perspectives like those of a single-minded individual or a single literary mode would categorically prescribe one reality and exclude the others. Shakespeare keeps all of his options open in *As*

*You Like It* by simultaneously enjoying and exposing the folly and the loveliness, the artificiality and the naturalness of all of these conventional games and rituals, these related feignings of man and of art.

Nowhere is this attitude more obvious than in the play's own amused self-criticism. Jaques and Touchstone have pointed out some of its aesthetic follies, but they have characteristically assumed that they shared none of them. In contrast to their uninvolved parody, and more like Rosalind's spirited role-playing, *As You Like It* gamely tries on the foolish, conventional, ritualistic garb of the comic and the romantic and even the satiric stage, and seeks to incorporate all of their shreds and patches into a new, comprehensive comic vision. Since the form of burlesque suggests that no single perspective—be it romantic, pastoral, idyllic, melodramatic, satiric, ironic, mythic, or what you will—can adequately express the complexity of reality, perhaps a blend of them, a comprehensive comic vision to match the comprehensiveness of reality itself, is the only adequate perspective. Shakespeare seems in *As You Like It* to be confirming his belief in the truth of the feignings of composite artistic conventions and modes by exposing the relative dishonesty of each of them individually, and then including valid parts of each perspective into his larger vision. This is so widely acknowledged a characteristic of the play that only a brief survey of its pertinence to our thesis will be presented here.

The play is full of aesthetic follies so grotesque and obvious that they must be calling attention to their own absurdity. It flaunts its folly by exaggerating its conventionality. The first scene, for example, begins and ends with a long, dreary piece of prose exposition, much like Prospero's speeches to Miranda in Act I, Scene ii of *The Tempest*. Rosalind's epilogue makes fun of this inauspicious beginning. The whole play is also strangely devoid of developing action, as the series of tableaux in Act II makes clear. Time stands still in the forest for more reasons than the lack of a clock. Further, characters like Duke Frederick and Oliver are so unabashedly villainous as to be mere humors of jealous ambition. Perhaps that is why they can be so easily converted when they enter the forest of Arden. The pastoral excesses in Duke Senior's first scene ("Sweet are the uses of adversity") are equally obvious as flauntings of the follies of the dramatic and pastoral modes. The bathetic responses to the sobbing, sentient deer, whose "big round tears / Coursed one another down his innocent nose / In piteous chase" (ii.i.38–40), like the moralizing on those "native burghers," is foolish enough for many readers to catch a jangling note of absurdity before Jaques's obvious parody to come. But if this sentimental moralizing is pretty foolish, so is the overblown ideality, language, and sentiment of the prelapsarian Adam, the perfect pastoral servant, talking to his equally perfect master Orlando: "O my gentle master, O my sweet master, O, . . ." etc. (ii.iii.2–4). He will follow Orlando "to the last gasp." We may also gasp at this, but not for admiration alone. Still, with many of these pastoral and dramatic excesses there is delight in indulging our sentimentality and our pastoralism, even while we recognize its folly. We relish the "tongues in trees, books in the running brooks, sermons in stones, and good in everything" even as we know that it is not quite true, a pastoral feigning in style and content. The same might be said of the anaphoric exchange of Orlando and Duke Senior in Act II, Scene vii (ll. 113–23). Part of the magic of *As You Like It* is that we can have it either way, critically or conventionally, or even both ways at once. In a similar celebration of its aesthetic folly, the play just stops for Jaques's oration "All the world's a stage" in Act II, Scene vii. For all of its rhetorical beauty it is a thoroughly conventional set-piece expressed with a naive cynicism. But at the same time, Jaques's evocation of the trope of the theater of the world, however accidentally, can reinforce our understanding of man's inevitable folly and his ultimate need for humility, his position as actor in a moral universe before an eternal auditor. The theme of humility in *The Tempest* derives from a similar use of the same trope by Prospero. Such aesthetic follies are legion in *As You Like It*, and they have been often observed. They parody the pastoral romance from which the play is descended while simultaneously including *As You Like It* securely within that genre and also securely within the community of folly.

In a similar combination of parody and celebration, Touchstone and Audrey and then Silvius and Phebe parody the romantic love of Rosalind and Orlando, but they also expand our understandings of its dimensions. For the extreme physicality of the clowns and the extreme conventionality of the pastoral figures are both true if feigning (and faining) aspects of the richer relationship of the primary pair. Like the love at first sight which we like in Orlando and Rosalind, and Oliver and Celia, but howl at in Phebe and Touchstone (or Olivia and Viola, or Bottom and Titania in related situations), we are forced to be aware of the "most feignings" of character, action, theme, and verse before we are allowed to celebrate their great truths as well. If we like it we can laugh at the follies and love the profundities at once. "For ever and a day" cannot be accepted uncritically into this vision. But it can be included, if it is willing to be criticized: "Say 'a day,' without the 'ever'" (iv.i.133). And so as audience we must always be *en garde* as well, lest we enjoy one of these conventional phrases, actions, sentiments, philosophies, too uncritically. This is a strenuous aesthetic vision that involves us in its wise humility. But it is also a joyous one.

Three of its cleverest manifestations come when Shakespeare connects the conventions of romance with highly conventional and ostensibly dramatic religious forms. We have already mentioned the faint echo of Communion in Touchstone's "sacrament" of the cods. Orlando and Rosalind also occasionally talk like the Student and Master of the Catechism during his instruction as a lover. Later they join Silvius and Phebe in an elaborate litany of love. These last two parallels deserve closer attention.

When Rosalind instructs Orlando "who Time ambles withal, who Time trots withal, who Time gallops withal," etc. (iii.ii.294–96), the style of questions and answers is clearly a parody of the catechism. The Master-Student relationship is part of that parody, but more important is the imitation of the unnatural style of the genre, a style itself based on the feigning of a dramatic situation. Orlando's lifeless questions about time ("Who doth he trot withal?," etc. (iii.ii. 297, 303, 309, 313)) are met by Rosalind's equally repetitive and unimaginative answers, paradoxically livelier here because they are so dull. Also like the catechism is the analysis of each answer into four- or six-part responses. They recall the familiar "How many parts hath the Lord's Prayer?" or "Into how many parts dost thou divide this whole confession of faith?"[9] One can imagine the frustration of schoolboys and girls trying to memorize such abstract and repetitive material. That experience is not likely to have been forgotten, or to have been remembered too fondly, either. "To answer in a catechism" is to answer predictable questions in dull and lifeless responses. Celia herself refers to this unpleasant if necessary conventionality during the same scene (III.ii.216–17), making sure that no one misses the parody to come. Paradoxically, even the flatness of this conventional religious form edifies and orders, and thereby justifies its own stilted aesthetic existence.

The highly conventional litany to love is sung by the four lovers just after Rosalind-Ganymede has promised to resolve all of the complexities that their feignings have wrought (v.ii.79–109).[10] Its hyperbolic conventionality, as well as its antiphonal form ("And I for Ganymede. / And I for Rosalind. / And I for no woman") is again grotesquely contrived. Can love possibly be all of these things, this incredible combination of outward signs and inward qualities? Could any lover be so dedicated? They are all posing, or lying, or exaggerating. And yet even the one who is consciously feigning, Rosalind-Ganymede, is only literally feigning. Secretly she is rejoicing with the rest, rejoicing even more because of her secret and the joy that she holds for them all. What of the conventionality of their litany? Is it so patently conventional? Notice the gradual transition from the artificial into the genuine, from the mechanical into the fluid. Notice the lovely crescendo as Silvius moves into the spirit of his hymn. It builds to "observance" and to "humbleness" and then the decrescendo begins, out of that moment of ultimate reality and ultimate convention, back to the conventionally juxtaposed "patience and impatience," back to the pure and passionless "trial" and the repeated "observance." That repetition combined with the awful, fourfold, later refrain ("If this be so, why blame you me to love you?") suggests on the one hand that the litany is running down. But simultaneously, repeating "observance" emphasizes the importance of observance not only to love but to any type of ritualized celebration. Observance makes the abstract concrete, expresses the inexpressible, like art, like ritual, like these words of Silvius. The conflicting and hyperbolical qualities of love are qualities confirmed by and contained in his litany. Likewise the direction of the celebration is carefully contrived: from sighs and tears to faith and service; from symptom to symbol; from fantasy to faith; from belief to worship; from protestation to celebration, the observance of belief, its manifestation. This characteristic moment has much to say of romantic faith and romantic folly, of the truth as well as the falsehood of the rituals and the conventionality of humankind.

One of the most outlandish of all the aesthetic conventions in *As You Like It* is the appearance of Hymen, a *deus ex machina,* in the final scene. The natural magic of Rosalind would have been quite sufficient, thank you, for the resolution of the plot. Like our first reaction to Adam's praise of his master, Orlando's catechism, or the lovers' litany, we may want to gasp or laugh out loud at the audacious folly of this moment. But while the appearance of such a figure makes fun of all conventionally contrived romantic endings, it also leads the audience, in the spirit of humility that permeates *As You Like It,* through its own ritual of romantic celebration, just as Silvius earlier led the lovers' litany. This most conventional dramatic creature, a feigning, a mere symbol, a figure of speech upon the stage, encourages us to celebrate the reality that we have learned to perceive in conventionality, games, and all of the playlike ritualistic qualities that enrich and direct human life. Laughable as Hymen is, a patent feigning, he still represents and embodies the audience's common and charitable wish for successful love and general comic happiness.[11] Such an "embodiment," such a "representation," might be all Hymen was ever supposed to stand for, as a god or a dramatic character. The greatest feigning is again the truest. Placing as it does the audience's most festive and charitable wishes before them on the stage, it merges stage and audience, confirming again the frequency of romantic and dramatic miracles, and the impossibility of expressing great truths without little lies.

But best of all of these moments of aesthetic self-criticism is Rosalind's epilogue, which once and for all explicitly admits the play's folly and its feignings and rejoices in it. First, it bluntly reminds us that the play also started with Orlando's long, undramatic prose passage, and criticizes both conventions: "It is not the fashion to see the lady the epilogue, but it is no more unhandsome than to see the lord the prologue" (ll. 1–3). She continues in this vein with her analogy between good wines and good plays: "If it be true that good wine needs no bush, 'tis true that a good play needs no epilogue; yet to good wine they do use good bushes, and good plays prove the better by the help of good epilogues." From the obvious humility of considering the play no better than a good wine, Rosalind goes even further into the play's folly. It is neither a good epilogue nor a good play: "What a case am I in then, that am neither a good epilogue nor cannot insinuate with you in the behalf of a good play!" Still, she will not be a beggar on behalf of this foolish play. Rather she will be true to its title by asking her audience merely to like as much of it as pleases them. Playfully, she suggests that the play, and the pleasure, can be understood in more than one way when she asks that "between you and the women the play may please" "for the love you bear to women." And then comes that most magical moment of all, when Rosalind exposes the play's last and best "feigning" and admits the folly of her pretended womanhood: "If I were a woman I would kiss as many of you as had beards that pleased me, complexions that liked me, and breaths that I defied not." But she is not a woman, in spite of our belief in that most faining, a belief that has ripened almost into love by the magic of Shakespeare's conjuring. She is a boy actor who has been playing a woman playing a young man, and now she is a boy actor again. And so we must bid farewell to her false "case" with the rest of the dramatic illusions. This last piece of dramatic self-criticism is also the best. For it takes us right to the center of the folly and the wisdom of the imaginative contract between the audience and the play. Rosalind's final, literal stripping away of dramatic conventions confirms and celebrates the intricate conventionality of man, in love, in art, in society. Her profound foolishness, like Touchstone's, encourages us to understand how the rituals of any society may contain their most elusive truths. If they are sometimes the "most faining" it is because they are intricately allied to the least.

It is a paradox with Erasmian and Pauline precedent that characters like Bottom and Touchstone stumble forth in Shakespearean comedy to lead us to its profoundest truths. In *A Midsummer Night's Dream* the lovers are all mad, but they are also divinely mad. In *As*

*You Like It* the lovers and the poet are all liars, but the audience is gladly fooled. In *The Praise of Folie* Erasmus cites St. Paul's authority when he reminds us that romantic dreamers and religious visionaries are "nere sybbe" in their madness and in their bliss. Harry Caplan suggests that like other Neoplatonists, Pico della Mirandola knows the possible folly of the imagination. But he also acknowledges its occasional necessity: "Higher faculties . . . cannot do without it; only let them guide it therefore, and it may act as the lens through which the intellect beholds the truth, it may prove to be the instrument of good prophesy, it may have part in the revelations of faith, and on it, as on wings, the mind may rise to contemplation of things divine."[12]

Touchstone has tried to tell us something like that in *As You Like It*. The lovers and the play itself are the imaginative pearls within the foul oysters of romantic and pastoral conventions. The audience is asked to share this humility by knowing how much it needs such feignings to understand such truths. But however we respond to the follies the play parades before us, we cannot criticize them condescendingly. For the play's aesthetic humility disarms that criticism by anticipating it, much as a character's ethical humility disarms the arsenal of the fool. Only the observer who must be condescending, like Jaques, remains immune to its festive happiness. And even Jaques is included in its wide-armed embrace of folly.

## iii. The Folly of the Lovers

Touchstone's blundering philosophizing and Rosalind's epilogue leave little doubt that *As You Like It* is intensely interested in the realities that transcend the greatest feignings of fools, lovers, and artists. Man requires conventional rituals and roles to embody otherwise inexpressible feelings and truths, and to convey them to others.[13] But absurdity can result from an inadequate understanding of this conventionality. Touchstone is one extreme exemplar of such folly. He tries on as many roles as he has observed—lover, traveller, courtier, scholar, literary critic, philosopher, duellist, husband—but he can only be an insensitive parodist, a fool, a stone, in each of them. On the other extreme is the contemplative Jaques, who anatomizes but resists all roles. As a result he remains a mere observer of life, uninvolved in most of the follies and the joys of its earnest if foolish conventionality. He is even more a fool, as Rosalind tries to tell him, for this uninvolvement. But he recognizes his folly even less than Touchstone, and he would not change it.

Unlike Touchstone, the other characters, according to their capacities, reveal even while they experience it the complex truth which underlies their conventional feignings. The vision of *As You Like It* is not the satiric *Narrenschiff* Jaques might have presented but an affirmative celebration of man's follies and his potentialities. The widespread roleplaying that goes on among most of them heightens the positive, creative connections between psychological and aesthetic conventions. And these connections, paradoxically, are highlighted by the character, Jaques, who seems to understand them least, during his cynical anatomy of the world as a stage. The others discover what he may never know, that all of the roles people (or artists) play can be creative as well as static, profound as well as foolish, and are often both at once. But when they work, these aesthetic or romantic conventions, these rituals and roles of artists and lovers, can lead to expressions and understandings of otherwise inaccessible truths. Their mutual feignings thus emerge from the comic vision of *As You Like It* as legitimate and essential ways to understand and cope with the humbling reality of man's finitude.

Orlando and Rosalind are the most realistic pair of characters in the play, but they engage us also as the most feigning. That their elaborately conventional behavior both edifies them and enriches their characterization illustrates how central the concept of "most faining" is to the play's vision of the wisdom of folly. It is precisely because the emotions and impulses of love are so erratic, so powerful, and so confusing that love's seemingly foolish rituals and conventions, like those of art and religion, can serve such vital functions. Each of these feignings channels chaotic impulses into creative, acceptable, and comprehensible patterns, patterns which do not have to be rediscovered by each new lover, but which rather are the common legacy of all. Their gamelike, ritualized behavior in Arden thus frees Orlando and Rosalind from the stumbling, tongue-tied attempts at communication that they undergo at their first meeting. It simultaneously frees them from embarrassing frankness, from the "base truth" of their physical impulses, and from the threat of its direct, nonfigurative, sexual gratification. Orlando is given a voice by these formal and prescribed rituals and games, even if for a while it is a foolish voice. Rosalind as Ganymede is given a protective if foolish disguise against her lover and herself. Their feignings, their romantic rituals, are therefore true in many ways. They control their love, making it more formal than it really is—more orderly—giving it a prescribed, repeatable, and socially acceptable form of expression. They direct their intensely personal, even idiosyncratic emotion into a universalized form, which grants it dignity and importance. And they remind the lovers of their continuing folly while allowing them to express and refine their enduring love.

That they can embrace the folly of this feigning as well as its exhilarating joy attests to their unusual comic wisdom. It also points to their role in the play's analogous aesthetic vision. Like the play, and unlike Jaques, both Rosalind and Orlando are fully aware of their own folly and of the inescapable folly of love. Also like the play, as Mark Van Doren notices, both of them delight in that folly without ever becoming cynical about it.[14] J. D. Palmer has recently suggested that the lovers' unusual awareness of their own folly is connected to the play's theme of universal feigning: "There is a general agreement in the play that, as the song puts it, 'most loving is folly,' and accordingly Rosalind's counterfeit wooing is intended not merely to ridicule the foolishness of lovers, herself included, but to make it fully aware of itself in terms of a charade, a pretense, in which it is foolish to be wise."[15] Orlando "will chide no breather in the world but myself, against whom I know most faults" (III.ii.267–68). Rosalind knows that if "love is merely a madness . . . the lunacy is so ordinary that the whippers are in love too" (III.ii.376–80). They obviously share a joyous understanding that love, like faith, is a manner of madness. That understanding is surely related to Erasmian and Pauline paradoxes.

Orlando loves Rosalind at first sight, and he continues to love her throughout the whole play. The "heavenly Rosalind" of their first meeting is a faith from which he never substantially wavers, through all of the tests his love must encounter. But that first faith is strengthened by the conventional postures, the feignings, that both Orlando and Rosalind go on to assume. On their first meeting he can say nothing:

> Can I not say 'I thank you'? My better parts
> Are all thrown down, and that which here stands up
> Is but a quintain, a mere lifeless block.
>
> (I.ii.230–32)

By the time he has reached Arden, he says far too much, in bad verses pasted upon every tree:

> O Rosalind! these trees shall be my books,
> And in their barks my thoughts I'll character.
>
> (III.ii.5–6)

But this howling, love-struck, tree-carving Petrarchan lover, like the earlier speechless one, will be laughed out of his excessive conventionality by the criticism of Touchstone and Jaques as well as Celia and Rosalind, so that by the beginning of Act IV he will have only a single line of blank verse: "Good day and happiness, dear Rosalind" (IV.i.27). This is still too much for Jaques, but it represents a considerable moderation in Orlando's excessively conventional and foolish behavior.

Orlando's sudden change into the humor of a Petrarchan lover continues to parody the play's literary heritage and its own conventionality. But it also reveals a momentary narcissism and a reluctance to grow up that Orlando must overcome. Like the antics of the gentlemen of *Love's Labor's Lost,* Orlando's false pose is too much surface and too little substance, therefore an impediment to both growth and self-expression. Orlando must learn that he can "live no longer by thinking" (V.ii.48), at least like this, too conventionally, in ways that obscure emotions and spirit rather than expressing them. Certainly the courtly pose is far less deeply ingrained in Orlando than it is in Berowne, and therefore more easily cured by Rosalind. But Orlando's immaculate dress, like his belief that a perfect woman loves him, must bother Rosalind; both excesses betray too much self-love, not just a conventional posture. Paradoxically, Rosalind's disguise, her feigning as Ganymede, functions to erode the false surface of Orlando's courtly humor and his narcissism at once, and thus frees him to love her more truly. This contrast between productive and unproductive folly, like the change finally effected in Orlando, is nicely opposed to Jaques's static anatomy of the seven ages of man. Man is not doomed to be the lover, though he may have to learn just how much of the lover to avoid and how much to keep by trying on the whole role briefly. Folly like Orlando's can free as well as enslave, especially if a Rosalind is around.

Much like his satiric counterpart, Silvius, Orlando is also something less than a man in his courtly pose. As Rosalind justly asks Celia of his versifying, "Is it a man?" Celia's answer, "And a chain that you once wore, about his neck" (III.ii.172), reminds us that Orlando is, indeed, a man, victorious over both Charles and Rosalind. But it also suggests distressing if amusing changes since then. Even before his effeminate and immature courtliness, Orlando's love of Rosalind seems to have cost him some manliness. If he has overthrown more than his enemies, he is also left somewhat impotent in Rosalind's presence after the wrestling:

> My better parts
> Are all thrown down, and that which here stands up
> Is but a quintain, a mere lifeless block.
> (I.ii.230–32)

Silvius is similarly emasculated by Phebe's scorn. As Rosalind admonishes him, "Well, go your way to her, for I see love hath made thee a tame snake" (IV.iii.70–71). That both of them finally become better men through Rosalind's feigning intervention as a man, and that Rosalind and Phebe also become less masculine through the same contrivance suggest that Shakespeare is having a bit of fun with their androgynous relationships. A similar interest in shifting sexual roles in Rosalind's epilogue suggests its relationship to the whole play. Like the other roles and elements the play depicts and satirizes—fools, philosophers, the artistic form—so even the most basic human roles of male and female are never absolute. On the most basic physiological level of Touchstone's relationship to Audrey, the man needs the woman, the woman the man, for sexual satisfaction. In another sense, there is some yin and yang, some *res extensa* and some *res cogitans,* some dominance and some submissiveness, in all of us. Especially is this ambivalence true during adolescence, "as a squash is before 'tis a peascod, or a codling when 'tis almost an apple" (*Twelfth Night,* I, v.151–52). Having to court another man—an effeminate one at that, appropriately called "Ganymede"—is the perfect purgative to drive out Orlando's excessive courtliness and his immaturity, along with his sexual ambivalence. But neither Orlando nor Rosalind can reject all such ambivalence, or they would both become as simplistic as a Charles or an Audrey, a virtuous Adam or a villainous Frederick. The sorting out, the juggling, never completely end. One can never be completely male, or mature, or natural, without becoming as static as the frozen portraits of Jaques's ages. If such ambivalence, social or sexual, is embarrassing, it is also an inevitable folly of the maturing personality. Shakespeare has ingeniously woven these ideas into the roles and disguises in *As You Like It.*

Orlando's related conventional assumptions about "the beloved" are also moderated by the edification of Rosalind-Ganymede, who has more than academic reasons for wanting to dispel his extremest expectations of his lover. Even Rosalind could never live up to his image of her perfection, and she would reject it if she could. For such a static posture of Platonic perfection is really no role at all for her; it is rather a non-role, another meaningless convention. Nor could Rosalind ever live with a rhapsodic sap who thinks that people die for love. So she tells Orlando, "Men have died from time to time, and worms have eaten them, but not for love" (IV.i.96–98). The stories to the contrary are "all lies," most feignings. Still, it must be pleasant and flattering for Rosalind to have a lover who momentarily believes in them, or one who would not be cured of his love except to prove his faith (III.ii.449). It is likewise both silly and exciting for her to find those verses everywhere. Orlando is proving himself a good Petrarchan lover and a good man even as he is being cured of the worst excesses of his tribe. And Rosalind, in spite of her own good taste, rather likes it.

Another important lesson for them both is the lesson of the horns that Benedick and Beatrice also grapple with in *Much Ado about Nothing*. No woman is perfect; many are quite imperfect. Orlando must at least acknowledge the possibility of imperfection in Rosalind before his edification is complete. Their love-game will dispel his excessively conventional faith in all women; but at the same time it will intensify his faith in one woman, Rosalind. We never seriously think, despite her warnings, that he will have any reason to repent this faith.

She begins her lesson during their first meeting in the forest. Women are "touched with so many giddy offenses" (III.ii.330) that they can hardly be recounted. Among them are many of the roles Rosalind-Ganymede will play in the courting game:

> changeable, longing and liking, proud, fantastical, apish, shallow, inconstant, full of tears, full of smiles; for every passion something and for no passion truly anything, as boys and women are for the most part cattle of this color; would now like him, now loathe him; then entertain him, then forswear him; now weep for him, then spit at him. (III.ii.385–91)

Of Rosalind's actual relationship to these roles we shall have more to say later, but we can see that their catalogue here is designed to disillusion the excessively trustful Petrarchan lover of his naive image of the beloved. She is likely to prove less than perfect, if better than this.

Specifically, she is likely to cuckold him. This threatening imperfection is the focus of Ganymede's assault on Orlando's continued faith in their next meeting. The destiny of any husband is "horns; which such as you are fain to be beholding to your wives for" (IV.i.54–55). Orlando is sure to meet "your wife's wit going to your neighbor's bed" (IV.i.155). And he will find her ever changeable:

> Maids are May when they are maids, but the sky changes when they are wives. I will be more jealous of thee than a Barbary cock-pigeon over his hen, more clamorous than a parrot against rain, more newfangled than an ape, more giddy in my desires than a monkey. I will weep for nothing . . . when you are disposed to be merry; I will laugh like a hyen, . . . when thou art inclined to sleep.
> (IV.i.135–42)

In short, she might be jealous, henpecking, fashion-conscious, lecherous, opposite in all things—the perfect shrew. Of course she will not, but she could be any or all of these things at one time or another, and Orlando no less than Benedick must at least be aware of the possibilities to appreciate what he actually gets, and to be forewarned of what could be his. If Benedick fears too much of this, Orlando fears it too little, and Rosalind's game is an important corrective for his naiveté. The song of the foresters about horns (Act IV, Scene ii), the constant, blessed state of cuckoldry, is a conventional statement of the same truth about human imperfection.[16] Without that awareness, Orlando will never be ready to wed, for he will be unable to expect, let alone cherish, the imperfection that is his, hers, and everyone's.

Rosalind also becomes more worthy of love and more aware of herself as a result of the games that she plays with Orlando and the Petrarchan masks that she tries on. In fact, there is an extremely complex character behind the feignings of her role. Her disguise as Ganymede results from expediency, to be sure. It also betrays to a degree her own reluctance to mature and a decided enjoyment of controlling the action, of dominating events and people. She looks forward, for example, to playing a man:

> Were it not better,
> Because that I am more than common tall,
> That I did suit me all points like a man?
> A gallant curtal-axe upon my thigh,
> A boar-spear in my hand.    (I.iii.111–15)

She has also promised Orlando that she will try to dominate him once they are wed. There is some truth in her role and her promise, and Orlando had better heed it.

The ritualized courting of Rosalind and Orlando, while certainly a game they both enjoy, grants her the proper courting she deserves as the daughter of the Duke. It also provides a civilized context she can control even though she is in Arden. For while they go through those conventional, even silly paces of boy courting boy, she is truly well-courted and Orlando well-trained in courting. Both are also thus protected from the potential folly of their unchecked passion. Further, as

Rosalind enacts the conventions and rituals of the disdainful maiden—scorn, indifference, impatience, haughtiness, jealousy, spite, sarcasm, cynicism, and most of the others—she is doing more than parodying the conventional Petrarchan woman, though she is certainly doing that. She is also trying those postures on in a context in which she cannot be held accountable, much as the lovers in *A Midsummer Night's Dream* can behave madly, violently, and cruelly without personal blame because of Puck's magic potion. Rosalind is evaluating, like Orlando, the excessive postures of the courted woman, and approaching womanhood and the *via media* as a result of their game.

A good example of the complexity of her feigning occurs during her response to Orlando's verses. Though she can lament the lame feet and the tedious homily of his words as she plays the traditionally disdainful maid, she can also be secretly delighted that they are written to her. Thus Touchstone's assault on their "false gallop" and their "bad fruit" is aimed more at Rosalind's edification than at Orlando's: "If the cat will after kind, / So be sure will Rosalinde." Her kind, Touchstone is saying, is the nutty fool of love: "Sweetest nut hath sourest rind, / Such a nut is Rosalinde" (III.ii. 98–99, 104–5). Her folly in loving the verses while she pretends to criticize them is especially clear when she tries lamely to defend them and herself against Touchstone's criticisms: "Out, fool! . . . Peace, you dull fool! I found them on a tree" (III.ii. 94, 110). As the fool says of these attempts to avoid embarrassment, "You have said; but whether wisely or no, let the forest judge" (III.ii.116–17). This is one of his few chances to expose unacknowledged folly in the play, and he does it brilliantly. For the nuts who read and secretly love such bad verses are of the same kind as the nuts who write them. And "truly, the tree yields bad fruit" (III.ii.111). Though that is momentarily an embarrassing folly for Rosalind to bear, it is also a joyous one.

Its joy becomes obvious in her later exchange with Celia, which she begins by feigning indifference and scorn towards the poet. But after Rosalind's criticism of the tedious and lame verses ("I was never so berhymed since Pythagoras' time that I was an Irish rat, which I can hardly remember" [III.ii.168–69]), she is soon beside herself to find out who wrote them, and to confirm her hope that it is Orlando:

> I prithee tell me who is it quickly, and speak apace. I would thou
> couldst stammer, that thou mightst pour this concealed man out of
> thy mouth. . . . Is he of God's making? What manner of man? Is
> his head worth a hat? or his chin worth a beard?
>
> (III.ii.188–96 passim)

And then when it is confirmed, this recently and soon-again-to-be
disdainful maiden sputters out her joy and her love in a foolish and
delightful explosion of questions too many for Gargantua's mouth to
answer:

> Alas the day! what shall I do with my doublet and hose? What did
> he when thou saw'st him? What said he? How looked he? Wherein
> went he? What makes he here? Did he ask for me? Where remains
> he? How parted he with thee? and when shalt thou see him again?
> Answer me in one word. (III.ii.208–13)

Because this delicious exuberance, this high folly, this near madness
of her womanly love bursts quite through her feignings both as Ganymede and as the haughty mistress, we are never in any doubt that
Rosalind is truer than Ganymede: "Good my complexion! Dost thou
think, though I am caparisoned like a man, I have a doublet and hose
in my disposition?" (III.ii.185–87). Fortunately for us and for Orlando, even her most feigning is never that true. Here, and when she
faints at the sight of the handkerchief, the true folly of her great love
is most manifest. The folly and the joy are both conveyed again just
after this exchange by the continued images of nuts and fruits. Celia
answers Rosalind, "I found him under a tree, like a dropped acorn."
And though Rosalind can hardly have forgotten Touchstone's recent
chiding, she has little doubt about the quality of the fruit this oak tree
bears: "It may well be called Jove's tree when it drops forth such
fruit" (III.ii.225–26). When she later says in the most horribly conventional Petrarchan style, "he comes to kill my heart," we see that
Rosalind and Orlando are nuts of the same tree, and we smile and are
delighted.

There are other brilliant glimpses of the true Rosalind through her
feigning with Orlando, and we consistently see her womanhood better
because she is playing the man. When, for example, she questions Or-

lando's lack of the proper symptoms of love, "lean cheek," sunken eye, "beard neglected," "shoe untied" and the rest (III.ii.352ff.), she is reciting romantic conventions that don't always represent reality. But she is also a bit distressed that Orlando does not conform more exactly with the textbook lover, and voices that distress through her feigning. She is still a little unsure of him; do those neat clothes suggest vestiges of narcissism? In a similar way her test of his faith is a real test as well as a game. She enjoys the excuse to be around Orlando, but she would also like to be as sure of his love as possible. Of course absolute surety is not vouchsafed to the true lovers in Shakespearean comedy. Hazard is a major ingredient of love's folly and its faith. And Rosalind always has some sense of hazard, though Orlando is as sure a bet as Shakespeare will depict.

Rosalind's distrust, her fear of imperfection, surfaces more clearly when we see Rosalind-Ganymede again. She "will weep," even if "tears do not become a man," because Orlando is late. "His very hair is of the dissembling color" she says, and yet, "I'faith, his hair is of a good color." Celia chides her with more of the nut joke: "An excellent color. Your chestnut was ever the only color. . . . But why did he swear he would come this morning, and comes not?" A question to be asked. For Rosalind, no less than Orlando, must learn of her mate's possible imperfections as she tests his faith in her. Perhaps he is a "worm-eaten nut," without "verity in love" (III.iv.1–23 passim). As Celia says, you are a fool to believe in a brave young man, especially in Arden:

> O, that's a brave man; he writes brave verses, speaks brave words, swears brave oaths, and breaks them bravely, quite traverse, athwart the heart of his lover, as a puisny tilter, that spurs his horse but on one side, breaks his staff like a noble goose. But all's brave that youth mounts and folly guides. (III.iv.36–41)

But Rosalind chooses to be that fool, despite her doubts; so later does Celia with the tarnished but redeemed Oliver. Their choice of such folly represents a faith in more than feigning, and it is destined to end happily for both of them.

C. L. Barber comments best on this paradoxical lesson on their mutual fallibility that Orlando and Rosalind must both undergo:

> As Rosalind rides the crest of a wave of happy fulfillment, . . . we find her describing with delight, almost in triumph, not the virtues of marriage, but its fallibility. . . . Ordinarily, these would be strange sentiments to proclaim with joy at such a time. But as Rosalind says them, they clinch the achievement of the humor's purpose. Love has been made independent of illusions without becoming any the less intense; it is therefore inoculated against life's unromantic contradictions.[17]

That they can both learn so much of their folly and simultaneously strengthen their faith in one another through the charade Rosalind-Ganymede conjures for them in the forest is one of the great achievements of Shakespeare's art. It continues to draw strength from the Erasmian and Pauline paradoxes about faith and folly that lie behind it, even though those paradoxes are more deeply submerged than they were in *Love's Labor's Lost, A Midsummer Night's Dream,* or *Much Ado about Nothing.*

Rosalind's upbraiding of Orlando for being an hour late is also more than a mere feigning, though she quickly enough forgives him for his snail's pace. After all, he has only stood up a stand-in, and so he can hardly be blamed for making light of the transgression. Though we know better, this whole relationship seems to him a feigning pure and simple, and it is one that he will increasingly tire of. In the sequence that follows, Rosalind directs her own courting, and edifies Orlando as well as she can concerning the Petrarchan excesses he still exhibits, especially his naiveté about perfect women. Her playful feigning ends with another promise to meet in the forest. After Orlando's departure, she reminds us again of the true love that lies behind her feigned cynicism: "O coz, coz, coz, my pretty little coz, that thou didst know how many fathom deep I am in love!" (IV.i.189–90).

Then she almost destroys her cover by swooning over the bloody napkin (IV.iii.157). And Orlando finally does tire of the feigning: "I can live no longer by thinking" (V.ii.48). The conventions of lovers are supposed to free as well as restrict. Their rituals are supposed to allow the lovers to express inexpressible feelings, to perceive imperceivable truth, and to sense their communion with all past and future lovers. Like the conventions of religion or of art, the lovers' observances can make them larger than themselves, at least momentarily. But they are also feignings that are less than life, and finally their celebrants must return to the world of the body as well as the mind. For none of us can live forever by thinking, and least of all can lovers, unless they are of the hopelessly ethereal kind (like Orsino through most of *Twelfth Night*). Even he must finally see Viola in her woman's weeds, as must Orlando now in *As You Like It*. His feignings, like Rosalind's, were "most true"; but because of that they must finally be superseded by that elusive experience we like to call "real life." That return to the literal is also the thrust of Rosalind's epilogue. The fools have paradoxically deprived themselves of this joy by remaining oblivious to their own folly. The play has revelled in its absurd conventionality, and found there its "greatest poetry." The lovers, by embracing the follies of their feignings with an analogous joy, have evidenced the spiritual health they share with the play's attitude toward itself. They have also equipped themselves for the vicissitudes, as well as the joys, of life ever after. Their delicious balancing of play and seriousness, artifice and realism, folly and profundity, defines and emphasizes the atmosphere of humility in which the whole play must be understood.

Again, this strenuous comic vision demands an unusual degree of assent from the audience. Shakespeare and his audience must share a healthy sense of their mutual inabilities to express or understand the inexpressible and the inconceivable for the play to work fully. J. D. Palmer has already suggested that the self-conscious role-playing of the lovers and Shakespeare's playfulness with his art both involve the audience in "the equivocal relations between fiction and reality, game and earnest, folly and wisdom."[18] The blundering foolery of Touchstone and Jaques also contributes to this vision, especially when Touchstone discusses the "most faining" of artists and lovers. So, we will recall, did Bottom's Pauline allusions and the lovers' Erasmian ones as they awoke to a new wisdom in *A Midsummer Night's Dream*. Both plays, because they display an interest in the limits of human understanding and expression, would naturally have drawn upon and suggested such familiar and analogous Erasmian and Pauline paradoxes about foolish wits and wise fools.

## iv. The Folly of the Liturgy

We have seen, through the folly of the fools, the lovers, and the play itself, how completely *As You Like It* investigates the realities that lie behind the conventions and rituals of human behavior and the aesthetic experience. We have suggested the epistemological dimensions of these interests and their Pauline and Erasmian contexts. But David Bevington, Jonas Barish, and Russell Fraser have also argued that the play touches, however obliquely, a heated Renaissance liturgical controversy. All three of them understand the play, partially, in terms of the contemporaneous Puritan-Anglican conflict between asceticism and artifice. To them, and to me, this widely fought controversy seems analogous to the distrust of artistic and psychological "feignings" we have found expressed so overtly and so ironically by Touchstone in the middle of *As You Like It*. We lack the numerous explicit allusions which invited us to pursue and understand the pertinence of another doctrinal controversy in *Love's Labor's Lost*. But in *As You Like It* a persistent interest in the ritualism that characterizes so much human activity, be it romantic or aesthetic, plus Touchstone's glance at a central issue of the controversy, the concept of "most faining," encourage us to pursue at least a few general parallels.

Fraser argues that the Puritans distrust the religious rituals and rites of the Anglican church (music, vestments, candles, crosses, genuflection, and the like) because they, like Touchstone, are unimaginative Platonists. They cannot see that these "most fainings" might be attempts to express or represent the "greatest poetry" of faith, as something "more than pure reason ever comprehends." To the Puritan mind any concrete representation of spiritual or abstract truth must be suspect because it feigns man's ability to perceive the ineffable.[19] David Bevington suggests how broadly such a dispute could have applied to the age and the play:

Shakespeare insists . . . on the fallacy of oversimplifying the appeal to withdrawal, whether to courtly artifice or to ascetic plainness. . . . Man cannot turn his back on social rituals of legal contract, hierarchy, and divine worship. The appearance of the outcast Orlando in the forest prompts Duke Senior to think not of society's ingratitude, but of their joint need for the dignified forms of civilization that must be reclaimed.[20]

And so the duke invites Orlando, and Old Adam too, to share their communal feast: "Sit down and feed, and welcome to our table" (II. vii.104). Such sharing reminds both of them of similar shared social rites and rituals in better times. Both Duke Senior and Orlando have

> with holy bell been knolled to church,
> And sat at good men's feasts, and wiped our eyes
> Of drops that sacred pity hath engend'red.
> (II.vii.121–23)

Barish takes this demonstration one important step further by showing that the distrusted religious ritual is often explicitly compared by the Puritan controversialists to the equally abhorred feignings of the stage:

From Tyndale onward, through the writings of the anti-vestiarian polemicists, the controverters of the mass, the anti-episcopal satirists, the admonishers and apologists and animadverters, expounders of doctrine and compilers of cases of conscience, popish liturgy is scornfully likened to the theater, and much picturesque invective mustered to drive the point home. For Thomas Becon, the priests come to the altar like "game-players" to a stage, in "Hickscorners apparrell," in "gay, gawdie gallant, gorgious game-players garments." For the conciliatory Bishop Jewel, the "scenic apparatus of divine worship" is a "tawdry" thing which Christians should be able to do without; the sacraments should cease to be ministered "like a masquery or a stage play." For John Foxe, the decay of the primitive church meant that Christ's true votaries were supplanted by "a new sort of players, to furnish the stage, as school-doctors, canonists, and four orders of friars." Ridley informed his superiors that the prescribed ministering garments were "abhominable and foolishe, & to fonde for a vice in a playe," and when Hooper, in 1551, to the disgust of the zealous, consented to preach in them, he was said to have come forth "as a new player in a strange apparel . . . cometh forth on the stage." . . . And John Rainolds, inveighing against the stage, finds room for particular censure of "the profane and wicked toyes of *Passion-playes*, . . . procured by *Popish Priests*," who, "as they have transformed the celebrating of the Sacrament of the *Lords supper* into a *Masse-game*, and all other partes of the *Ecclesiasticall service* into *theatricall sights*; so, in steede of *preaching the word*, they caused it to be played." [21]

His vivid details illustrate both the customary outrage of the Puritan controversialists and their repeatedly pejorative references to the "playing," the feigning rituals, the games that mar the pure worship of God. In this contemporaneous play that is persistently interested in both the truth and the folly that underlies the "playing" of lovers and artists, Touchstone talks to Audrey about the feignings of both groups, and tells her that "the greatest poetry is the most faining." And Jaques tells us in a set-piece that "all the world's a stage." Such interests at a moment when drama as well as ritual was under severe Puritan attack suggest intriguing if elusive parallels between the play and the controversy. Speaking of such parallels, Fraser sees *As You Like It* only as a "bucolic lament for an age already and irremediably past." [22] But Bevington finds the play tactfully committed to the preservation and defense of many "social rituals." The play argues through being rather than through rhetoric that a man, like a work of art, needs psychological, social, political, legal, and religious rituals if he is to remain fully a man, and fully civilized. [23] I am persuaded by his argument and by the argument of the play that Bevington is correct. If he is, the religious dimensions of Shakespeare's treatment of faith and folly in *As You Like It* would have been all the more visible for his audience.

A discussion of general relationships between art and liturgy by Romano Guardini in *The Spirit of the Liturgy* suggests in conclusion how natural it would be for a play like *As You Like It* to reflect issues of the liturgical discussion through the paradox of the wisdom of folly. Appropriately, his discussion begins with the intuitive wisdom of the child. Child-play at its spontaneous, affirmative best is analogous to art or ritual, but precedes them both in time. It is a type of prelapsarian art or ritual, "purposeless but full of meaning nevertheless." "Because it does not aim at anything in particular, because it streams unbroken and spontaneously forth, its utterance will be harmonious, its form clear and fine; its expression will of itself become picture and dance, rhyme, melody and song. That is what play means; it is life, pouring itself forth without an aim, seizing upon riches from its own abundant store, significant through the fact of its existence" (p. 179). Art and liturgy, to Guardini, must try to recreate this intuitive wisdom of the child. To do so they would both teach profound truths indirectly rather than directly, by "being," in Bevington's term. They would immerse the audience, like the child at play, in the aura of truth itself: "The liturgy wishes to teach, but not by means of an artificial system of aim-conscious educational influences; it simply creates an entire spiritual world in which the soul can live according to the requirements of its nature. . . . [Like art] it is not a means which is adapted to attain a certain end—it is an end in itself" (p. 177).

But art, finally, can only attempt to represent "the higher life of which [man] stands in need, and to which in actuality he has only approximately attained. The artist merely wants . . . to give external form to the inner truth." The liturgy, though it uses many of the forms and methods of art, can actually re-create something of the lost wisdom of the child:

> In it man, with the aid of grace, is given the opportunity of realizing his fundamental essence, of really becoming that which according to divine destiny he should be . . . a child of God. . . . Because the life of the liturgy is higher than that to which customary reality gives both the opportunity and form of expression, it adopts suitable forms and methods from that sphere in which they are to be found, . . . from art. It speaks measuredly and melodiously; it employs formal, rhythmic gestures; it is clothed in colours and garments foreign to everyday life; it is carried out in places and at hours which have been co-ordinated and systemised according to sublimer laws than ours. It is in the highest sense the life of a child, in which everything is picture, melody and song.
> Such is the wonderful fact which the liturgy demonstrates; it unites art and reality in a supernatural childhood before God.
> (Pp. 180–81)

This analysis of the relationships between art and liturgy inevitably brings to mind the vision of both of Shakespeare's epistemologically oriented comedies, *A Midsummer Night's Dream* and *As You Like It*. What Mircea Eliade has said of religious symbols is equally true of the feignings of these two plays: "They unveil the miraculous, inexplicable side of life, and at the same time the sacramental dimensions of human existence."[24] Hymen is as useful in the latter as the fairies are in the former in representing this miraculous dimension of human experience. Bottom and Touchstone help us understand our epistemological folly in relationship to it. For man's imagination can be as erratic and as undisciplined as his behavior, as Pico, Erasmus, and St. Paul all suggest.[25] But that imagination, for all its madness, is also partly divine. Through this faculty man can contemplate the transcendental, and devise liturgical and artistic rituals to aid that contemplation. In such a context Jaques's "all the world's a stage," and Touchstone's "the truest poetry is the most faining," like Bottom's "most rare vision," are as relevant as they are naive. If they are obviously foolish as they grope toward these profoundest awarenesses, so are we all most foolish when we attempt to transcend our own finitude. At such moments our epistemological kinship to these Erasmian fools is almost inescapable.

A recent critic of relationships between comedy and Christianity, Nelvin Vos, reminds us how traditional and how timeless this Erasmian and Pauline identification of such folly and such wisdom really is. He asserts that comedy has always combined the incarnational view of man (only human) with the eschatological one (more than human). We laugh both at and with the comic victor/victim because he is "the image of dignity intermingled with frailty." He both unmasks "the incongruous involvement of the finite and the infinite" and also affirms it. In so doing, the fool—the Touchstone and the Jaques, the Feste, the Falstaff, the Bottom—helps us see "that the grossly human and the grandly sublime" are "wonderfully and repugnantly mixed" within us.[26] The wisdom of such folly is not the whole truth of *As You Like It*. But it is an important part of that truth. We have ignored the play's Erasmian Touchstones long enough.

# CHAPTER VI

# "Man's Estate"
# The Festival of Folly in *Twelfth Night*

*Twelfth Night* offers an embarrassment of riches to the student of faith and folly in Shakespeare's romantic comedies. Feste's donning of the curate's robes in his ministry to Malvolio could have invited Shakespeare's audience to recall the familiar Erasmian and Pauline identification of the fool and the curate. It could also have suggested again their paradoxical reversals of folly and wisdom. Prodding that memory, Feste and Viola allude pointedly to such paradoxes when they talk about the task of bringing their friends to a humility that enables them to love one another and rejoice in their shared folly. As in *Much Ado about Nothing,* edifying humiliation again has a central place in Shakespeare's comic action. When Feste's Epilogue alludes to St. Paul's most famous passage about folly and maturity ("when I was a childe"), we are directly invited to understand the attempted edification of Orsino, Olivia, and Malvolio within this doctrinal context. Liturgy, like art, can lift a man to the wisdom of a child. But the willful childishness of a spoiled brat, St. Paul seems to say, must be replaced by humble maturity if one is ever to reach "man's estate." The Pauline passage is therefore as central to the self-willed isolation and eventual cure of Orsino and Olivia as it is to Malvolio's refusal to grow into humility, and his resultant absence from felicity. Folly is more central than faith to this comic vision. Illyria, unlike Arden, is chock full of unacknowledged fools. But when Sebastian glories like Erasmus in his romantic madness just when Malvolio madly refuses to acknowledge his share of folly, we understand how faith and folly are again thematic confederates. In fact, the opposition of Sebastian's faith and Malvolio's is the basic structural and thematic principle of the fourth act.

Further, the play's festival title reinforces these Pauline and Erasmian allusions and analogies. If the play has the fitting amount of festival misrule, it has as well its share of appropriate festival regeneration. Not surprisingly, there has already been some critical interest in the liturgical context of *Twelfth Night*. C. L. Barber and John Hollander, for example, have demonstrated that the play incorporates the Saturnalian form and spirit of the Christmastide social festival, particularly in its use of "a 'Festus' or 'Lord of Misrule' to preside over the maskings, interludes, music, song, and other merrymaking." Other critics have debated Leslie Hotson's intriguing but generally unaccepted thesis that the play might actually have entertained the English court on Epiphany, 1601.[1] But only two, Marion Bodwell Smith and Barbara Lewalski, have paid much attention to the possible parallels between the play and the religious season its festival title also suggests. Their observations suggest that both the liturgical festival and the play embody Erasmian and Pauline reversals of folly and wisdom to a degree that warrants further consideration.

Lewalski finds Illyria widely troubled by the flaws of ill-will and self-love. Malvolio, whose name literally means "ill-will," manifests both flaws in his refusal to forgive his enemies and in his denial of all Christmastide revelry. Toby Belch loves himself too much, but is named for his Saturnalian overindulgence, his excess of good will. Olivia and Orsino, in their overabundant refinement and self-esteem, and in their preposterous and self-indulgent vows about love and grief, are, like them, severely flawed. Sebastian and Viola, on the other hand, are by Lewalski's account two outsiders miraculously delivered from death who will minister to these imperfect Illyrians. They both embody and teach the basic values of the play and the season—good will and selfless love, forgiveness and humility. Viola's love of Orsino is exemplary and finally edifying in its selflessness; with her considerable help, Sebastian inspires a similar love in Olivia, and exemplifies it himself. With the possible exception of one brief moment in Act V, I do not follow Lewalski's argument that these two characters are light comic types of the incarnate Christ. I do, however, agree that the attempt to edify the prideful characters of Illyria without losing their good will is a central challenge of the comedy, and an appropriate action for a comedy named after the eve of Epiphany.[2]

Smith's most important contribution to my understanding of relationships between the liturgical occasion, the play, and Pauline and Erasmian paradoxes about faith and folly comes when he associates *Twelfth Night* the play and Twelfth Night the festival with the Feast of Fools and its traditional praise of folly. In playing the curate, Smith continues, Feste may suggest the role-reversals associated with the church's Feast of Fools, a celebration commonly occurring on Epiphany in such cathedrals as Lincoln and Berkeley: "Feste, of course, reverses the rite: the fool plays the curate, not the curate the fool, but the transition, as his rapid alternation of roles indicates, is an easy one."[3] In addition to this second, ecclesiastical Lord of Misrule, the play also shares with the festival many speeches in praise of folly: "A set speech in praise of folly [like Viola's, III.i.57–65] was a common feature of Christmas celebrations. . . . Feste . . . garners tributes . . . from almost everyone but Malvolio. However, Sir Toby's justification of his turning night into day, the Duke's glorification of his foolish love, Olivia's soliloquy of love for Cesario, and Malvolio's of self-admiration, are also instances of the praise of folly by fools" (p. 115). These ironic instances, we might add, are also reminiscent of Touchstone and Jaques in *As You Like It*.

Lewalski, Barber, Hollander, and Smith all link several strands of sociological, ecclesiastical, and theological traditions associated with Epiphany to the fabric of its dramatic namesake, *Twelfth Night*. The most important of them are also pertinent to this study of the Pauline and Erasmian paradox of celebrated folly in Shakespeare's romantic comedies. As Smith says in concluding his chapter, "the comic inversions of *Twelfth Night* have demonstrated, each in its appropriate time and place, the folly of wisdom and the wisdom of folly" (p. 122). Both Lewalski and Smith associate the festival's motif of enlightenment with the play's movement towards clarification. But neither of them gives enough emphasis to the festival's secondary theme of the humility of Christ and the humiliation of mankind, a theme that defines the nature of that clarification in this and other Shakespearean comedies. This would be a good time to consider that influence.

Epiphany celebrates the revelation of Christ's deity and his hu-

manity to the Gentile world, represented by the Magi. It also celebrates the effects of the Incarnation, mankind's rebirth into humility
and concord. The Collect, the Gospel story of the journey of the Magi,
and both Lessons for the day, Isaiah 49 and 60, all use imagery of
glorious light to stress the brightness of Christ's coming and its agency
in man's enlightenment.[4] "Arise, shine, for thy light is come, and the
glory of the Lord is risen upon thee," a text for Handel's "The Messiah," is probably the most familiar of these passages today.[5] Through
this great light man can escape the impure blackness of his ignorance
and sin, "the darknesse & cloude [which] covereth the earth and the
people" (Is. 60:2). Light was also the first creation in Genesis, and
the sign which drew the wise men to Christ.

But this Christ was a child in a manger, not a king in a palace.
Humility is as prominent a part of the Epiphany celebration as exal-
tation. Christ's humiliation, God's condescension to become man that
He might become manifest to man is one of the great paradoxes of the
Incarnation. As Donne says, "Hee suffered his *Divine nature* to ap-
peare and shine thorough his *flesh,* and not to swallow, or annihilate
that flesh." To profit from this great light, then, man must both
humble himself before Christ's brilliance and embrace the paradox of
His humility. Christ's blessings are available, Donne continues, only
"If with that little candle [scripture] thou canst creep humbly into
low and poore places, if thou canst finde thy Saviour in a *Manger,* and
in his *swathing clouts,* in his humiliation, and blesse God for that
beginning" (3:360).[6] Lancelot Andrewes emphasizes the same paradox of Epiphany in many of his Christmas sermons: "Humility then:
we shall find Him by that sign, where we find humility, and not fail;
and where that is not, be sure we shall never find Him."[7] The theological and the psychological reasons for this lie in the fall of Adam:
"By pride he perished. . . . Then, by humility to be recovered, according to the rule, *Contraria curantur contrariis"* (1:206). Horton
Davies emphasizes the prominence of this tradition in Renaissance
England: "At the heart of Anglican piety there was the awed wonder
at the condescension of the God-man, sheer adoring amazement at the
humility of the Incarnation."[8] It is interesting, then, that humility, so

central a virtue of the festival, is also central to the comedy whose title invites associations with Epiphany.

Feste also deserves a much closer look than he has previously received. He does represent the Christmastide spirit of good will, as Lewalski and Smith suggest. But his sharp consciousness of his curate's role in edifying the other fools in Illyria and his clear understanding of its Erasmian and Pauline contexts suggest that he, with Viola, embodies and facilitates a wise festivity that transcends his merely Saturnalian name.[9] Unlike Touchstone and Jaques, his naive counterparts in *As You Like It,* Feste knows just what he is about, and he does it well. Of course, he is not frustrated, as they were, by an abundance of humility. Unacknowledged folly is almost everywhere in Illyria; humility is a rare commodity, at least until Viola and Feste have taught Orsino and Olivia their catechisms of folly by the end of the play. Only Malvolio will be immune to these lessonings, and his exclusion from the final festivity is defined by his unwillingness to admit his great folly. Sebastian is his opposite. By glorying in Act IV in his infirmities, his divine madness, he wills himself great joy. "What you will" is what you get in this festive comedy. Looking more closely than Lewalski or Smith at the attempted edifications of Orsino, Olivia, and Malvolio, Feste's disguise as curate, and Sebastian's unusual humility should increase our appreciation of the significant role of acknowledged and celebrated folly in Shakespeare's romantic comedies. It should also strengthen our sense of the ties between that comic vision and the words of St. Paul and Erasmus. For both of them receive prominent acknowledgment again in *Twelfth Night.*

## i. Olivia and Orsino

Lewalski and Smith rightly assume that the enlightenment of Olivia and Orsino are directly apposite to the festival of Epiphany. Of course their humiliating edification, their final acknowledgment of their common follies, has equally important roots in the Pauline and Erasmian traditions. Both characters begin the play in love with themselves. Olivia's pride takes the form of her self-indulgent posturing as a grief-stricken sister. Orsino's is embodied in his self-indulgent poses as a Petrarchan lover. The thrust of much of their comic action in *Twelfth Night* is designed to disabuse them of their amusing but ultimately anti-festive attitudes, embodied in their extremest forms in Malvolio's pride and Toby's self-indulgence.

As Hollander suggests, Olivia's intended monasticism is an emblem of her absurdity. She is "no true anchorite, but, despite herself, a private glutton." Instead of a charitable commitment to God or the service of others, her literal taking of the veil is an "immersion in committed self-indulgence."[10] She perfectly complements Orsino's hunger for the foods of love in the same scene (i.i.1–4). Feste attacks this folly and her sin of self-love as soon as she appears on the stage. In fact, he catechizes her in order to initiate her acknowledgment of folly, the basis of comic and Christian joy:

> CLOWN.        Good my mouse of virtue, answer me.
> OLIVIA. Well sir, for want of other idleness, I'll bide your proof.
> CLOWN. Good madonna, why mourn'st thou?
> OLIVIA. Good fool, for my brother's death.
> CLOWN. I think his soul is in hell, madonna.
> OLIVIA. I know his soul is in heaven, fool.
> CLOWN. The more fool, madonna, to mourn for your brother's soul, being in heaven. Take away the fool, gentlemen.        (i.v.57–67)

This well-known passage reflects Feste's approach to the folly of pride throughout the play. Give it enough rope and it will hang itself; give it enough exposure and it will mend. His method is at the same time comically cathartic; as the priest of folly he brings his victims, who become his beneficiaries, to goodnatured admissions of their own folly by making them enact it for themselves. This is also the manner in which he handles Malvolio's "catechism" later. But Malvolio is neither honest nor humble enough to mend. Because Olivia is even now able to smile at her folly and laugh at his wit, her edification is already underway.

She even asks Malvolio, "What think you of this fool, Malvolio?

Doth he not mend?" (i.v.68–69). Her metaphor of the tailor comes from Feste's use of the same figure at the beginning of the scene. He is, by his own anatomy, a botcher of souls, his motley dress botched by and illustrative of his own acknowledged human imperfection:

> Bid the dishonest man mend himself: if he mend, he is no longer dishonest; if he cannot, let the botcher mend him. Anything that's mended is but patched; virtue that transgresses is but patched with sin, and sin that amends is but patched with virtue.　　(i.v.40–44)

We are all patched men; all of us are imperfect. Only when Olivia realizes this consistently about herself will she be free to marry wisely and join the community of patched men in festive humility.

Viola has her fool's turn with Olivia too, and the mistakes that arise from their relationship humiliate Olivia until they make her humble. Unlike Feste's ministry to folly, Viola's is less conscious and less contrived. In part she conveys it simply by being selfless in love; in part her disguise as page to Orsino forces the role upon her, since Olivia can only humiliate herself by begging for the love of a page, not to mention a woman. But Viola understands her role as Olivia's fool, just as she knows how to praise Feste's folly. That praise of folly, so rich in Erasmian overtones and so much a part of Epiphany, is also so well known as to require no commentary:

> This fellow is wise enough to play the fool,
> And to do that well craves a kind of wit.
> He must observe their mood on whom he jests,
> The quality of persons, and the time;
> And like the haggard, check at every feather
> That comes before his eye. This is a practice
> As full of labor as the wise man's art;
> For folly that he wisely shows, is fit;
> But wise men, folly-fall'n, quite taint their wit.
> 　　　　　　　(iii.i.58–66)

As with the lovers in *As You Like It*, it is the wisdom of Viola's humility that usually protects her from the fool's talons. Just before this praise of Feste's folly she has had to parry his thrust herself ("I think I saw your wisdom there," he says, invitingly). Because of her humility she is able to parry with "Nay, an thou pass upon me, I'll no more with thee" (III.i.40–42). Of course, her disguise is her inescapable folly; but though she knows this, even her humility cannot extricate her from the humiliating duel that arises with Sir Andrew. And so she is challenged to "strip [her] sword stark naked, . . . or forswear to wear iron" (III.iv.234–36). Providence will extricate her from this moment of folly, but her involvement with Antonio, the sea captain, will still take a while to run its embarrassing course.

Just after Viola parries Feste's exploratory thrusts, and praises his folly, she in turn must play Olivia's fool. As she does so she is clearly aware of her role as fool, and actually analyzes it for us. Olivia, hopeless now in her love for Cesario as well as her continuing vanity, again asks to be proven a fool, this time by commanding the page: "Tell me what thou think'st of me." Viola's response is as effective a ministry to her pride as anything Feste can muster:

> VIOLA. That you do think you are not what you are.
> OLIVIA. If I think so, I think the same of you.
> VIOLA. Then think you right. I am not what I am.
> OLIVIA. I would you were as I would have you be.
> VIOLA. Would it be better, madam, than I am?
> I wish it might, for now I am your fool.
> (III.i.136–41)

The first thrust is directed at Olivia's pride in her personal appearance as well as her sense of deserving. She assumes that she can have any man she wants, and have him on her own terms. Witness the haughty if playful "inventory" of her beauty earlier (I.v.230–35). Even that early, Viola replies, "I see you what you are; you are too proud; / But if you were the devil, you are fair" (I.v.236–37). Viola the fool stalks on. Checking at every feather of pride, she acknowledges her own foolish disguise while asking Olivia to share such humility with her. Instead, Olivia reveals another of the keys to her folly. Like Beatrice, she distrusts love's dispensations and would therefore re-create a perfect husband or suitor, "as I would have you be." This distrust must explain her absurd position of courting one alter ego, another woman, or grieving for another, her brother. Olivia thinks she wants a lover made in her own image, or worse, one totally subservient to her will. Viola-Cesario is the closest thing to the first of those perverse wishes to have come along. The weak-willed fop Sir Andrew, heaven forbid, is the closest to the second in Illyria. Olivia's fool gently reproves these errors of pride in her final question. But in concluding her anatomy of Olivia's folly by calling herself a fool, Viola is also trying to tell Olivia that she is making an even bigger fool of herself. Olivia continues to do so through the rest of the scene, but her extremest folly has almost run its course. Repeated humiliations have a way of correcting false pride, however lovely its victim, if that victim has the wit and the humor to change. Olivia has both.

There are two other important examples of Viola's ministry to the foolish pride of this charming woman. At the end of this same scene, just after their exchange about folly, Olivia tries to give herself away to Cesario. This debases her currency terribly, of course. But it also evidences a new humility, born of desperation, and a new ability to abandon herself to another:

> I love thee so that, maugre all thy pride,
> Nor wit nor reason can my passion hide.
> Do not extort thy reasons from this clause,
> For that I woo, thou therefore hast no cause;
> But rather reason thus with reason fetter,
> Love sought is good, but given unsought is better.
> (III.i.148–53)

Thus debased and exposed, Olivia must then suffer the further humiliation of refusal. She is being punished for being in love with herself by falling in love with her mirror image—another woman. But she is simultaneously being trained to accept with the wisdom of folly whatever dispensation love has in store for her. In Shakespeare's romantic comedy, her reward will be great.

But Olivia has yet another humiliation to suffer, and this one is public. She has been brought from the gamelike admission of folly with Feste, through the semiprivate anatomy of her folly and the refusal of Cesario, to this last and most embarrassing moment before all of Illyria. But its public nature, while heightening Olivia's embarrassment, also heightens the commonness of her folly, and therefore makes it the more bearable. For almost everyone is being humiliated at this moment in the play. Thinking she has married Viola-Cesario, she reminds him of his duty to her. Instead of affirmation, she receives the now nearly intolerable disappointment of another denial. Viola is again its agent, and her unconscious foolery is Olivia's final lesson in humiliation:

> OLIVIA. Where goes Cesario?
> VIOLA.                   After him I love
> More than I love these eyes, more than my life,
> More, by all mores, than e'er I shall love wife.
>                                    (v.i.128–30)

First Olivia could not give herself away. Now she finds that her assumed husband prefers a posturing Orsino, a man, to her own exquisite love. What on earth has she chosen to marry? She is allowed to live with that humiliating uncertainty through much of the final act.

We all recognize the association of Olivia's name with the olive branch and thus with peace. Feste even has some fun with this association when he enters Olivia's house and Malvolio's prison with the words, "peace be to this house." Several biblical commonplaces, two of them Pauline, suggest that Olivia's name could have been identified with three other metaphoric equivalents, potential fruitfulness, successful grafting, and the body of Christian believers. Such a connotation argues that Olivia's name predicts her successful humbling, connects it with the Christian tradition of edifying humiliation, and therefore makes her intended monasticism even more richly ironic in *Twelfth Night*.

Several biblical phrases illustrate the common identification of the olive and fruitfulness. Jeremiah 11:16, for example, promises, "the Lord called thee a greene olive tree, a faire one, a fruitful one, a goodlye one." The Psalmist has two similar references to the fruitful olive: "The wife shalbe as a fruitfull vine: upon the sides of thyne house. Thy children [shalbe] like olive branches: rounde about thy table" (128:3–4); also, "I am lyke a greene olive tree in the house of the Lorde" (52:8) refers to an obvious reward for fidelity. St. Paul in Romans 11:17 invokes the "fatnesse [bounty] of the Olive tre."

The ironic relationship between Olivia's name and her personality is already obvious. Olivia is belying her namesake by refusing to marry and increase. Thus her vows and her mourning, not to mention her love for Viola, pervert her natural function as a woman. Viola once upbraids her directly:

> Lady, you are the cruell'st she alive
> If you will lead these graces to the grave,
> And leave the world no copy. (I.v.227–29)

A joke in the same scene makes Olivia's fruitlessness even more obvious. Viola says, "I bring no overture of war, no taxation of homage. I hold the olive in my hand. My words are as full of peace as matter" (I.v.198–200). Viola puns on "peace," of course, but she is carrying fruitfulness, if Olivia will accept it, in the form of Orsino's suit. That neither lady wants that suit to bear fruit enhances the joke.

*As You Like It* also jokes about this commonplace, and for similar reasons. It too contains girls who cannot become fruitful until they become women. Thus Rosalind, with irony but also with frustration, directs Phebe to "my house, / 'Tis at the tuft of olives, here hard by" (III.v.74). Later Oliver, aptly named it turns out, inquires about "a sheepcote, fenced about with olive trees" (IV.iii.78). Oliver, of course, is about to make Celia fruitful.

Shakespearean comedy consistently concludes with young men and women celebrating their coming of age in a festival of potential fruitfulness. In *Twelfth Night* the celebration certainly has a Christian context as strong as this mythic one. The tree for which Olivia is named is associated with peace and with fruitfulness. It is also St. Paul's metaphor for the congregation of the Christian faithful. That the metaphor was well known is evidenced by its elaborate use in a notorious published sermon by John Foxe, entitled, "A Sermon Preached at the Christening of a Certaine Jew." It was also used in one of the prescribed homilies.[11] Finally, the extended analogies in this same biblical context to repairing barren or broken branches with purified "naturall braunches, . . . graffed in their owne olive tree," seems particularly applicable to Olivia's charitable humiliation. She is being mended by two master botchers of souls. I do not mean to suggest by these associations that Olivia might have become in *Twelfth Night* an allegorical embodiment of the Christian congregation (although she is ideally suited in her imperfection for such an embodiment). I do mean to suggest that Shakespeare's audience would have known the olive metaphor, and could have applied it discreetly in relating her edifying humiliation, received at the hands of her two wise fools Viola and Feste, to the Christian tradition that must have generated that action. The other Pauline and Erasmian allusions in the play, as well as its festival title, would have heightened the possibility of that association.

Orsino's edification into a regenerative humility is less a process than a sudden conversion. Because of the immensity of his self-love and the opaqueness of his mind, it cannot be as gradual, as charming, or as convincing as it is in Olivia. She smiles at the Fool's first catechism of her folly; Orsino misunderstands even his last. She suffers the repeated humiliations of Viola's rejections until she can embrace the miracle of Sebastian's acceptance. But Orsino is a slower study. Olivia rejects him again and again, yet still his self-esteem seems unaffected. His mind is truly a "very opal," as Feste once tries to tell him (II.iv.74), characteristically to no avail.

In the space of one scene in the middle of the play Orsino contradicts himself time and again concerning the relationship between male and female love. First he tells Viola that men's fancies are weaker:

> more giddy and unfirm,
> More longing, wavering, sooner lost and worn,
> Than women's are.         (II.iv.32–34)

Then he says that they are stronger:

> There is no woman's sides
> Can bide the beating of so strong a passion
> As love doth give my heart.   (II.iv.92–94)

The reason: "They lack retention," and suffer "surfeit, cloyment, and revolt." Therefore, he concludes,

> Make no compare
> Between that love a woman can bear me
> And that I owe Olivia.   (II.iv.100–102)

Of course, Viola doesn't have to. Orsino has already done it, and come up with diametrically opposite conclusions of which he is completely unaware. His mind is indeed a very opal. The submerged sexual references here and elsewhere suggest as well that he knows as little about the physical as he does about the psychological aspects of love (see, e.g., i.iv.31–34). In the same scene he reveals this naiveté still further in his stunning, thoughtless admission that he can love only young virgins:

> For women are as roses, whose fair flow'r,
> Being once displayed, doth fall that very hour.
>
> (ii.iv.37–38)

Viola has to suffer this "changeable taffeta" of his mind throughout the play; miraculously she loves him in spite of such folly. She even tries to tell him of her love at the end of this very scene of his great folly. Her history includes a touching reference to that ruined rose Orsino has so callously referred to in the image of "the worm i' the bud." Is Viola's love "not love indeed?" Orsino sees none of it, even when it is staring him in the face. Her "history," as he calls it, belongs with Feste's song of tragic love. Both feed his vain fancies of himself as the greatest of lovers; both also reveal him wallowing in the masochistic joy of unrequited love. Feste tries several times to penetrate this darkness. To highlight Orsino's foolish posturing and its self-indulgence, Feste reminds Orsino that a tragic song is only a song: "No pains, sir. I take pleasure in singing, sir" (ii.iv.67). Orsino's obliviousness to the joke casts Feste into his only bad mood of the play: "I would have men of such constancy put to sea" (ii.iv.74–75).

The problem is that Orsino is too vain ever to imagine an insult. Not even Malvolio is that much in love with himself (he knows when he is being made a fool of, though he never likes it). In the final scene of the play Feste tries another catechism to enlighten Orsino concerning his own folly. Enemies are friends because they expose folly; friends like Valentine and Curio are enemies because they flatter it. This is Feste's most pointed assault on Orsino's lack of self-knowledge and humility:

> Marry, sir, they [friends] praise me and make an ass of me. Now my foes tell me plainly I am an ass; so that by my foes, sir, I profit in the knowledge of myself, and by my friends I am abused.
>
> (v.i.15–18)

Notice Feste's clear assumption of universal imperfection, universal
folly, and the consequent need for humility. To this wise fool, as to
Erasmus and St. Paul, the true knowledge of self must produce humility. We are all patched men. But comic characters, like most of us
in real life, learn largely by their own errors, seldom by precept. And
so again Orsino misses the point. First he becomes one of Feste's
friends, when what Feste wants are better enemies ("though it pleases
you to be one of my friends"). Then he curses and threatens Viola,
the selfless lamb, the dove, who has loved and served only Orsino
throughout the play, even when he asks her to undertake the absurd
embassage to Olivia. He imagines her infidelity, of all things. And so
he makes an absolute fool of himself in public, right after Olivia's
parallel public humiliation, and banishes forever from his sight the
only person who could have loved this arrogant, blind, old Orsino.
Paradoxically, he is finally most blessed in this humiliation, for it allows him to prove himself a fool where Feste could not. And that
proof admits him to the comic community of joy. But before that joy,
Shakespeare lets him, like Olivia, lie for a while on the uncomfortable
bed of his own pride.

Of course Olivia's real husband is not effeminate, nor has Orsino
lost Viola. Sebastian will soon enter to make all well. Olivia will have
learned through her public and private humiliations how little she deserves Sebastian's love, and she will cherish it therefore all the more.
Orsino will finally, if belatedly, accept and embrace his folly and its
paradoxical joy. Viola's incredibly selfless love at the moment of Orsino's selfishness makes his present folly and his future joy most obvious to us: "And I, most jocund, apt, and willingly, / To do you rest
a thousand deaths would die" (v.i.126–27). By embodying a self-
sacrificing, Christlike humility that is most appropriate for Epiphany,
Viola has become Orsino's best fool. Smith is especially good in inter-
preting Orsino's final conversion into a wise fool and therefore a
proper reveller at Epiphany through her example and his own folly:

> Having been proved wrong about women in love, he is willing to
> accept that proof at the cost of proving equally wrong in what he
> had said about the love of men, and especially about the eternal
> constancy of his love for Olivia. His declaration to Viola is couched

in language appropriate to the seasonal rite of exchanged services.
. . . Jest becomes earnest as the Feast of Folly gives place to the Feast
of Love.                                                    (P. 120)

In calling Viola "your master's mistress" and later "Orsino's mistress
and his fancy's queen," Orsino has signified for us by laughing at himself his final release from the bondage of self-indulgence and self-love.
In wanting to hold her woman's hand and see Viola in her "woman's
weeds," Orsino shows that he, like Orlando, can "live no longer by
thinking." His immature pose as an unrequited lover is finally over.
Now he too can finally enter "man's estate." His proposal of marriage
is the last "proof" of his maturation. The regeneration is sudden, to
be sure, and it is therefore less convincing than Olivia's slow schooling
in humility. But he gains something at least of a "natural perspective"
on his own folly in the final scene, and is richly rewarded for it. So
Jack will have Jill, and if he keeps his head on right he might even
be allowed to keep her happily and forever. Neither Orsino nor Olivia
deserves such joy, such grace. Knowing their undeserving folly and
finding such joy in spite of it is a romantic experience of the first
order. It is an experience common to many of Shakespeare's romantic
comedies. Both the Pauline and Erasmian paradoxes of celebrated folly
and the festival of Epiphany lie close to the heart of that joy.

## ii. Malvolio and Sebastian

Like Viola, but more self-consciously, Feste has much to do with the
systematic humiliation of Olivia and Orsino in *Twelfth Night*. He
helps to teach them both the wisdom of acknowledged folly, though
their own absurdity and their relationships with Viola offer potent instruction as well. Feste and Maria even achieve a modicum of success
with Sir Toby. With the help of a good blow on the head as inflicted
by Sebastian and the ingenuity of Maria's plot against Malvolio, Toby
too comes to renounce the old man, the "drunken rogue" he was, and
decides to marry Maria. Feste knew it would happen all along, if only
he "would leave drinking" (I.v.25).

Neither Feste the Curate nor Maria is as successful at reforming

Malvolio, but even here *Twelfth Night* displays its analogies to Paul, Erasmus, and the feast of Epiphany. We might have expected such a failure as early as Maria's judgment of Malvolio as a hypocrite or a "time-pleaser; an affectioned ass" (ii.iii.135). The prospects would be dim indeed of reforming any character so well "persuaded of himself; so crammed, as he thinks, with excellencies that it is his grounds of faith that all that look on him love him" (ii.iii.137–40). Feste's jokes about his demonic possession, especially epithets like "goodman Devil" and "dishonest Satan" in Act IV, Scene ii, even suggest that Malvolio is given over to the devil, an intense worship of himself, as his only grounds of faith. There is also no dispute that Maria's plot against Malvolio is motivated as much by revenge as by a desire to enlighten him. Malvolio is almost everyone's enemy in *Twelfth Night*. But by exposing his folly Maria demonstrates as well the truth of Feste's paradox to Orsino: the enemy can prove a true friend if the enemy's victim can hear his detractions and put them to mending. "My foes tell me plainly I am an ass; . . . by my foes, sir, I profit in the knowledge of myself" (v.i.15–18). The homilist tells us that no man, however vicious, is irredeemable, and both Maria and Feste seem to operate on that assumption. So does Shakespearean comedy, but never beyond all probability. For Malvolio *will not* be edified into humility by Maria's excellent practice, however much he is humiliated by it.[12] Humiliation is not always equal to humility, even in Shakespearean comedy. The cure depends on "what you will." Thus Malvolio is left to Feste–Sir Thopas the Curate, who is given one last chance to cure him of his devilish madness of self-love.

In the homiletic tradition the curate is the mediator of grace through enlightenment.[13] Feste–Sir Thopas, in blessing Malvolio's new house ("peace in this prison"), brings to mind the Renaissance tradition of blessing houses on Epiphany.[14] But much more pertinent to Epiphany is the quibbling which follows the blessing (iv.ii.29–46) about the darkness of Malvolio's prison. Malvolio, characteristically, imputes that darkness to others: "They have laid me here in hideous darkness." He is literally right, of course; the prison is unquestionably dark, and he would be as wrong to accept the nonsense of Feste's contrary opinion as he would be to embrace the opinion of Pythagoras concerning the transmigration of souls.

But even as he is being silly, Feste may also be trying as curate and wise fool to prod Malvolio into acknowledging that the literal darkness symbolizes an inner darkness, a prison or sickness of his own making. To the fool the house is bright: "It hath bay windows transparent as barricadoes, and the clerestories toward the south north are as lustrous as ebony." At the very least, such strange testimony might make Malvolio distrust his own physical senses, thus admitting on that simple level his own fallibility. But Malvolio will not see his own folly; he denies the fool's wisdom: "I say this house is as dark as ignorance, though ignorance were as dark as hell." Feste has cleverly led Malvolio to stumble upon the truth of his own ignorance in this second statement by suggesting himself that "there is no darkness but ignorance" (IV.ii.42). But though he stumbles into the right words, Malvolio will not acknowledge their relationship to the darkness of his own obdurate pride. Indeed, he later complains about Sir Thopas's ministry, "They have here propertied me; keep me in darkness, send ministers to me, asses, and do all they can to face me out of my wits" (IV.ii.89–91). The ass, like the fool or the curate, is not a bad minister of folly; witness the feast of fools. In fact, Feste talks about "the picture of We Three" in an earlier scene with Sir Toby and Sir Andrew, and they readily grasp how they "make a third" (II.iii. 16, 159–60) with the two asses in the frame. But though Maria tells Malvolio in the same scene to "go shake your ears" (II.iii.115), he never gets the point. He likely never will.

This obliviousness to his own folly is never more obvious than when Malvolio calls Feste "fool" no less than twelve times after he replaces Sir Thopas in Act IV, Scene ii. "Fool, fool, fool," "Good fool," Malvolio calls out again and again. But he can never call himself "fool." This failure predicts the eventual result of their long interview. Feste may make a fool of Malvolio, but he will never bring him to admit his folly. There are superficial, forced admissions, to be sure. Once Malvolio declares, "I am as well in my wits, fool, as thou art," and again, "I am as well in my wits as any man in Illyria." Feste counters the first with edifying wit: "Then you are mad indeed, if you be no better in your wits than a fool" (IV.ii.87–88). But by the second he has almost given up his futile ministry to this sick and imprisoned man: "Well-a-day that you were, sir" (IV.ii.105). He tries once more to get Malvolio to admit his folly with the impossible question, "are you not mad indeed? or do you but counterfeit?" (IV.ii.110–11). But like Jaques, Malvolio will not reply with wisdom, humility, or humor. Malvolio ironically calls for light throughout the scene. But while we laugh at such ritualistic admissions of his folly, he can never laugh at himself.[15] Unlike Olivia with Feste earlier in the play and Orsino with Viola at the end Malvolio will never enact this comic equivalent of wisdom and salvation; he will never escape from the dark sickness of his imprisoning pride.

Malvolio's darkness also suggests Epiphany because it is the festival of enlightenment. *The Annotated Book of Common Prayer* mentions how much light imagery characterizes the lessons and epistles for this festival. Such light invites mankind in Isaiah 60 to celebrate the bright manifestation of Christ's truth:

> Get thee up betimes, and be bright [O Hierusalem] for thy light commeth and the glorie of the Lord is risen upon thee. For lo, whyle the darknesse & cloude covereth the earth and the people, the Lorde shall shewe thee light, and his glorie shalbe seene in thee. And Gentiles shall come to thy light, & Kings to the brightnesse that springeth foorth upon thee. Lift up thine eyes, and loke rounde about thee. . . . Then shalt thou see this and be glorious. . . . Thine heart shalbe opened.

Equally appropriate to *Twelfth Night* is the second Lesson, Isaiah 49, concerning the remaining prisoners in darkness: "That thou mayest say unto the prisoners, Go foorth, and to them that are in darknesse, come into the light. . . . Lift up thine eyes and loke about thee." In the Epiphany Epistle, Ephesians 3:10, St. Paul plays the fool by reversing this prison imagery. He is the "prisoner of Jesue Christ," who tries, like Feste and Viola, "to make all men see what is the fellowship of the mystery" of Incarnation and humility. Malvolio's darkness and the jokes about his madness are thus closely associated in image and theme to his alienation from the Christian enlightenment that the Twelfth Day festival celebrates.

William Tyndale provides a clearer understanding of the Christian context of Malvolio's fate in his prologue to St. Paul's Epistle to the Romans:

> The apostle . . . rebuketh all those holy people . . . which . . . live well outwardly in the face of the world, and condemn others gladly; as the nature of all hypocrites is, to think themselves pure in respect of open sinners, and yet they hate the law inwardly, and are full of covetousness, and envy, and of all uncleanness. . . . Furthermore, St. Paul, as a true expounder of the law, . . . calleth them hardhearted, and such as cannot repent.[16]

How clearly Malvolio's reaction to Toby and Andrew is predicted; how closely he conforms in this passage with Maria's description of him. One could hardly find a more penetrating analysis of Malvolio's severance from comic grace.

Malvolio's inability to forgive his enemies or profit from his humiliation at their hands help explain his exclusion from the final festivity. John Donne's explication of Romans 12:20, a Pauline text on the benefits that can be derived from such humiliation, also serves as a gloss to his exclusion. The coals of humiliation's fire can purify or punish. Their function depends upon the will of their recipient:

> If he have any gold, any pure metall in him, this fire of this kindness will purge out the drosse, and there is a friend made. If he be nothing but straw and stubble, combustible still, still ready to take fire against thee, this fire . . . will . . . assure thee, that he, whom so many benefits cannot reconcile, is irreconcileable.     (3:386–87)

Orsino is finally humiliated into true love by Viola's selflessness and his own considerable folly. Olivia's humiliating love for the unattainable Viola-Cesario lets her embrace Sebastian with relief and happiness. Even Toby finally hates the "drunken rogue" he once was. But Malvolio can only say, "I am not of your element" (III.iv.116). Since Maria's element is gold, "my metal of India" (II.v.11–12), and since Viola's and Olivia's must be equally rare and pure, this admission is further evidence that Malvolio is pitiable only in his irreconcilable will.

The structure of Act IV establishes a sharp contrast between Malvolio's unacknowledged folly, which Feste calls madness, and Sebastian's madness, which he himself joyously admits to be folly. Feste's ministry to Malvolio's devilish pride is framed in Scenes i and iii by Sebastian's blessed humility. Scene i ends, in fact, with Sebastian's affirmation of the transcendent sanity of his madness:

> What relish is in this? How runs the stream?
> Or I am mad, or else this is a dream.
> Let fancy still my sense in Lethe steep;
> If it be thus to dream, still let me sleep!
> (IV.i.56–59)

And Scene iii begins with his further celebration of this paradoxical wisdom:

> For though my soul disputes well with my sense
> That this may be some error, but no madness,
> Yet doth this accident and flood of fortune
> So far exceed all instance, all discourse,
> That I am ready to distrust mine eyes
> And wrangle with my reason that persuades me
> To any other trust but that I am mad,
> Or else the lady's mad.          (IV.iii.9–16)

They're both mad, of course, mad with a humility that Malvolio never achieves. That madness is their greatest blessing and their profoundest sanity.

This response is too closely analogous to the madness of religious ecstasy described by Erasmus in *The Praise of Folie* to be dismissed as completely coincidental. Sebastian's soul tells him to distrust his senses and his reason with their scientific, worldly evidence and embrace this sapiential blessing that exceeds "all instance, all discourse." As Erasmus paraphrases St. Paul, "was never mans eie sawe, nor eare heard," (pp. 127–28) such evidence as this. Like Erasmus's holy fools, Sebastian is first befuddled by his romantic good fortune, thinking it a dream:

> In sort that whan a little after thei come againe to their former
> wittes, thei denie plainly thei wote where thei became, or whether

168

thei were than in theyr bodies, or out of theyr bodies, wakyng or slepyng: remembring also as little, either what they heard, saw, saied, or did than, savyng as it were through a cloude, or by a dreame. (P. 128)

Sebastian's romantic faith, however, tells him that this madness, if it is madness, is also the greatest sanity he has ever known. Again his response recalls Erasmus describing the similar madness of religious faith:

This thei know certainely, that whiles their mindes so roved and wandred, thei were most happie and blisfull, so that they lament and wepe at theyr retourne unto theyr former senses, as who saieth, nothyng were leefer unto theim than continually to rave and be deteigned with suche a spece of madnesse. (P. 128)

Erasmus himself connects these two species of romantic and religious witraving by analogy:

PLATO . . . wrote, *that the passion and extreme rage of fervent lovers was to be desired and embrased, as a thing above all others most blisfull:* because that a vehement lover liveth not now in hym selfe, but rather in that that he loveth. . . . Whiche so beyng that soules yet pinned within these bodily foldes maie smacke a little of suche a felicitee, consider ye than what a life the sainctes soules leade in heaven? (P. 126)

In both lovers and believers, great humility and great faith promise great joy. Sebastian exemplifies this paradox even more obviously than the lovers in the woods outside of Athens at the moment of dawn. But as in that play, Shakespeare has again called upon the Erasmian and Pauline paradoxes about the wondrous madness and humility of religious faith to elucidate his comic interests in the analogous madness and humility of romantic love. Sebastian has the good sense to distrust his senses and embrace this folly; Malvolio never comes close to such an epiphany in *Twelfth Night*.

## iii.  Feste the Curate and St. Paul the Fool

Feste's regenerative efforts, like Sebastian's moment of admitted madness, are consistently reminiscent of Pauline and Erasmian paradoxes concerning the wisdom of folly. That reminiscence is brought into focus in *Twelfth Night* by the pointed allusions of Viola, Sebastian, and Feste to some of these paradoxes. It is heightened by Feste's "dissemblance" of the curate with Malvolio. For he is persistently trying to correct unacknowledged follies in the play, trying to transform them into humility. In his best moments he proves Orsino an ass (v.i.16–18: "My foes tell me plainly I am an ass," while my friends "praise me and make an ass of me") and Olivia a fool (i.v.67: "Take away the fool"). Unlike Malvolio they finally accept his patchings and mend. Interestingly, St. Paul was known to William Tyndale and the Protestant reformers as the corrector of personal and doctrinal faults. Tyndale says of St. Paul, casually, as all commonplaces are stated, "If they err from the word, then may whomsoever God moveth his heart, play Paul, and correct him." Elsewhere Tyndale says, "Paul corrected Peter, when he walked not the straight way after the truth of the Gospel." [17] So Feste, playing the curate in *Twelfth Night* and playing the fool, is also "playing Paul," as Tyndale puts it, playing the corrector of personal if not theological errors. That is, after all, what wise fools are supposed to do.

But Feste's connection to St. Paul is more intimate still. For Feste directly alludes to the Apostle in his famous epilogue:

> When that I was and a little tiny boy,
>     With hey, ho, the wind and the rain,
> A foolish thing was but a toy;
>     For the rain it raineth every day.
> But when I came to man's estate,
>     With hey, ho, the wind and the rain,
> Gainst knaves and thieves men shut their gate,
>     For the rain it raineth every day.
>                                     (v.i.378–86)

Richmond Noble rather cautiously assigns this echo to First Corinthians 13:11, which is almost certainly the source. Combining the three most common versions of Paul's famous words, we see how closely Feste's voice conforms to St. Paul's here:[18]

When I was a childe, I spake as a childe, I understood as a childe,

170

I imagined as a childe: but assoone as I was a man, I put away
childishnesse.                                                (Bishops')

I thoght as a childe: but when I became a man, I put away childish
things.                                                      (Geneva)

When I was a litle one, I spake as a litle one, I understood as a litle
one, I thought as a litle one. But when I was made a man, I did
away the things that belonged to a litle one.                (Rheims)

Renaissance comments about this famous passage intensify our understanding of St. Paul's relationship to *Twelfth Night* and all of
Shakespeare's romantic comedies. Nowell's catechism, for example,
uses the thirteenth chapter of First Corinthians as the text to illustrate
that "we be by nature most inclined to the love of ourselves." Another gloss to the chapter in Nowell's Communion section confirms
that "full perfection in all points, wherein nothing may be lacking,
cannot be found in man so long as he abideth in this world. . . . Yea,
if we were perfect, there should be no more need of . . . the Lord's
Supper among us." [19] Malvolio, clearly besought by Feste to become a
communicant by growing up and admitting his membership in imperfect humanity, refuses to do so. In that refusal he isolates himself
not only from the comic community but from the Christian community,
the community of repentance and forgiveness of which most of Shakespeare's comic characters partake, as well. Another quotation from
Nowell's catechism explains this phenomenon in a Christian context
that provides an especially appropriate explanation for Malvolio's
eventual isolation from festivity and fellowship:

> As for them that do not confess that they have sinned, nor do crave
> pardon of their defaults, but with that Pharisee do glory in their
> innocency and righteousness before God, or rather against God, they
> exclude themselves from the fellowship of the faithful.[20]

All the major characters except Malvolio begin at least to grow out
of their childishness into Christian maturity. In accepting the fool,
Feste, into their community, they signify their acceptance of their own
foolishness. An exchange with Viola in the middle of the play reveals
how clearly Feste understands this symbolic dimension of his role. He
embodies the folly of those around him. Viola says of him, "I saw thee

late at the Count Orsino's." He responds, with all of his fool's wisdom,

> Foolery, sir, does walk about the orb like the sun; it shines every-
> where. I would be sorry, sir, but the fool should be as oft with your
> master as with my mistress.                                    (III.i.37–40)

Where the fool walks, there walks folly.

With similar wisdom, Feste says of Olivia that she will have no fool until she has a husband:

> VIOLA. Art not thou the Lady Olivia's fool?
> FESTE. No, indeed, sir. The Lady Olivia has no folly. She will
> keep no fool, sir, till she be married.                      (III.i.30–32)

Besides the effective pun on sexual folly, which is also called "will," the act of marriage is a movement toward selflessness and mature responsibility, and away from childishness.[21] It is also an affirmation of faith in flawed humankind and in flawed self. To be aware of one's own imperfection and of the imperfection of one's beloved, and still to "give and hazard all"[22]—that is an act of faith which Shakespeare's lovers are continually called upon to make, in *Love's Labor's Lost, A Midsummer Night's Dream, Much Ado about Nothing,* and *As You Like It,* as here. It is no coincidence that Malvolio remains unmarried in *Twelfth Night,* or Jaques in *As You Like It.* Paradoxically, in the last comedy we will consider and the one that gives us that quotation about hazard, *The Merchant of Venice,* the lovers do not have to perform that act of faith, for they never realize their shared imperfections. That the audience does realize them creates enduring ironies.

In his epilogue, then, Feste is appropriately paraphrasing St. Paul, whose spirit he variously embodies in *Twelfth Night.* He is most fully a fool when he can play the corrector of follies rather than the "corrupter of words" (III.i.35) he has had to be since Orsino's and Olivia's majorities. That he not only embodies Pauline and Erasmian paradoxes about the wisdom of folly but also understands and even discusses these paradoxes of humility is all the more evident when we hear both Feste and Viola paraphrase First Corinthians 3:18–19 into secular wisdom. First St. Paul: "If any man among you seem to be wise in this worlde, let hym be a foole, that he may be wyse. For the wisdome of this worlde, is foolishnesse with God." Feste understands this well: "Those wits that think they have thee [wisdom] do very oft prove fools, and I that am sure I lack thee may pass for a wise man" (I.v.30–32). Viola, also aware of this Erasmian and Pauline commonplace, praises Feste in precisely these terms:

> This is a practice
> As full of labor as a wise man's art;
> For folly that he wisely shows, is fit;
> But wise men, folly-fall'n, quite taint their wit.
> (III.i.63–66)

Even Touchstone (*As You Like It,* V.i.30–31) and Jaques (*As You Like It,* II.vii.42–51) have heard of the commonplace,[23] but they both misapply it.

Preachers are also placed by St. Paul, Erasmus, and their commentators into this context of the foolishness of simplicity and truth. As Colet translates First Corinthians 1:21, "it pleased God by the foolishness of preaching [to] save them that believe."[24] Additionally, William Fulke in "A Comfortable Sermon of Faith" tells us, "as Saint Paule sayth . . . For by this foolishness of preachyng the wysedome, power, and goodnes of God appeareth greatest, and woorketh most effectually in them that are the children of God."[25] But it is John Donne in an unusually witty sermon on First Corinthians, "Be Ye Reconciled to God," who convinces us of the extensiveness of the paradoxical jointure of priest as fool and fool as priest. Notice the two meanings of "foole" as perceiver of simple truth and exposer of human flaws as Donne speaks with appropriate humility:

> Mad men have some flashes, some twilights, some returns of sense and reason, but the *foole* hath none; And, *we are fools for Christ,* says the Apostle; And not onely we, the persons, but the ministration it self, the function it self is *foolishnesse; It pleased God by the foolishnesse of preaching to save them that beleeve.* . . . We are *fooles* for Christ, and pretend nothing to work by, but the foolishnesse of preaching. Lower then this, we cannot be cast, and higher then this we offer not to climbe.                (10:125)

In *The Praise of Folie,* as we have seen, Erasmus explains for us most completely the intimate connection between St. Paul, Christian folly, and Christ himself. Commenting on the same Pauline phrase, "we are fools for Christ's sake," Erasmus's Stultitia[26] exults, "Dooe you here now how great praises of Foly this so great an autour alleageth, yea and that more is, he plainely enjoygneth Folie unto us, for a thyng most necessarie, and right importyng to salvacion" (p. 116). Christ preceded St. Paul in exalting the simple (lambes, shepe, culver, and faunes). In addition, "Christ hym selfe mindyng the relefe and redempcion of mankyndes folie, although he was the ineffable wisedome of the father, became yet a maner foole, wheras takyng mans nature upn hym, he was founde bothe in fourme and habite lyke unto other men" (p. 118). Erasmus here relates the paradoxical humiliation of the preacher to the shepherd Christ's own humiliation at Epiphany. Twelfth Night, the eve of that festival, could hardly have seen a fitter entertainment.

Walter Jacob Kaiser's excellent study of Erasmus, *Praisers of Folly,* paraphrases the essentials of Erasmus's influence upon the Renaissance perception of folly in terms of this same theological paradox: "We must be fools for Christ's sake, for the mind of the fool is not closed to Him by *sapientia mundana*." "The highest folly, and indeed, the Christian's greatest reward, is a transcendent, mystical theolepsy." "The final state of folly is to lose oneself in God." Finally, "it is toward this portrait of the Fool in Christ that all Stultitia's foolery has been directed."[27] Such a widely known precedent makes it unlikely that Shakespeare's Christian contemporaries would have failed to recognize the noble, almost divine calling of Feste in *Twelfth Night*.[28]

We are fools for Christ, says the Apostle—simple articulators of simple truths, edifiers of others into their own simplicity and humility, exemplifiers of humility to teach it. We are fools for Christ. Just as surely as Feste and Viola explicitly allude to those paradoxes of Erasmus and St. Paul they are also playing the curate's most conventional role of fool throughout *Twelfth Night*. It is no great leap from that awareness to the acknowledgment that Shakespeare's comic form itself, by urging self-knowledge and humility upon its characters and its audience, becomes another foolish, humble corrector, another vital member of this Pauline and Erasmian category. Feste even disclaims pretensions for the play or the playwright, so that as in *As You Like It* they too can join the humility and the festivity: "But that's all one, our play is done, / And we'll strive to please you every day." Shakespeare's complex linking of Sebastian, Viola, and Feste to these Renaissance religious commonplaces indicates how fully he was aware of the Christian dimensions of his comic art. The Epilogue's invitation to perceive St. Paul in the play is also an invitation to the audience to participate in an experience not unlike that of the Christian communion and the festival of Epiphany. Humbly aware of shared errors, the festive society of *Twelfth Night* rejoices in that communion and anticipates its new life with maturity and hope. Comic festivity thus achieves its fullest potential in *Twelfth Night*, by becoming associated with both the sacrament and the festival of Christian humility and Christian love.

# CHAPTER VII

# "I Stand for Sacrifice": Frustrated Communion in *The Merchant of Venice*

THE REVELS ACCOUNTS for the court of King James I records two performances of *The Merchant of Venice* during Shrovetide, 1605, the second of which the king himself apparently commanded.[1] Such a repeat performance on a festival occasion is quite rare in the annals of English drama, and suggests that *The Merchant of Venice*, like *Twelfth Night*, may have close ties with a major festival of the church year. A glance at the liturgical tradition of Shrovetide should determine what light if any it can shed on the treatment of the wisdom of folly in Shakespeare's most perplexing romantic comedy.

Like *Love's Labor's Lost*, *The Merchant of Venice* is also touched by interesting strands of doctrinal controversy. Unlike the former play, whose controversial allusions were frequent, explicit, and basically celebratory, in *The Merchant of Venice* they are infrequent, submerged and ironic. Verbal allusions are harder to demonstrate. Further, instead of reinforcing and explaining the play's festivity, the undercurrents of doctrinal controversy in *The Merchant of Venice* seem to run counter to the play's predominantly romantic experience. Like the Shrovetide context in which the play may also be understood, the Protestant-Catholic controversy concerning the Communion "sacrifice" first directs us to ironic connections between Antonio and Shylock and then helps us formulate our slight but perplexing dissatisfactions with Portia and the play's festivity. Following these doctrinal undercurrents in *The Merchant of Venice* will complete our study of the paradoxical reversal of folly and wisdom in Shakespeare's romantic comedies by revealing how severely the absence of the wisdom of humility among the comic revellers in Belmont, even Portia, affects the quality of their final joy.

# i. The Shrovetide Setting

Like *The Merchant of Venice,* Shrovetide contains a mixture of incongruent qualities. It is on the one hand a time for self-scrutiny, confession, penance, and absolution, "that time when, preparatory to the Lenten season, the faithful were shriven."[2] But Shrove Tuesday is simultaneously a day of extraordinary license in Renaissance and Jacobean England, called "carnival," farewell to the flesh, because it hosts a final outburst of riotous merrymaking just before the penitential restraints of Lent.[3] A. R. Wright describes this characteristic dichotomy: "For many centuries Shrovetide was the time for confessing and shriving, but its chief features were feasting and boisterous hilarity."[4]

The prescribed biblical passages for Shrovetide reflect this same dichotomy. *The Prayer Book Dictionary* finds in these passages a celebration of "the grace of love." In the Epistle (I Cor. 13) St. Paul describes love's superiority to the other Christian virtues. In the Gospel (Luke 18:31–43) Christ loves the blind man, even as He approaches certain death. The Lessons portray God's love to Abraham (Gen. 12) and Noah (Gen. 9); "Genesis 13 contains a striking example of man's self-denying love to his fellow man." Finally, the Collect invokes "that moste excellent gift of charitie."[5]

However, implicit in these same biblical passages is man's penitential awareness of his need for "the grace of love," his inevitable imperfection. We remember Launcelot Gobbo's cruel treatment of Old Gobbo when we learn that Genesis 9 is also about Ham's "derision & contempt for his father." We think even more readily of Shylock's cruel bond when we find the same passage forbidding the eating of living flesh: "But flesh with the life thereof, I meane with the blood thereof, shal ye not eat." The Geneva note explains, "That is, living creatures and the flesh of beastes that are strangled: and hereby all crueltie is forbidden." Likewise, Abraham responds to God's grace with moral cowardice and distrust, and his kindness to Lot is tempered by the prediction that Lot's people as well as his inheritance will be destroyed. Even the Collect for Shrovetide warns against good works unaccompanied by the proper spirit of charity.[6]

Donne's Lenten sermons are especially aware of this paradoxical conflict of attitudes during Shrovetide. Man's Lenten meditations on his immense imperfections should not overwhelm him with despair; neither should he presume sufficient righteousness or sufficient grace. Purity, like righteousness, can be vicious as well as virtuous. He should strive therefore to blend during Shrovetide holy day and holiday, feasting and fasting, as difficult as that blending might be: "All Lent is *Easter Eve;* And though the *Eve* be a *Fasting Day,* yet the *Eve* is a halfe-holiday too. God, by our Ministery, would so exercise you in a spirituall *Fast,* in a sober consideration of sinne, and the sad Consequences thereof, as that in the *Eve* you might see the *holy day;* in the *Lent,* your *Easter;* in the sight of your sinnes, the cheerefulnesse of his good will towards you."[7] Such a precarious Shrovetide balance is a commonplace of Renaissance theologians: "The great souls are those who yield neither to presumption nor despair, who know that the good they aim at is too difficult for complacent human strength, but not beyond the divine attainment."[8]

This homiletic and liturgical material helps us understand how *The Merchant of Venice* might have been thought relevant to Shrovetide by James I in 1605. There is inarguably plenty of joy and festivity in the play, and nothing sinister about most of it. Appropriately for Shrovetide, that joy is the joy of love's wealth, the grace of love. Bassanio exhibits it when he chooses aright; Antonio gives and hazards all for his friend; Portia too loves well enough to hazard the casket plot, and even tries to save Shylock's vicious soul. Lorenzo and Jessica, Christian and Jew, are symbolically joined together in Belmont in the final act. There is, then, considerable love for these explicitly Christian characters to celebrate at play's end, and also some sense of grace. For they have been delivered from severe hazards and will now, we must assume, live happily ever after.[9]

But where are the paradoxical Lenten aspects of Shrovetide, penitence and imperfect charity, presumption and despair, "fasting, and sober consideration of sinne"? As we shall see in the discussion to follow, the absence of this darker side of the Shrovetide vision among the Christians in the play is the flaw that separates them from all of Shakespeare's other major comic characters, and that invites an ironic perspective to coexist with the romantic one.[10] Though they live in the most self-consciously Christian society in the romantic comedies, these characters never understand the inevitable imperfections of even their best-intended actions. Antonio's attempt to play Christ is incongruously combined with a self-righteousness that spits upon a sinner instead of forgiving or loving him. Shylock receives a mercy and a justice that leaves many of us uneasy. There is even a slight breach between Portia's lovely precepts and Christian practice. Because no wise fool inhabits Venice or Belmont, there is no counterpart to Feste or Viola or even Touchstone to lead these erring Christian characters to the wisdom of humility. Thus they are all vulnerable to the unique Shrovetide sins of presumption and despair. A sure Lenten knowledge of the lack of deserving enriches the festive celebrations of the grace of love in each of the other comedies. That awareness is largely absent in Belmont. Donne's Lenten sermon restates the paradox of fortunate folly: "in the *Lent* . . . [you see] your *Easter;* in the sight of your sinnes, the cheerefulnesse of his good will towards you." His perspective can enrich the festive experience of *The Merchant of Venice* only because its absence among the festive celebrants forces the audience to understand and to celebrate, alone for once and therefore ironically, a profounder if more muted joy.

In her first scene Portia alludes to the familiar Pauline commonplace of the breach between Christian precept and practice. Like its Shrovetide context, this allusion suggests a rich doctrinal basis for the play's ironies. Her familiar comment reads,

> If to do were as easy as to know what were good to do, chapels had been churches, and poor men's cottages princes' palaces. It is a good divine that follows his own instructions; I can easier teach twenty what were good to be done than to be one of the twenty to follow mine own teaching. (I.ii.12–17)

Such an allusion would probably have suggested either the phraseology of the General Confession or its Pauline source in Romans. The former would have been extremely familiar to an Anglican: "We have left undone those thinges whiche we ought to have done, and we have done those thinges which we ought not to have done, and there is no health in us" (p. 42). Its Pauline source is in Romans 7:18–19: "For I know, that in mee (that is to say in my flesh) dwelleth no good thing. For to will, is present with me: but I finde no meanes to performe that which is good. For the good that I would, doe I not: but the evil which I would not, that do I." Man's dilemma is not only doing what he knows to be right, but knowing what that righteousness is.[11] Such a dilemma should ideally lead a Christian to that humility we have so often associated with folly and faith in Shakespeare's comic vision. In Belmont it does not.

Portia's allusion thus alerts us to the incomplete Christian vision of Belmont. It also spotlights its source, St. Paul's Letter to the Romans, which was understood by Catholic and Protestant commentators alike to urge the attainment of peace between Jew and Gentile, by their unity in the death and sacrifice of Christ for all men.[12] The bond that leads both Jew and Gentile to this common grace is the same Shrovetide bond that Antonio and his friends fail to recognize, their shared imperfection. Colet glosses the very passage Portia alludes to in precisely these terms: "St. Paul concludes that none of them, whether Jew or Gentile, ought to accuse another; but that each one should acknowledge his sin, and hasten to repent of his own wickedness, and not abuse the forbearance of God."[13] That Romans was also known for its distinctions between the old law and the new, and between the letter and the spirit of the law[14] adds to the aptness of this early Pauline allusion in *The Merchant of Venice*. Such an allusion challenges us to look closely at relationships between Christian precept and Christian practice throughout the play.

But let us not judge the Christians too harshly. If Antonio and his company are somewhat presumptuous of their goodness and righteousness, Shylock, though we may pity him, viciously embodies that Shrovetide sin in his self-assured pursuit of the "rightful" bond. A Renaissance audience enjoying this Shrovetide entertainment just before the penitential rigors of Lent might thus have been edified by both Belmont's facile joy and Shylock's obdurate pride. They might have understood that Belmont's carnival is not sufficiently Lenten, its feast a surfeiting of joy unmitigated by fasting, its holiday insufficiently holy.[15] Enid Welsford's descriptions of the momerie as another Shrovetide tradition—with public masking, parading through the streets, and dancing in neighbors' houses—further intensifies the connections between the play and its liturgical occasion.[16] That occasion encourages us to make the traditionally polar critical positions toward the play complementary. One can celebrate the grace of love's wealth in *The Merchant of Venice* and accept without despair the severity of Shylock's shriving; but one must simultaneously resist the presumption that the grace is ever deserved by maintaining an ironic distance from the attractive but still naive revellers. If Shrovetide encourages such a balanced perspective, so do the elusive hints of a prominent doctrinal controversy in the play, one involved like Shrovetide in the ironies of scapegoating and "sacrifice."

## ii. Antonio's "Sacrifice" and his Righteousness

Antonio's self-righteousness and his apparent desire literally to stand for sacrifice to the Jew and exemplify the perfect Christian life is particularly ambiguous in light of the Christian assumptions just mentioned, as well as Shakespeare's usual comic insistence on recognized and celebrated imperfection. That several of his own words and those of others describe this "sacrifice" in terms reminiscent of Christian Communion makes it possible that Shakespeare's contemporaries would have seen refracted through Antonio's portrayal key issues of the vigorous Renaissance doctrinal controversy concerning the nature and efficacy of the Eucharist. Few Renaissance Christians, Protestant or Catholic, would have been ignorant of the major outlines of this controversy,[17] though of course the differences appear more pronounced among the polemicists than they actually were among moderate churchmen. But while Shakespeare used similar controversial issues so genially in *Love's Labor's Lost* as to heal rather than open old wounds, here the effect is not quite the same. By touching ever so lightly the still-raw edges of the well-known Communion controversy, Shakespeare seems again to accentuate the ironic if inevitable gap between Christian precept and Christian practice, in Belmont and in the world beyond. The audience does not have to "take sides" to appreciate this irony; that would be far too divisive, and also beside the point. But there is little question that some issues of the controversy are suggested by the play and can, with our Shrovetide understandings, help define Antonio's precarious heroism.

Antonio is without question Bassanio's noble, brave, and generous friend. He is also a good and righteous Christian man. As such, however, he illustrates throughout *The Merchant of Venice* the moral dilemma ascribed to the Renaissance Puritan by C. H. and Katherine George—the precarious morality of a righteous Christian in an imperfect world. For this type, evidently increasingly common in late sixteenth- and early seventeenth-century England, it became almost impossible to accommodate the two Christian injunctions of righteousness and humility.[18] Put another way in *The Interpreter's Bible*'s gloss of a prescribed passage for Shrovetide, "the great souls are those who yield neither to presumption nor despair, who know that the good they aim at is too difficult for complacent human strength, but not beyond the divine attainment."[19] Antonio lacks this Shrovetide wisdom about himself, his friends, and his enemies. Nowhere is this lack more obvious than in his relationship to Shylock. In fact, of the six stereotypical Puritan character traits Siegel attributes to Shylock, Antonio has at least five: intolerance, hypocrisy, usury (in love), a sense of election, and self-righteousness.[20] The sin of presumption is thus his inevitable companion in the play. Paradoxically, he is also accompanied by its fellow, despair. Surely that mysterious sadness he first exhibits represents at least in part Antonio's deep dissatisfaction with a corrupt business community that seems immune to grace. Of course Antonio is not Shylock. His basic virtue is just barely tainted by such Shrovetide sins, while Shylock's obvious vices are only touched with humanity. Still, that the two evidence any similarities at all is an interesting irony. It reminds us throughout the play of the moral ambiguity and the naiveté of the whole Christian community.

Antonio's self-righteousness is the burden as well as the wonder of friends and enemies alike. Even courteous social hypocrisy (i.i.63–64) or a missed appointment (ii.vi.62–64) elicits his righteous chastisement. Salanio and Salarino with equal parts of pain and respect refer to "the good Antonio, the honest Antonio—O that I had a title good enough to keep his name company!" (III.i.12–13). But his dealings with Shylock are the real proof of his intolerant self-righteousness. Nothing in their relationship suggests a glimmer of humility or charity. In fact, the habitual and arrogant physical and mental insults we hear Antonio proudly admit (I.iii.107–30 passim) are damaging attributes of an otherwise good man. As much as Shylock, he is citing Scripture to justify his own questionable activities. Choking on the cruelty and corruption of his merchant world as they are embodied in Shylock, Antonio seems to lose sight of their paradoxical place in a comic or a Christian world that is also infused with grace.[21] According to the Pauline and liturgical passages quoted above, it is man's universal imperfection which makes God's grace amazing. However, Antonio seems so obsessed by his own perfection and the imperfection of others that he has no conception of grace. Paradoxically, his counterparts the festive Belmontians seem to rejoice almost exclusively in their grace without perceiving their imperfection. Shylock knows their mutual presumptuousness, but as a stage Jew he can only demand vengeance for it. Thus all of them possess pieces of the complete comic and Christian formula, but none of them can put it together properly.

Antonio's impossible love for Bassanio also dramatizes Belmont's and Antonio's imperfect relationships to the Christian and the comic ideals. His attempts at "greater love" are inevitably frustrated again and again because he is but a man living in an imperfect world. Antonio would sacrifice himself to win Portia's love for his friend. He would even renounce the entire world for this selfless love: "I think he only loves the world for him" (II.viii.50). But inevitably his gift of love loses Bassanio as well, confirming only the bitter half of Christ's famous paradox: "Hee that findeth his life, shall lose it: and hee that loseth his life for my sake, shall finde it" (Matt. 10:39). While Antonio's charity, like his "sacrifice," is unquestionably noble, it is also at least doubly flawed. It is partly selfish, demanding usury, recompense; and it is directed only towards one man, not all. His happiness for Bassanio in the final scene is tempered by the sadness of loss that marriage occasions, as well as the comic unnaturalness of Antonio's single state.[22]

Of course, neither his friends nor his enemies infer anything sordid in Antonio's love for Bassanio,[23] though much of the jesting that pervades the final festivity reminds us of sexual perversion. Rather, his love for Bassanio, like his abortive attempt at self-sacrifice, suggests all varieties of human folly, the inevitable breach between the Christian ideal and its limited realization among men. No one can perfectly play Christ, in love or in sacrifice. Because the doctrinal controversy about Communion and Christ's unique sacrifice includes this impossibility as a central issue, let us see how much light it can shed on the inevitable irony of Antonio's "sacrifice."

Two verbal allusions first alert us to the controversial subject of "sacrifice" and Communion during the pivotal scene of Bassanio's choice of the caskets. The second is more immediately obvious to us today. Bassanio, having just won Portia's hand, interprets Antonio's letter and his plight in terms which compare his sacrifice to Christ's as it is described in the Communion service:

> Here is a letter, lady,
> The paper as the body of my friend,
> And every word in it a gaping wound,
> Issuing lifeblood.           (III.ii.263–66)

Even a twentieth-century audience is surprised by the extravagance of the comparison. Bassanio seems momentarily to have interpreted Antonio's acts of "greater love" as Christlike; implicitly, he seems to have compared the paper and the words of the letter to the body and the blood of the Christian Communion. Emphasizing this startling moment for Shakespeare's Christian audience, and properly directing its significance, Portia earlier in the scene describes her offering of herself for Bassanio by using the pivotal term in the Catholic-Protestant-Puritan controversy concerning Communion: "I stand for sacrifice" (III.ii.57). In that controversy "sacrifice" refers to Christ's sacrifice, "once only" offered for man according to the Anglican controversialists. It also refers to the mystical functions of the Catholic priest during the Communion service, his reenactment on the altar of Christ's sacrifice, and his mediation of grace to the congregation. Relevant cognate issues concern the doctrine of transubstantiation, the denial of the cup to the laity, the impossibility of future offers of sacrifice, and even the place of Jews in the controversy. Occurring together as they do at prominent moments during the turning point of the play, and pointing so obviously to Antonio's sacrifice by Shylock, these two allusions to Communion and "sacrifice" should have alerted Shakespeare's audience that this second most important Reformational controversy[24] might have further relevance to *The Merchant of Venice*.

As we established in the chapter on *Love's Labor's Lost*, most Renaissance Christians would acknowledge Christ to be the only perfect sacrifice. Only Christ could have fulfilled the Law of the Old Testament; only Christ, therefore, could have liberated mankind to try and follow His new commandment of love and forgiveness.[25] Though every Christian can symbolically participate in the communal offering of himself to God, no man can stand for sacrifice, because no man can ever perfectly perform good works. As we also recall from that chapter, the Protestant controversialists would have made much more of this inevitable imperfection of good works than the Catholic, since such imperfection can be used to support their doctrine of salvation by faith. William Fulke counters Gregory Martin's argument that St. Paul prefers charity (love) to faith with just this argument: "Wee never sawe the man, nor ever shall, that loved his neighbour as himselfe. Therefore unperfect love doth not perfectly fulfill the law."[26] Luther, Tyndale, and Bullinger all take a similar position.[27] The imperfect love and forgiveness of a self-righteous Christian (Antonio) trying to stand for sacrifice through a Christlike act of greater love might well have suggested this basic issue of the doctrinal controversy.

An even more impressive connection between the play and the controversy concerns the position that Christ's sacrifice, once enacted, never again occurs literally, even during Communion. Such a belief diminishes for the Protestant controversialist the importance of both the Mass and the Priest as mystical intermediaries between man and God. It also challenges the doctrine of transubstantiation; the body and blood are not sacrificed again and again, but "once onely." Nowell's catechism, addressing these issues, advises that Christ alone could offer to die for the sins of the world. Antonio's posturing notwithstanding, we can neither reenact his sacrifice sacramentally nor perform it ourselves in life: "As for the prerogative of offering for sins, it pertaineth to Christ alone, as to him which is the eternal Priest; which also when he died upon the cross, once made that only and everlasting sacrifice for our salvation, and fully performed the same for ever. For us there is nothing left to do, but to take the use and benefit of that eternal sacrifice bequeathed us by the Lord himself, which we chiefly do in the Lord's Supper."[28] The emphasis is strikingly redundant here and in the *Book of Common Prayer: "once* made that *only* and *everlasting* sacrifice for our salvation, and *fully* performed the same *forever"* (my italics). The homilist is just as emphatic: "He hath made upon his Crosse a full and sufficient sacrifice for thee, a perfect cleansing of thy sins, so that thou acknowledgest no other Saviour, Redeemer, Mediatour, Advocate, Intercessour, but Christ onely, and that thou mayest say with the Apostle, that he loved thee, and gave himselfe for thee."[29] Notice the prominence of *sacrifice* in both quotations. The word is stressed to counter the Catholic use of *sacrifice* to describe the priest's mystical and mediative function during the Mass. He was considered to be reenacting, ritually and corporeally, Christ's sacrifice for salvation, and mediating its benefits to the layman.[30]

In contrast to Christ's literal sacrifice of his life is the spiritual sacrifice required of the Christian communicant: "And here we offer and presente unto the, O Lord, our selves, our soules, and bodies, to be a reasonable, holy, and lively sacrifice unto the."[31] Neither its Pauline source nor commentary by Augustine or the Geneva marginal gloss allows any confusion between this symbolic, living sacrifice and Christ's literal, dying one. In Romans 12:1 we read, "Give up your bodies a living sacrifice, holie, acceptable unto God, *which is* your reasonable serving of God" (Geneva). Sacrifice is service, not death, and certainly not a symbolic execution. Augustine explains that the term is metaphoric: "Every work of mercy towards others or ourselves, if it be directed to God, is truly sacrifice. Every person consecrated to God is a sacrifice." Aquinas calls this "sacrifice" an "inner human act of conscious conformity to the divine will."[32] The Geneva commentary's gloss of the passage in Romans is understandably even more emphatic: "In stede of dead beasts, livelie sacrifice: in stede of the blood of beastes which was but a shadowe & pleased not God of it self, the acceptable sacrifice of the spiritual man, framed by faith to godlines and charitie." This spiritual signification of a living sacrifice, the faith or love that does not die, would have been granted by both Protestants and Catholics. Theologically speaking, there is no confusing this sacrifice with Christ's. The only controversial issue here concerns whether the priest literally performs the sacrifice again during Communion. But Antonio's Christian friends, and possibly even Antonio himself, ironically if briefly make that first mistake.

Their most preposterous exaggeration of Antonio's self-image occurs during the casket scene in Belmont. But Antonio himself either shares or encourages such confusion between his sacrifice and Christ's.[33] The best evidence of this occurs during the trial scene. There Antonio self-consciously plays the sacrificial victim, and embellishes his role with a continuous if unconscious false humility. Antonio must know that his friends are awed by his goodness, not his weakness; still he can say,

> I am a tainted wether of the flock,
> Meetest for death. The weakest kind of fruit
> Drops earliest to the ground, and so let me.
> (IV.i.114–16)

The pun on his own meetness for death is also of liturgical origin, and could have reminded any imaginative listener of the Anglican Communion service. During its antiphonal responses, the congregation responds to the priest who is about to bless their sacramental meal, "It is mete and right so to do." To this the priest responds, "It is very mete, right, and our bounden duety . . ." (pp. 103, 101). Such a punning reference to his appropriately sacrificial flesh further emphasizes Antonio's inflated self-image, his presumptuous likeness to Christ. Its liturgical echoes tighten the connections between the Shrovetide context, the Communion controversy, and the play's ironies. Further, Antonio cannot enact the "sacrifice," the ultimate, Christlike act of "greater love"[34] selflessly. Antonio implores Bassanio first to witness the act, distrusting him in the process (III.ii.320), then to "write mine epitaph" (IV.i.118). Of course, there is nothing monstrous in this imperfect love, which cannot "give and hazard all" without the "interest" of acknowledgment and reverence. But martyrs do not usually appoint themselves or their chroniclers, nor do they proclaim, even with humility, their "meetness" for sacrifice. Antonio does.

When Bassanio hears in Belmont that Antonio's bond to the Jew is forfeit, and when he recalls the image of likeness to Christ Antonio has so carefully cultivated for himself, Bassanio naturally thinks with reverence that Antonio is dying a redemptive death to insure his comic happiness. Antonio seems to be reenacting Christ's "only and sufficient" sacrifice, or at least its sacrament. Bassanio clearly draws the comparison:

> I have engaged myself to a dear friend,
> Engaged my friend to his mere enemy
> To feed my means. Here is a letter, lady,
> The paper as the body of my friend,
> And every word in it a gaping wound
> Issuing lifeblood.          (III.ii.261–66)

Like the bread of Communion, the paper is the body of Antonio. Like the wine, the words are the sacrificial wounds, "issuing lifeblood." Like Christ's engagement to Death and Satan to deliver erring man, Antonio has engaged himself to his "mere enemy," the "devil incarnation" (II.ii.28), Shylock, "to feed" Bassanio's "means." These associations recur during the trial scene, when Bassanio offers to take Antonio's place. That place again is clearly both sacrificial and redemptive.

> I would lose all, ay sacrifice them all
> Here to this devil, to deliver you.
>                    (IV.i.284–85)

Portia is justifiably a little dismayed at the extravagance of Bassanio's offer of both of them for "sacrifice." But we might recall that she has proudly said of herself, "I stand for sacrifice," at the beginning of the casket scene, a scene which ends with the confusion of Antonio's sacrifice and Christ's. Thus Antonio, Bassanio, and Portia are all ironically involved in Christlike roles of sacrifice. Shakespeare twice calls attention to the irony of their impulse by using the key controversial word *sacrifice* to highlight it. Antonio's punning on his "meetness" for sacrificial death solidifies the connection. And Bassanio's interpretation of Antonio's letter in expressly communal terms makes it almost unavoidable. The words and the paper become "seal" and "symbol" of that great sacrifice they would all play out, but cannot.

When we then see Shylock enact his own ill-fated role in Venice by trying to extract the body and blood of his Christian scapegoat, and when we watch the Christians punish him in turn for his grievous error that is so much like their own, we sense the full dimensions of the play's ironies. For Shylock's lust for the living flesh of this exemplary Christian is an understandable if monstrous distortion of the Christians' own presumptuous misconceptions concerning both human perfection and Antonio's attempted "sacrifice." Lovely as they sound, even Portia's Christian precepts may betray the naive moral optimism that slightly taints the whole Christian community of Belmont. The ambiguous imagery of imperfect love during the festive conclusion thus seems the inevitable consequence of all of these imperfect relationships to the ideal of wise humility so common to Shakespearean comedy and its Christian heritage. Such threads of irony, glossed by the Shrovetide context as well as the Communion controversy in *The Merchant of Venice*, do not greatly alter the basic fabric of romance of which the play is woven. Nor do they approximate the richer ironies of *Measure for Measure*, where Angelo and Isabella exhibit flaws only dimly present in Antonio and Portia. But in Venice and in Belmont, such ironies cannot be totally ignored.

## iii. Shylock's Frustrated Communion

Though they are vastly different characters, Shylock and Antonio are spiritual communicants in their common Hebraic and Puritanical self-righteousness and in their related dependence upon fulfilling the Law. Their similarity is enhanced when each becomes the other's scapegoat. Since Antonio exemplifies both the best and the worst of the Christian community in the eyes of his adversary, he is most meet for Shylock's sacrificial knife. Assured of his own righteousness, Antonio seems ethically as much a stage Jew as a Christian throughout the play, but especially when he spits out uncharitably upon Shylock in the Rialto. Shylock is just as obviously Antonio's scapegoat and ours, embodying as he does both the vices of the Venetian business community and those of the comic *alazon*.[35] When he is expelled after the fourth act, poetic justice and the form of New Comedy are admirably fulfilled and we are glad to see him thwarted. But the Christian idealism that has been coexisting with the comic structure suffers something of a setback. For again, the Christian community should need no other scapegoat than Christ, once only offered for the remission of the sins of all men. Punishing and expelling Shylock in the guise of baptising him is thus a failure without parallel in Shakespeare's comedies. At worst it is blasphemous. But it is at least an act devoid of Shrovetide humility, forgiveness, and the communal Christian acknowledgment of universal human imperfection. To St. Paul shared human error should unite, not separate, Jew and Gentile. Here, because the Christians cannot perceive their communion in imperfection with the Jew, he is baptized literally but never spiritually. His absence in Act V makes that failure clear to all of us.[36]

Shylock shares the literal-mindedness and the self-righteousness of his Christian enemies, even though he cannot share their sacraments. As Antonio tries literally to fulfill the law and stand for sacrifice, so Shylock pursues the bloody, literal sacrifice of the old covenant. As he himself interprets his actions:

> The villainy you teach me I will execute, and it shall go hard but I
> will better the instruction. (III.i.62–64)

Additional exegesis of Romans 12:1, the passage Portia alludes to when she remarks on the breach between Christian precept and Christian practice, indicates how well-equipped Shylock might have been as a Jew to better their instruction. According to Colet, St. Paul, in urging the Romans to present their bodies as living sacrifices, "is covertly reproving the sacrifices of . . . the Jews, who . . . were accustomed to make oblations of victims on festival days by slaughtering thousands of sheep, and to glut the whole temple with blood; thinking that by this act they gave great pleasure to God."[37]

But if such bloody sacrifice could be associated with Colet with the

Jews, and therefore by Shakespeare's audience with Shylock's literal attempt upon the body and blood of a Christian, it could also be cited by William Tyndale to attack the Catholic doctrine of transubstantiation. According to Tyndale, the Jews abhorred the eating of Christ because they "could not see that Christ's flesh, broken and crucified, and not bodily eaten, should be our salvation and this spiritual meat." But the Catholics, continues Tyndale, who believe in "sacrifice" and transubstantiation, have even less faith than the Jews: "Our fleshy Papists (being of the Jews' carnal opinion) yet abhor it not, neither cease they daily to crucify and offer him up again, which was once for ever and all offered, as Paul testifieth."[38] Embarrassing as such polemics might seem today, they were the stock-in-trade of Reformation sectarian exchanges. They were readily available to Shakespeare's contemporaries, in texts like Tyndale's, in sermons, and in the catechism. *Certaine Sermons or Homilies*, for example, calls this Catholic belief in sacrifice and transubstantiation "a grosse carnall feeding, basely objecting and binding ourselves to the elements and creatures" (pp. 200–201); "we must then take heed," the homily says elsewhere, "lest of the memory, it be made a sacrifice, lest of a communion, it be made a private eating" (p. 198). Nowell's *Catechism* says transubstantiation would "fill them with abhorring that receive the sacrament, if we should imagine his body . . . to be enclosed in so narrow a room, . . . or his flesh to be chawed in our mouth with our teeth, and to be bitten small, and eaten as other meat" (p. 216). The literal and repeated sacrifice of flesh and blood relates both to the frequent sectarian debates about the nature of the sacrament and to the relationships of Jews, Catholics, and Anglicans. That the key term, *sacrifice,* is alluded to and key issues enacted in *The Merchant of Venice* suggests again that Shakespeare was using this well-known controversy to investigate the complicated ironies of an imperfect but self-satisfied Christian community and a Jew whose lust for Antonio's body and blood could finally be satisfied neither literally nor symbolically.

Reinforcing such undercurrents of the controversy are the play's repeated references to eating and starving. To suggest like Coriat that Shylock's problem is anal-erotic[39] makes little sense in the context of the dramatic actions or the understandings of Shakespeare's contemporaries. But to suggest that because he is persistently spurned by the Christian community he is driven in revenge to enact a bloody sacrifice reminiscent of Christian Communion is directly within the spirit of the play. Denied all spiritual communion by the Christians (who stole Jessica) as well as by his own villainy, he pursues in his hunger a literal anti-Communion instead,[40] one encouraged further by Antonio's own misunderstandings of "sacrifice" and righteousness. As a Jew Shylock might well commit a bloody, literal, vengeful sacrifice, a "grosse carnall feeding," a "private eating." For as Shylock finally tells Jessica, he would "feed upon" this "prodigal Christian" in hate if he cannot dine with Christians in love. Such references to the "meals" of Jew and Christian fill out the symbolic dimensions of Shylock's obsessive appetite for Antonio's body and blood. They also suggest that Shylock's final revenge upon the Christians is his exposure of their own imperfect treatment of a bitter enemy, and their unawareness of that imperfection.

At Shylock's first appearance in the play his language unconsciously expresses a perverse hunger. Almost immediately he says about Antonio,

> If I can catch him once upon the hip,
> I will feed fat the ancient grudge I bear him.
> (I.iii.42–43)

Antonio's appearance is then greeted by the most astonishing "Freudian slip" in Shakespeare:

> Rest you fair, good signior!
> Your worship was the last man in our mouths."
> (I.iii.55–56)

When Shylock is invited to dinner with the Christians earlier in the scene, he categorically turns it down, showing his conscious disgust over eating with them. Simultaneously, however, his language indicates how closely Shylock associates Christian dining and Christian worship: "I will not eat with you, drink with you, nor pray with you" (I.iii.33–34). In these ways, feasting and flesh consistently relate to the human communion which Shylock desperately needs and will never experience, and the mystical Christian Communion he does not understand.

They also suggest the universal communion with foolish, imperfect mankind that this Christian community never achieves.

Shylock is consistently uneasy when he tries to explain his desire for the strange terms of the bond. In many scenes he is dumbfounded and irritated by his own irrational and thriftless behavior (1.iii.161–63; III.i.44–47). As late as the trial Shylock responds to the question of his desire for Antonio's flesh with a defiant and evasive reply:

> You'll ask me why I rather choose to have
> A weight of carrion flesh than to receive
> Three thousand ducats. I'll not answer that,
> But say it is my humor.          (IV.i.40–43)

Incapable of understanding the impulse himself, incapable of explaining how a Jew would prefer worthless, carrion flesh to so much money, beset by a perplexing symbolic condition he can neither explain nor comprehend, Shylock evades the question, publicly and personally. All Shylock knows, and all he can communicate, is that he desires the body and the blood of a Christian.

Shylock's complex attitude toward the Christians' dinners furthers our sense that dinners have communal implications in the play. As in no other Shakespearean play, characters so frequently refer to dining together that such dining becomes our sense of the natural Christian condition. Dinners are consistently focal points for celebration and companionship. For example, Lorenzo promises to meet Gratiano after dinner (1.i.104), and Portia delays Morocco's hazard until the same time (II.i.44). Gratiano promises to meet Bassanio at suppertime (II.ii.192). The Duke celebrates the trial's happy conclusion by inviting Portia to dinner (IV.i.399); his generosity is almost ritually followed by Gratiano's similar invitation of Portia to a celebratory meal (IV.ii.7–8). Lorenzo, Launcelot, and Jessica joke at length about diners and festivity (III.v.39–83). Finally, Bassanio deems an elegant dinner the reward for love: "I do feast tonight / My best esteemed acquaintance" (II.ii.158–59). Like Communion these dinners celebrate and reward shared love.

Shylock, in contrast, is niggardly with his food. His skinny servant must laugh hollowly when his master upbraids him for eating too much: "Thou shalt not gormandize / As thou hast done with me" (II.v.3–4). Shylock seems to have starved his whole household in his material and spiritual thrift. Jessica, for example, mentions the "taste of tediousness" (II.iii.3) that pervades their house. But though Shylock instinctively refuses his one invitation to dine with the Christians (I.ii.31–34), he then compulsively and ambiguously reverses his decision and decides to attend:

> I am bid forth to supper, Jessica.
> There are my keys. But wherefore should I go?
> I am not bid for love—they flatter me—
> But yet I'll go in hate to feed upon
> The prodigal Christian.            (II.v.11–15)

Here Shylock almost articulates for us the submerged irony of his compulsion to eat with—nay, "upon"—the Christian. His supper will not be one of love, that communal meal shared by Christians and traditionally called "love" in the homily and the catechism.[41] Instead it will be a supper celebrating their hatred for him and his for them, a complete reversal of the sacrament of Communion and the image of Christian dining established elsewhere in the play. Even worse, while he dines with Antonio and Bassanio, their Christian friends steal away with Shylock's last remnant of human communion, his daughter Jessica. The meal is doubly prodigal: Shylock is hypocritical to attend thus in hatred, but his hosts share his hypocrisy and as Christians should perceive this common error much more readily than Shylock. They never do.

Of course, Shylock does not get the chance to carve out Antonio's body and blood, even in hatred. Portia mercifully tricks him, after first arousing him to a feverish expectation during the trial. The Duke recalls an old law against aliens, and strips him of his wealth. And then Shylock is given literally what he never knew he wanted. He is forced to join the Christian community after all. The Shrovetide and Communion ironies intensify again in this scene. Antonio wants only to stand for sacrifice and exhibit perfect, Christlike love. Consequently he has renounced the world and prepared himself to die. Instead he is given the life and later the goods he had willingly resigned. Simultaneously, his attempts to act Christlike have made him less so, more presumptuous, more contemptuous of imperfection. Shylock pursues a literal, bloody, ritualistic Communion of retribution upon the greatest Christian in his community. He is diverted from his literal bond only to be made through baptism a Christian communicant, a fellow of enemies who seem no more capable of forgiving him than he can forgive them. Ostensibly their forced conversion is merciful, directing a monstrous cannibalism to the Table of our Lord.[42] But the aesthetic sense of the moment is one of defeat and exclusion, not Shylock's salvation. That is why so many readers, viewers, and actors have found the moment unsatisfactorily slick. When Portia denies Shylock the blood and offers him only the flesh (IV.i.304), Shakespeare may remind us of the Communion controversy once again: the Catholic communicant, unlike the Protestant, is given the wafer but not the wine.[43] When the Christians have to resort to the letter of the law, it seems that they have joined the Jew rather than defeating him. In fact, Shylock's absence from the fellowship of Act V announces the negative thrust of their partial and ironic victory. Both Antonio and Shylock, two central and occasionally parallel characters, suffer the same imperfect mercy at the end of the play, and its festivity is the more ambiguous because their fates are so similar.

## iv.  Portia and the Ironic Festivity of Belmont

Antonio tries to play Christ in *The Merchant of Venice*, but inevitably he is not quite up to the role. Similarly, Portia is the play's attractive Christian apologist, but she too cannot quite live up to her own idealism. Her plea for mercy is justly called by Bradbrook "the most purely religious utterance [in all of Shakespeare]—the most directly based upon Christian teaching, with its echoes of the Lord's Prayer, the Christian doctrine of salvation, and the words of Ecclesiasticus 35.20— 'Mercy is seasonable in time of affliction, as clouds of rain in the time of drouth.' "[44] She is certainly closer to perfection than Antonio, young and charming in her lively speech, "rich and pure in poetic feeling." To Mrs. Kemble she is the "ideal of a perfect woman. . . . Laughter-loving, light-hearted, true-hearted, deep-hearted, . . . full of

. keen perception, of active efficiency, of wisdom prompted by love, of tenderest unselfishness, of generous magnanimity." Mrs. Jameson ranks her first among Shakespeare's women for her "high mental powers, her enthusiasm of temperament, her decision of purpose, and her bouyancy of spirit."[45] Portia deserves much of this praise, but not all.

For like Antonio she also leaves some readers puzzled or dissatisfied by her elusive imperfections. Some find her only a "a trifle colorless" or overly conventional. To others she is affected, pedantic, and even prejudiced.[46] They are uneasy with her treatment of her suitors as well as her direction of the trial scene, and uncertain how to take either her manipulation of Bassanio's choice of the leaden casket or the ambiguities of the festivity she conducts at the play's conclusion. A glance at these moments will reveal that Portia's bondage lies, like Antonio's, in a persistent if slight imperfection that Portia twice acknowledges preceptually but never quite embraces as her own. Thus her small share of Shrovetide presumptuousness also contributes to the play's undercurrents of irony.

There is no question that Portia knows the precept of universal human imperfection. Her first words to Nerissa remind all of us of the inevitable breach between precept and practice: "If to do were as easy as to know what were good to do, chapels had been churches, and poor mens' cottages princes' palaces. It is a good divine that follows his own instructions" (I.ii.12–15). Her most memorable speech presents the quality of mercy in similar terms: "In the course of justice none of us / Should see salvation" (IV.i.197–98). For this reason must Christians try to forgive their enemies; for this reason also they take the sacrament commemorating Christ's only sacrifice for the remission of their sins. But between these moments of apparent Christian and comic wisdom, Portia seems, like the divine she referred to in Act I, incapable of applying her own instruction to herself. She seems unaware of her prejudice towards the suitors, unaware that she is cheating just a little during the casket scene, and unaware that the Jew cannot possibly understand her Christian arguments during the trial. This naiveté makes her less compassionate towards others than Grebanier suggests (p. 232). "Her awareness of her own fallibility" would "endear her to us" if only she carried it more consistently with her, or applied it more directly to the minor flaws she occasionally if inevitably exhibits.

Olivia in *Twelfth Night*, Beatrice in *Much Ado*, Rosalind in *As You Like It*, and Helena and Hermia in *A Midsummer Night's Dream* all learn the wisdom of such humility as their play proceeds; Viola and the ladies of *Love's Labor's Lost* seem to have it from the start, and gradually teach it to their lords. Beatrice's discovery of the wisdom of folly in *Much Ado* is a culminating moment of the play:

> Stand I condemned for pride and scorn so much?
> Contempt, farewell! and maiden pride adieu!
> (III.i.108–9)

Such paradoxical wisdom is central to their joy and happiness throughout the rest of the play. Rosalind too has this wisdom: "Love is merely a madness . . . [but] the lunacy is so ordinary that the whippers are in love too" (III.ii.376–79). Like Orlando, ("I will chide no breather in the world but myself, against whom I know most faults" [III.ii.267–68]), Rosalind is never far from the comic and Christian wisdom of folly as she plays out her many roles with humor in Arden. Viola too knows better than to take herself too seriously as a man or a woman. When Feste tries to get her to praise herself, she parries his thrust with wit and humility:

> CLOWN. I think I saw your wisdom there.
> VIOLA. Nay, an thou pass upon me, I'll no more with thee.
> (III.i.40–41)

Further, both of them charm us when they let their "weaker" womanliness slip through their masculine roles. Viola, when she is amusingly challenged to strip her sword stark naked, readily admits:

> I am one that had rather go with sir priest than sir knight. I care not who knows so much of my mettle. (III.iv.255–56)

And Rosalind actually faints upon seeing the bloody handkerchief ("how well I counterfeited" [IV.iii.168]). As she has said, "Dost thou think, though I am caparisoned like a man, I have a doublet and hose in my disposition?" (III.ii.185–87). We are glad the answer is no.

Though Portia speaks the wisdom of such folly, she neither carries this lively awareness of her own imperfection with her nor does she try to transmit it to others. There are no funny, foolish slips when she plays the man; there are also no charming lapses into girlhood. Thus her machinations as a man, unlike Rosalind's or Viola's, seem too powerful, too sure. In the trial scene and the ring plot that follows it this lack of balance makes her seem vengeful as well as edifying, too dominant, and not a little selfish or petulant. She may, as Bryant has suggested in a recent article, grow a little out of this selfishness as the play progresses, but she doesn't grow much. She may, as Dessen argues, even have taught Antonio and the Duke some of her precepts of mercy and forgiveness,[47] if not quite enough. Yet even if they are right, her measure of the wisdom of humility is still much less than that of Shakespeare's other comic heroines. That shortcoming is far less serious than Antonio's self-righteous attempt to stand for sacrifice. It is certainly not monstrous, like Shylock's vicious desire to prosecute his vengeful bond. But because Portia so seldom laughs at herself, or even knows when to do so, still more irony enters this basically romantic play. It could be that in Portia and Antonio Shakespeare is merely trying to draw idealized romantic characters without his usual comic complexity. But their mutual lack of the wisdom of folly has a great deal to do with the play's final effect. Let us look briefly at the moments when Portia most obviously lacks that wisdom.

Portia's witty jesting with Nerissa about the various infirmities of her first four suitors is a lively introduction to her and the casket plot. But as Portia herself admits, it is also a little uncharitable: "In truth, I know it is a sin to be a mocker" (1.ii.53). We need only think how seldom any of Shakespeare's other comic women are mockers to realize how much of a comic sin this must be. As Rosaline reprimands the lords, "I dare not call them fools" (Love's Labors Lost, v.ii.372). Portia continues to do it in spite of her precept. In fact, when she goes on in the same scene to refer to the black face of the fifth suitor, Morocco, as "the complexion of a devil" (1.ii.121), the theme of racial prejudice slips, however lightly, into Belmont. Right afterwards, in Venice, we experience Shylock's violent hatred of Antonio because he is a Christian; we also see Antonio's ugly self-righteousness towards the Jew. The juxtaposition is instructive. Morocco's defeat occasions an earlier racial slur from fair Portia's lips: "Let all of his complexion choose me so" (II.vii.78–79). Again the Jew's hatred and the Christians' in Venice follow hard upon this scene in Belmont and envelop it a little in irony. Lamenting the loss of "my ducats and my daughter," Shylock shouts, "Fled with a Christian! O my Christian ducats!" But as he rants against the Christians, one of them, Salanio, calls him "the dog Jew" (II.viii.14–18 passim). Racial prejudice is rarer and gentler in idyllic Belmont than it is in the urban harshness of Venice. But there is some prejudice in Belmont too, and no one seems particularly concerned.

Grebanier also finds Portia's gentle direction of Bassanio's choice of the leaden casket charming, and so it is. But for the highborn maiden of outspoken Christian values, it is also at least a bit ambiguous. Portia heightens this ambiguity at the beginning of the scene by telling us that she has resisted the temptation to cheat:

> I could teach you
> How to choose right, but I am then forsworn;
> So will I never be."           (III.ii.10–12)

In these middle scenes of the other comedies, Shakespeare's comic maidens are joyfully coming to acknowledge their share of folly. Portia's wavering from her absolute moral position as her scene is played out is delightfully human, and we can cherish that humanity as part of her excitement and her confusion. But Portia would make us much more comfortable with that folly if she simply admitted it to herself or to us. Instead, she protests again that she will not be forsworn: "You'll make me wish a sin / That I had been forsworn"; "Let fortune go to hell for it, not I" (III.ii.13–14, 21). And then she is forsworn. Bassanio would have to be a slow lad indeed to miss the well-known hints she lays out for him. "Pause a day or two / Before you hazard" is but the first of several reminders of the casket's inscription ("Who chooseth me must give and hazard all he hath"). "Venture" is not far off. Nor is that familiar "I stand for sacrifice" (III.ii.57) a bad hint either. But there is more. "But 'tis to peize the time" (III.ii.22) can suggest either lead weights or the lead peizing between panes of stained glass. The insistent rhymes of her accompanying song, "Tell me where is fancy bred" are "bred," "head," "nourishèd," and "fed"; all rhyme with "lead." And finally the song itself, about disdaining outward show, things of the eyes, for higher values, is no mean clue either. Grebanier, who has assembled all these clues, is delighted by their cleverness: "No *man*, of course, would know how to break a vow and keep it at the same time."[48] This may be so. But amidst the lavish romanticism and obvious joy of the scene, there is also some uneasiness. Portia's hypocrisy may be charming, but it is still hypocrisy, especially since she has just proclaimed her total innocence. Bassanio naively directs us to this ambiguity when he says,

> So may the outward shows be least themselves;
> The world is still deceived with ornament.
> (III.ii.73–74)

We see what we want to see in the mirrors of this scene, and of the world. But there is surely a leaden irony to be reflected here as well as the gold and silver beauty of romance. Unless we see both images, we are not seeing the whole play.

Even the image of "love's wealth" that permeates the scene is partly ironic. Portia is "something of merchandize" in this young Jason's eyes; she even images herself forth in monetary terms:

> I would be trebled twenty times myself,
> A thousand times more fair, ten thousand times more rich,
> That only to stand high in your account
> I might in virtues, beauties, livings, friends,
> Exceed account.      (III.ii.153–57)

Her humility is impressive at this moment; so is her sense of great wealth as the beloved of Bassanio and the mistress of Belmont. This incredible wealth, this boundless grace of love and riches, must stand in spirit as it does in words behind Portia's naive and uncompassionate assumption that she can make adequate reparation to the Jew:

> What, no more?
> Pay him six thousand, and deface the bond.
> Double six thousand and then treble that,

Before a friend of this description
Shall lose a hair through Bassanio's fault.
(III.ii.298–302)

But as we have seen in the ugly dimensions of Antonio's self-righteous treatment of the Jew, and in Shylock's agonized response to his lost daughter, it is no "petty debt" they owe the Jew. Their joy, like their assurance that Antonio can be "redeemed" with money, has an uncomfortably metallic clink. Portia and Bassanio sound momentarily like Daisy and Tom over in East Egg. Like them too, this pair will finally escape the city's ironic setting, and remain oblivious to their share of its meaning. The wisdom of Shrovetide and Communion seems to have no place in Belmont.

The trial scene follows. Though harsher than the casket scene, it is also basically celebratory. Few want Shylock to carve out Antonio's flesh and blood, and he is not allowed to do so. Most enjoy the poetic justice of a villain "hoist on his own petard," and exult with Gratiano when Portia turns the tables. Portia's speech on the quality of mercy is a ravishing statement of Christian precepts central to the play; her strategy to thwart Shylock only if she cannot make him merciful is both clever and charitable. One can even argue that the forced conversion at the end of the scene saves Shylock's obdurate soul, or that he could have remained a Jew and forfeited the other half of his wealth if his religion really mattered to him.[49] But because the whole scene hinges upon contrasts between the old law and the new, between Judaism and Christianity, so its effect, like the previously mentioned similarities between Antonio and Shylock, is complicated by continuing similarities between the Christians and the Jew. Most obvious in this regard are Portia's pointed references to the exemplary Christian mercy of Antonio and the duke: "Down therefore, and beg mercy of the duke," or "What mercy can you render him, Antonio?" (IV.i.361, 376). Similarly, the duke pardons him, "that thou shalt see the difference of our spirit." Reminiscent of Portia's own protestations of innocence during the casket scene, these presumptuous statements remind us again of a "Jewish" or a "Puritan" self-righteousness that is unaware of its own small share of imperfection. Even in the "quality of mercy" speech itself, Portia cannot avoid the irony of basing her argument to the Jew on Christian doctrines of God's forgiveness, Christ's sacrifice, and man's fortunate finitude, teachings that Shylock could hardly be expected to know, much less suddenly believe. He would have to be a Christian to understand her at all. Such ironies do not overwhelm the celebratory nature of the trial scene; they do make us uncomfortable with it.

These ironic similarities between the Christians and the Jew had some precedent in Renaissance drama before Shakespeare. Alan Dessen has recently established a "Renaissance habit of mind that could conceive of Jewishness as a spiritual or moral condition lurking behind the façade of orthodox Christian profession." Several plays, including Marlowe's *The Jew of Malta,* use the stage Jew to indict false Christians,[50] much like the Protestant controversialists used the stereotype of Jewish literal-mindedness and bloodiness to indict the Catholics in the Communion controversy. In this tradition Shakespeare has already had Shylock remind the Christians of his own humanity and their vengefulness (III.i.51–63). During the trial he exposes the breach between Christian precept and practice by discussing Christian slaveholding (IV.i.90–103). Then Gratiano emerges after Portia's defeat of Shylock (one depending on her precise legalism) as a "Jewish" Christian, baiting the stage Jew as he had baited Antonio, urging "a haltar gratis" and a rope for vengeance, braying his ill-will towards Shylock and his goodwill for Antonio in the same impulsive breath. To be fair, the scene also contains Portia's patient attempt to make Shylock merciful, the Duke's decision not to take his life, and Antonio's not to take all his wealth, if he will become a Christian. As Dessen says, "at least some of the figures on stage have listened and learned" (p. 243). But even this learning troubles us. For the Christians' relationship to Shylock during the trial scene fails in precisely the area of "sacrifice" that the living Christian could perform according to the Communion controversy, the merciful, charitable, selfless treatment of another in God's name. The Christians speak well of mercy, and they might believe that forcing Shylock into the Christian communion will save his soul. But because the merciful judgments of Antonio and the Duke can seem as punitive as merciful, their charity appears as much show as substance. "Mark, Jew," they seem to echo

Gratiano, "we know how to forgive even if you do not." Thus it might as well be a ceremony of exclusion as one of conversion that they conduct in Act IV. Indeed, the case can be made that the Christians are making Shylock "eat and drincke [his] owne dampnation" by forcing him to become an unworthy and unwilling Christian communicant.[51] Such imperfect charity may be inevitable in any attempt to deal mercifully with a Shylock. But its effect is still felt in Shylock's agonized exit from the trial and in his haunting absence from the play's festive conclusion. The Communion controversy, like the Shrovetide context of presumption and despair, continues to enrich the ironies of such moments. But the Christians, Portia included, are blissfully oblivious to such ironies. In their preoccupation with their own literal escape from Shylock's clutches, they have failed to grasp their inevitable spiritual kinship with him in imperfection. Bryant is correct when he says, "This selfish preoccupation is of the degree that characterizes most fallible, redeemable human beings" (p. 611). But in most of Shakespeare's romantic comedies the characters have begun to escape its bondage before the festive celebration can occur. In *The Merchant of Venice* they have not.

We can judge from Gratiano's taunting of the Jew and other ironies during the trial that the society of Venice is going to retain some of the characteristics it sought to dispel in its scapegoat Shylock.[52] Consequently, the only successful resolution in festivity must be achieved away from Venice in a retreat, in a green world such as Belmont. This need to escape the real world urges us again to re-examine the play's seemingly neat achievement of Christian love, mercy, and justice.[53] Ideally for Shakespearean festivity, the reconciliation of green world and real should either be promised or realized, as it is in every mature festive comedy except this one. But in *The Merchant of Venice* even Belmont is touched by Shrovetide reminders of perversion, guilt, hypocrisy, and infidelity. Shylock's memory and the unacknowledged imperfection of Antonio and Portia haunt the imagery and the jesting of the festive conclusion. The guilt which is carried back to Belmont is no greater, of course, than the guilt of all individuals and all cultures of all times. But it is still perplexing, especially within a self-contented Christian society. The unconsciously tainted society of Portia's Belmont joins Antonio's ironic likeness to Christ and Shylock's frustrated Communion in injecting important ambiguities into the concluding festivity.

The lyrical conversion of Lorenzo and Jessica carries the ambiguous tones of the trial back to Belmont. To be sure, these two lovers are as sympathetic a pair as Shakespeare draws in Venice or Belmont. Further, the love-pairings of Jessica and Lorenzo and those to follow represent at least superficially the reconciliation of Jew and Christian and Venice and Belmont.[54] But their language may simultaneously indict the remaining imperfections of both societies and the uneasiness of their jointure. The lovers recall past romantic figures, all of whom— Cressid, Thisbe, Dido, and Medea—connote tragedy and infidelity: fickleness, familial discord, unfaithfulness, and murder (v.i.1–14). The light joking that follows immediately, about Jessica's theft and desertion and Lorenzo's false vows of faith, further disturbs the romantic surface by faint undertones of falseness. As Lorenzo sings of love, other suggestions of past individual and social failures creep in through the predominantly romantic, tender veneer. In particular, the unheard music of the spheres reminds him of man's frailty and decay:

> But whilst this muddy vesture of decay
> Doth grossly close it in, we cannot hear it.
>
> (v.i.64–65)

Even the allusions to Diana suggest the failure of Endymion, man, to achieve her. Lorenzo explains Jessica's sadness by contrasting man's bestial savagery with his ideal potential (v.i.69–88), evoking once again in Belmont the memory of a world—Venice—where man is obviously imperfect. A melancholy sense of transitory, romantic joy accounts for some of the ironic imagery in this exchange. The unacknowledged imperfection of the Christian community gives it special emphasis.

Though it is equally engaging in its wit and playfulness, the ring plot also conveys undertones of irony. Its perplexing suggestions of the inevitable imperfections of finite love begin just after the trial's conclusion. Portia, exhilarated by her victory, demands her love-token back from Bassanio as payment for her services (IV.i.425–27). Antonio's plea seconds the disguised Portia's:

> My lord Bassanio, let him have the ring.
> Let his deservings, and my love withal,
> Be valued 'gainst your wife's commandèment.
>
> (IV.i.447–49)

Upon Antonio's urging Bassanio finally relents and becomes "unfaithful" to the letter of his wife's commandment, if not the spirit. Both pleas create the uncomfortable if amusing situation of two ostensible men pleading for the love and the love token given to another man by his wife. Back in Belmont, the ambiguity of Bassanio's dual relationship to his wife and his friend is further dramatized by his having to defend his "infidelity" to Portia—the very person who caused it. As a friend, Bassanio could act no other way. But as a lover he has failed, at least literally. Such frustrating finitude again suggests the larger ambiguity of Shylock's relationship to this festive group. His disposal was hardly a satisfactory blending of justice and mercy, just as the disposal of the rings could not possibly be judged moral or immoral, faithful or unfaithful. Letter and spirit are thus as ambiguously mixed in the Christians' foolish play as in their earnest business. But none of them seem to know it.

When Portia follows Lorenzo and Jessica into the final scene of the play, these ambiguities intensify. First, the light in darkness reminds her of a "naughty world" (v.i.91), but only superficially, since she is still oblivious to her own small but inevitable share of guilt. The imagery that follows is often romantic; it also contains many suggestions of infidelity and perversion. Gratiano grumbles about the lost ring, "Would he were gelt that had it, for my part" (v.i.144). This reference to geldings is paralleled when Nerissa responds "The clerk will ne'er wear hair on's face that had it!" (v.i.158). Men without their parts, like men without their beards, are strange bedfellows for the festive ending of a romantic comedy. So are transvestites. But Nerissa soon jokes, "Ay, if a woman live to be a man." After the ladies threaten a sexless marriage (v.i.190–93), they charge their husbands with infidelity: "I'll die for't but some woman had the ring!"; then they proudly proclaim their own unfaithfulness:

> PORTIA. Since he hath got the jewel that I loved,
> And that which you did swear to keep for me.
> I will become as liberal as you;
> I'll not deny him anything I have,
> No, not my body nor my husband's bed.
> (v.i.224–28)

Indeed, their husbands have already been cuckolded:

> PORTIA. For by this ring the doctor lay with me.
> NERISSA. And pardon me, my gentle Gratiano,
> For that same scrubbèd boy, the doctor's clerk,
> In lieu of this last night did lie with me.
> (v.i.259–62)

As poor Gratiano exclaims, "What, are we cuckolds ere we have deserved it?" Of course they are not. These riddles will be solved more easily than those on the caskets. But even the happy and conventional playfulness of such moments cannot completely negate their more serious suggestions that men and women, and society in general, are fickle and unpredictable, a fact that this society is only beginning to come to grips with. Orlando and Rosalind, Benedick and Beatrice finally come to celebrate the lesson of the horns as a basic element of the wisdom of folly. In Belmont such knowledge is still more a threat to happiness than a means to humility. It is thus as much a weapon of Portia's comic revenge as a vehicle for celebration or edification.

When the final note of infidelity is sounded (v.i.256–65), it is almost too late for another, less perplexing moral tone to supersede. A general sense of wonderment typically characterizes the last moments of the comic resolution, but the veneer of festivity in Belmont seems always to belie a dearth of awareness. In fact, it is almost at the very end of the play that Lorenzo, upon learning of the "special deed of gift . . . from the rich Jew," replies, "Fair ladies, you drop manna in the way / Of starvèd people (v.i.292–95). No one seems even vaguely aware of the grotesque inappropriateness of this last unfortunate thrust against Shylock and the Jews. In such a naive festivity Antonio's leaden "I am dumb!" (v.i.279) is almost as fitting a final word as the overabundant happiness around him.

The idea of the Christians' overabundance is not new to this scene. Nerissa discusses surfeiting in the same scene in which Portia alerts us to the inevitable breach between precept and practice. Her comments help us perceive again the common denominator between their naiveté and Shylock's hunger. Nerissa tells Portia, "they are as sick that surfeit with too much as they that starve with nothing" (i.ii.5–6). That this warning is pertinent to Portia's deliciously romantic condition is accentuated by its recurrence during the successful choice of the caskets in Act III, Scene i. There Portia rightfully offers a prayer which seems to go unanswered:

> O love, be moderate, allay thy ecstasy,
> In measure rain thy joy, scant this excess!
> I feel too much thy blessing. Make it less
> For fear I surfeit.        (iii.i.111–14)

Throughout the play, but especially in their escapist's paradise of Belmont, the Christians are so surfeited of their own love, wealth, righteousness, and communion, so presumptuous of comic grace, that they neither feel the spiritual hunger of others nor become aware of their own. They are not vicious characters, of course. But their ethical naiveté and their preoccupation with themselves color the play's final gaiety with ironic hues. The Christians are literally victorious in *The Merchant of Venice,* and Shylock gets about what he deserves. But Shakespeare's ideal comic festivity is usually spiritual, not physical; a festive state of mind, not a simplistic if colorful celebration; a sacrament, not a literal eating. It is ideally a communion of unworthiness, of imperfection, of humility, and of grace. Such Shrovetide wisdom has eluded the Christians in Belmont, in spite of their fair share of imperfections. Portia's precepts sound the familiar Erasmian and Pauline paradoxes that underlie Shakespeare's comic vision. But in practice neither she nor her Christian friends are yet blessed with the wisdom of their own folly.

# EPILOGUE

# "Good Wine Needs No Bush"

> If it be true that good wine needs no bush, 'tis true that a good play needs no epilogue; yet, to good wine they do use good bushes, and good plays prove the better by the help of good epilogues. What a case am I in then, that am neither a good epilogue, nor cannot insinuate with you in the behalf of a good play!     *As You Like It*

POSSIBLY BECAUSE epilogues have always been such a perfect place for the would-be wise to prove themselves begging or conjuring fools, both *As You Like It* and *The Praise of Folie* end by making fun of them. But even as they parody that convention, both epilogues also illustrate for one last time that the only way to be foolproof is to admit one's folly and gain the paradoxical freedom of humility. For "man is a giddy thing," after all, who must "vent his folly" more often than he would like, will he or nill he. Surely a book about Shakespearean comedy would be incomplete without a similar exercise. Let us look, then, briefly backwards and forwards, and finally, like Rosalind, make curtsy, and bid farewell.

This study has tried to demonstrate that Shakespeare's major romantic comedies employ with rich variety the paradoxical reversals of wisdom and folly most commonly associated in the Renaissance with the writings of St. Paul and Erasmus. In his Epistles, St. Paul instructs those who are overly proud of how much they know and how well they behave to glory instead in their infirmities. For "not one of them colde perceive by his owne wisdome this mysterie of Christ reveiled in the Gospel," or "acknowledge their owne follie & weakenes" and "beate downe [their] arrogancie."[1] Under considerable Pauline influence, the Christian liturgies contain this same paradox in the frequently reiterated doctrine of universal human imperfection, which is coupled with the promise that its acknowledgment and attempted amendment will be followed by the grace of God's forgiveness and love. Within such a Pauline or liturgical context it becomes most foolish to assume oneself wise, and most wise to know oneself foolish.

Man can know only in part; he can act only imperfectly in that knowledge. But if he knows and acknowledges such folly, he can find great joy.

Erasmus's notorious *The Praise of Folie* proudly acknowledges its own Pauline heritage. Crucially for us, it also bridges the considerable chasm between what is basically a theological paradox and the vision of Shakespeare's romantic comedies. First, Erasmus connects the theological concept of universal sin with the comic concept of universal folly, interchanging them frequently in his work (e.g., p. 119). Equally important, he takes the Pauline connection between the folly of madness and the ecstasy of religious faith and links it to the analogous madness of romantic love. In fact, Erasmus calls romantic and religious madness "nere sybbe" (pp. 122, 126–27). These theological and comic paradoxes have thus been connected by Erasmus long before Bottom alludes to St. Paul's famous description of the folly of faith in *A Midsummer Night's Dream,* or Feste alludes to St. Paul's equally famous passage about the childishness of unacknowledged folly in *Twelfth Night.*

William F. Lynch, V. A. Kolve, Nathan Scott, and O. B. Hardison all attest from different perspectives to the paradoxical "joy of finitude" that the comic and the Christian visions may thus both celebrate.[2] Its connection with Erasmus suggests how deeply this paradox is rooted in the Christian humanist tradition. Feste and Bottom voice only two of many pointed Erasmian, Pauline, and liturgical allusions and analogies in Shakespeare's romantic comedies. Shakespeare's comic theme of the wisdom of folly is enriched and indeed defined by a cluster of controversial Pauline allusions in *Love's Labor's Lost.* His parallel theme of the blessed madness of romantic faith profits equally from the lovers' Erasmian allusions in *A Midsummer Night's Dream.* In *Much Ado about Nothing* the romantic relationships of Benedick, Beatrice, and Claudio are so persistently compared to religious faith and skepticism, penance and repentance, that we are never allowed to ignore their delightful Pauline, Erasmian and liturgical dimensions. Touchstone and Jaques are two Erasmian fools in *As You Like It* whose frequent allusions to the paradox of the wisdom of folly usually indict only their own lack of humility; in contrast, the play shares the lovers' unusual humility by exposing and enjoying the great follies of art's feignings and the asinine but pretty rituals of lovers, their mutually foolish attempts to express the inexpressible. Feste's connected roles as wise fool and curate in *Twelfth Night* combine with Viola's traditional praise of folly, Sebastian's Erasmian embrace of the madness of love, and the play's festival interest in selfless love and edifying humiliation to suggest the frequent connections between its Christian and comic motifs. A major thrust of this culminating Shakespearean comedy is its movement towards acknowledged folly and the consequent achievement of great wisdom and great joy. The Shrovetide context of *The Merchant of Venice,* the ambiguous mixture of righteousness and self-righteousness instead of humility in its self-consciously Christian characters, and its intriguing allusions to the doctrinal controversy about the nature and efficacy of Communion make clearer and more intense its ironic relationship to these other comedies. In none of these plays is Shakespeare using allusions and analogies to teach his audience anything about Christian doctrine. He is instead depending upon their familiarity with contemporary doctrinal commonplaces and controversies to enrich and clarify his comic interest in the sanity of madness and the wisdom of folly.

Certain themes, character types, and actions unique to Shakespearean comedy would thus seem particularly influenced by their Pauline and Erasmian heritage. Most prominent is the theme of edification through humiliation. The lords in *Love's Labor's Lost,* the lovers in *A Midsummer Night's Dream,* Benedick, Claudio, and Beatrice in *Much Ado about Nothing,* Orlando and Rosalind in *As You Like It,* and Orsino, Olivia, Belch, Malvolio—virtually everyone in *Twelfth Night*—all need to be humiliated before they can love properly. The degree varies considerably, of course. The lords of *Love's Labor's Lost* need humility so badly they cannot be cured of their self-love by the end of the play. Orlando in *As You Like It* is much less flawed, but even he must suffer the embarrassments of speechlessness in Act I and Petrarchan effusiveness in Act III, the irreverent jesting of Rosalind and Jaques, and the long, ritualized courtship of Ganymede before he is finally proven ready for Hymen's grace. Rosalind, though playing instructive games with others through her disguise, must also learn to reject some of the unattractive poses she assumes. Her long waits in the forest may also teach her just how long she will wait for the right husband. Olivia is humiliated again and again in *Twelfth Night,* and must finally be rejected by her suitor and even her ostensible husband before she is finally ready to embrace love with humility and joy. Orsino just begins to embrace his folly as he embraces his new mistress, Viola, at play's end. Benedick and Beatrice in *Much Ado about Nothing* require an elaborate cure for their extreme pride, and Claudio requires deep humiliation, so foolishly do they all distrust their mates and trust their erring senses and reason when the play begins. And in *A Midsummer Night's Dream* the lovers outside of Athens are first loved, then shunned in the most formal version of this consistent comic purging of the lover's pride in what he knows and what he deserves. They finally learn, all of them, to welcome a love they neither deserve nor understand. This coming to accept love as a gift of grace transcending all understanding or merit is a Shakespearean theme closely related to the humble, communal acknowledgment of folly as a prerequisite to comic festivity. Sebastian in *Twelfth Night* and the lovers in *A Midsummer Night's Dream* most obviously and explicitly embrace the madness and absurdity of their good fortune, in words evocative of *The Praise of Folie.* But Olivia and Orsino in *Twelfth Night;* Claudio, Benedick, and Beatrice in *Much Ado;* and Orlando, Oliver, Rosalind, and Silvius in *As You Like It* all share facets of this same humility.

The heavy joking about infidelity and perversion in *The Merchant of Venice, As You Like It,* and *Much Ado,* and the addition of Olivia's falling for another woman in *Twelfth Night,* punctuate another side of this equation of humility and faith. The lovers must not only be purged of their own considerable pride; they must also become aware of the threatening possibility of imperfection in their beloved. Further, their faith in the beloved must then transcend this sure knowledge. They must not become skeptics. Claudio is the slowest of the lords to learn this difficult lesson. His experience is analogous to Orlando's confrontation of all of Rosalind's possible errors (through Ganymede and Jaques), Benedick's and Beatrice's final ability to marry in spite of the imperfect dust of which both sexes are made, and the lovers' nightmarish awareness of the unpredictability of love and lovers outside of Athens. Only in *Love's Labor's Lost* do the men fail to reach this level of sophistication. At the end of the play they have not yet acknowledged their own flaws, and are far from the more threatening but essential counterpart of that awareness, the concept of "sickness and health" that the marriage vow so insistently contains.

The imperfection of self-love and the need for humility are so pervasive in the romantic comedies that other characters, nonlovers or nonaristocrats, are even more seriously afflicted. Along with the nobler characters, we are saturated with their folly—and our own. Sometimes they are cured; sometimes not. Their catalogue reveals their consistency and their diversity: Armado, Holofernes, Bottom, Don John, Dogberry, everyone in Belmont, Jaques, Touchstone, Phebe, Oliver, Shylock, and Malvolio. How these characters are treated at the end of each of their respective plays determines the atmosphere of the celebration at the play's conclusion. Universal rejoicing over the perception of human imperfection represents the zenith of these treatments in *Much Ado, As You Like It,* and *Twelfth Night.* In each of these three plays fools and buffoons confound the wise, as St. Paul said they would; but by doing so they also offer them the greater wisdom of humility, if they will see themselves in the fool's glass. Viola, Feste, Touchstone, and Jaques all allude to their Erasmian and Pauline heritage in such a role, though they do not all understand it equally well. Even Dogberry's missayings are a more subtle, unconscious counterpart to his betters' misperceptions in *Much Ado.* Feste culminates the tradition when he dons the curate's robes in *Twelfth Night* and becomes the "foole for Christ" John Donne and St. Paul called all ministers of this paradoxical wisdom of folly. The lack of such an attitude of humility among the Christians in Belmont, like the absence of a wise fool, are two important indexes to the undercurrents of irony in that troublesome but fascinating play.

But as Viola's praise of folly suggests, the preceptor of these prideful comic characters need not be the only wise fool. Viola certainly has her successful go at bringing both Olivia and Orsino to the wisdom of folly. Rosalind consciously teaches Orlando something about a few of his Petrarchan absurdities, though she can never convince him not to love her. Most of the characters in *Much Ado* (even Don John, unintentionally) have a hand in teaching Benedick and Beatrice to have more faith in love, and to be less afraid of their own folly. Puck and Oberon in *A Midsummer Night's Dream* lead the lovers, Titania, and Bottom a merry chase for their own eventual good. And the Princess and her three ladies in *Love's Labor's Lost* spend much of the play trying to teach their thick-headed lords the wisdom of folly and the absurdity of self-love. Even Berowne may finally learn the lesson, if only after a year of penance.

Certain recurring actions in Shakespearean comedy also seem especially well-designed to teach erring mortals the wisdom of their own folly. Feste's catechising of Olivia and Orsino and his attempted ministry to Malvolio certainly belong in this category, as does Rosalind's catechising of Orlando about the passing of time. Both plays refer to the catechism by name at these moments, to make the connection clear. Penance is also prominent as a comic ritual to teach the wisdom of folly. The lords in *Love's Labor's Lost* are required by the Princess and her ladies to devote a year and a day learning their own unworthiness ("Teach the pained impotent to smile") and repenting their self-love. Only then might the play end like a comedy. And Claudio in *Much Ado* is directed in a parallel ritual of repentance by the father of the injured Hero. Perhaps after disrupting the ritual of marriage, Claudio must perform another ritual of repentance before he can be readmitted into the comic community.

Sometimes a play within the play conveys the wisdom of folly or the sanity of madness. In *Love's Labor's Lost* the Pageant of the Nine Worthies becomes a pageant of unworthiness, an unworthiness the lords will have to acknowledge before they can achieve festive happiness. In *A Midsummer Night's Dream* the literal, rational mistakes of Bottom's play remind us of the lovers' escape from the reasonable into a realm variously analogous to religious faith. In *Much Ado* a staged recital of their mutual faith and folly liberates Benedick and Beatrice from their twin follies of pride and faithlessness to a rebirth in humility and love. Witness the newly barbered Benedick! In *As You Like It* Rosalind and Celia can watch "a pageant truly played" that is not, finally, so far removed from their own "realistic" experience; then the play concludes with Rosalind as director of a preposterous drama in which everyone is matched and Hymen·blesses the country copulatives. It may be as we like it; it may make fun of our tastes and dramatic conventions. But these pageants clearly further the play's interest in the follies of lovers and art. In *Twelfth Night* Feste tries to cure Malvolio of his ill will and pride by playing a curate and a fool before him; unfortunately, Malvolio as audience is fool-proof and play-proof, and must go off and sulk alone while everyone else celebrates the liberating wisdom of folly and the sanity of madness. As with so many of these conventions, *The Merchant of Venice* is conspicuously different. The trial scene may be its playlet, but there Shylock is merely vanquished and humiliated. No one learns the more traditional wisdom of humility; no one carries it back to Belmont.

Shakespeare's comic artifice sometimes shares the wisdom of folly with his comic characters. *As You Like It,* like *A Midsummer Night's Dream,* is persistently about the folly of trying to dramatize romantic and aesthetic truths which surpass all understanding, a folly familiar to both St. Paul and Erasmus. *A Midsummer Night's Dream* stresses the receptive side of this question, the analogous roles of Bottom, the four lovers, Theseus, and the audience as imperfect beholders or interpreters of the transcendental. *As You Like It* emphasizes its expressive side, the foolish attempts of the lover or the artist, Orlando or Rosalind or Shakespeare himself, to convey transcendental truths. Both plays enrich this rather esoteric aesthetic interest with analogies between the rituals of true lovers and true believers. Both employ allusions like Bottom's or Touchstone's to connect their imaginative conventions and insights to the "most feignings" of all, the "most rare visions" of a St. Paul, which "eye hath not seen" and is not likely to see. Feste's epilogue, which admits that *Twelfth Night* is only a play, is also comfortable within this thematic context. In fact, all three plays end with epilogues in which Puck, Rosalind, and Feste remind us of the delicate fabric of their comic vision.

Most of these delightful motifs of characterization, theme, and action can probably be appreciated without an understanding of the Pauline and Erasmian paradoxes that lie behind them. But knowledge of Shakespeare's delicate use of the Christian heritage he shares with his contemporaries enriches our understanding of the plays, increases our pleasure in them, enhances our appreciation of Shakespeare's comic artistry, and enlarges our sense of the coherence of his comic vision. It also places that vision and that artistry squarely within the tradition of Renaissance humanism.

Though the focus of this study has been on six of Shakespeare's romantic comedies, its implications reach beyond these plays. Shakespeare's histories, problem plays, tragedies, and romances continue the comedies' interest in human imperfection, but that imperfection seems to have become both more sinister and more widespread. It has also become an increasingly important issue in the early seventeenth century. Douglas Bush, for example, notices a widening chasm around 1600 between "the pessimism inherent in evangelical Protestantism and the optimism inherent in Christian humanism" concerning the imperfect nature of man: "The Christian humanist of the Middle Ages or the Renaissance knew the inward things essential for the good life and what he did not know about the outer or even the inner world did not matter. For the seventeenth-century man both the outer and the inner world have become oppressively vast and dark, and the great question is 'What do I know?' "[3] In this brave new world of scientific rationalism man's finite ability to know or to do, his folly in the outer or the inner world, is becoming a dark threat rather than a paradoxical blessing. As Theodore Spencer has shown, Shakespeare's histories, his problem plays, and his tragedies seem to immerse themselves in this darker, more "modern" attitude toward human imperfection.[4] Only the final vision of Shakespeare's romances combines the severe and threatening imperfections of the middle plays with the comedies' paradoxical Pauline and Erasmian attitudes towards such imperfection. Let us look very briefly at these changes in perspective and consider their relationship to the vision of Shakespearean comedy.

In the major tetralogy of Shakespeare's history plays, especially *I* and *II Henry IV*, this awareness of imperfection seems pained and pessimistic, an ironic vision of ethical folly without forgiveness, and of epistemological confusion without ultimate truth. Their heroic-absurd structure is the most obvious manifestation of this ironic attitude. Ironic language, either the Rabelaisian "base comparisons" or the Pistollian fustian, also suggests a painful awareness of man's embarrassing imperfection and his lost and possibly irrecoverable potential. Language and structure thus both suggest a widening breach between the heroic and the ironic, the sacramental and the historic visions of man.[5] Similarly, though Hal would try to redeem the time, the shattered sacramental premises can be replaced only temporarily by effective ceremonials. Temporary also must be any effective political maneuvers based solely on personal leadership. Because Prince Hal, the *eiron*, understands these ironies, he can no more celebrate his folly in the tavern than he can embrace its embodiment in Falstaff after he becomes king. The Erasmian and Pauline paradoxes that would allow such an act have either been forgotten or judged irrelevant in this worldly world.

In the major problem plays, like *Measure for Measure* and *Troilus and Cressida*, Shakespeare seems again to have pushed his depiction of human imperfection beyond the limits of the comic perspective. Behavioral follies become more and more sinister, until they approach a viciousness that is difficult to accommodate within Shakespeare's comic spirit of forgiveness or regeneration. And that blessed madness which allows comic man to imagine and to express the unimaginable is almost completely absent from these plays. The resultant picture is even bleaker than that of the histories. For here we have comedies that are ironically unfunny, and an epic that is ironically antiheroic. These ugly imperfections either remain at the end of the play, or are cured through a regeneration that must be forced or contrived. The latter creates at best a shallow festivity; the former perpetual irony. We are unsure if any of the characters of *Measure for Measure* are unqualifiedly good, but fairly certain that some are redeemed by the end. But in *Troilus and Cressida* we are overwhelmed by the disgusting ulcer of universal human imperfection, and by a radically different attitude toward that imperfection. Thersites states that attitude quite clearly: "The common curse of mankind [is] folly and ignorance" (II.iii.25). In the romantic comedies folly and ignorance were symptoms of man's fortunate finitude, the admission of which could bring him great joy. In *Troilus and Cressida* they have become his "common curse." The juxtaposition of such diametrically different plays around 1601 is an astonishing testimony to the plasticity of Shakespeare's genius as well as its persistent interest in ethical and epistemological imperfection.

*Hamlet,* also a contemporary of these plays, shares the same thematic interest, but carries it in yet a third direction. Hamlet's discomfort with his mortality—with universal human imperfection—is a fundamental part of his character throughout the play. His encounter with human finitude thus becomes a fascinating way for us to understand his tragic experience. Dreams of dust, the "stamp of one defect," "some vicious mole of nature in them"—such disgusting visions of ruined human potentiality are all around him. But Hamlet is slow to acknowledge himself to be a part of this universal folly, nor does he seem to have a religious or a philosophic consolation for it. This is the most basic comic wisdom, and though he often plays the fool at Elsinore, Hamlet is far from understanding it. He is just as far from acknowledging his epistemological finiteness, and just as troubled by it, as the interrogative mood of the play eloquently testifies.[6] How can any man know enough about this life or the life beyond, about God's will or his own, to act with perfect certainty? Only in a Sidneyan golden world of art (Hamlet loves the theater) could such things be so. So Hamlet refrains from killing Claudius at prayer on the audacious assumption that he can guarantee another's damnation (or his own salvation). There will never be such a perfect moment in this world, and Hamlet would not know it if there were.

Paradoxically, only Hamlet's own commitments to flawed activity will lead him to understand the inevitable frailty his flesh and mind are heir to. He stabs Polonius behind the arras thinking him to be Claudius; he drives Ophelia mad. He leaps foolishly into her grave to pronounce with high folly the unbounded dimensions of his love. In the graveyard the wisdom of his folly is finally inescapable. We are as mortal in action and knowledge as we are mortal in time. We will all return to the dust, willy nilly. But of course in tragedy such a lessoning, such humiliation, leads not to celebration but to death. He may finally "let be" the questioning. He may accept the "special providence in the fall of a sparrow," and proclaim that "the readiness is all." But finally he can confirm his mortality only by dying, and by dying confirm only his own mortality. Still, to Hamlet at least the questions are finally beyond asking. "The rest is silence," and that silence will be a blessed rest after so many recriminations and so much uncertainty.

Like Hamlet, Lear has a Feste-like fool and an abundance of folly to learn. His humbling experience is thus analogous to Hamlet's as well as Olivia's in *Twelfth Night*. But Lear is so old, and has held the old personal and philosophic illusions so long, and his will is so stubborn, that the lessons of humility will come hard and slowly. Most of the teachers are nearly as cruel as the lessons: two compassionless daughters and an apparently blank and pitiless universe. Lear gradually learns that he has acted like a fool; the disappearance of his fool in Act III may signify the completion of this learning. And once he has mastered the ethical lesson the old man embarks on the even harder lesson of his epistemological folly—the ingrained but inadequate assumptions about the dignity of man in a comprehensible universe that he shares uneasily with so many of Shakespeare's contemporaries. Most would agree that Lear—and the audience with him—learns almost all there is to know about these things as well, namely, Montaigne's frightening assertion that he can know nothing at all. Edgar's "the ripeness is all" may thus be far more pessimistic than Hamlet's "the readiness is all" in this respect. But such an absolute humility does not necessarily postulate a meaningless universe. Lear's remaining dignity, his last exquisite hazarding of love, and his final, perplexing, but stirring response to the loss of Cordelia can suggest to those who survive him something far nobler about the nature of man and his universe—a personal and cosmic dignity that transcends all disillusioning and ennobles all suffering. One receives such impressions tentatively, humbly, in Lear's universe. But one receives them nevertheless.

*Antony and Cleopatra* has radically different things to say about Shakespeare's tragic interest in human imperfection. In fact, embodied in its tragic vision is something like a return to the comic paradoxes of faith and folly in which we have been most interested. The structure of the play, as well as the characters' eventual understanding of their earthly limitations, announce that "chance and change" are the inevitable ingredients of the human condition. Through Antony and Cleopatra we glimpse intimations of a human dignity that is inextricably bound up in human folly, and of a human finiteness that can only be transcended through death and rebirth. The victorious tone of Cleopatra's death is directly related to that paradox. This unusually affirmative tragic vision thus celebrates the connections between man's folly and his grandeur, his finitude and his infinitude.[7] In so doing it paves the way from the tragedies to the romances, where tragic errors lead, with time's slow assistance, to joyous comic regeneration.

The romances embrace the paradoxes of human folly with a celebratory spirit that falls between the vision of *Antony and Cleopatra* and that of the romantic comedies. Human imperfection is still sinister in these last plays. But it occurs within the vision of a forgiveness that can redeem it and a providence that can control its potential destructiveness. As Robert Hunter's *Shakespeare and the Comedy of Forgiveness* has shown, these last plays seem again to channel this imperfection through the familiar comic-Christian framework that allows its acknowledgment, its forgiveness, and even its occasional cure. Leontes errs grotesquely. But with Paulina's help and time's, he finally achieves the humility he sorely needed before. Joy is again the consequence of this acknowledged folly.

Much like *As You Like It*, *The Winter's Tale* shares the eventual humility of its main character. It exults in its own aesthetic folly, especially while exploiting the mixture of genres at its center. In that one crucial scene at the end of Act III, dead center in the play, the transition from tragic to comic occurs. Tragic strains are followed by sentimentality in Antigonus's speech. These are both followed by the bathos of the roaring bear and Antigonus's preposterous death. In fact, preposterous death is a fine image for this strange transition from tragedy to comedy. And then enter a shepherd talking first like Euphues, then gradually yielding to the vernacular impulse of the comic rather than the pastoral mode. The happy discovery of Perdita saves her from a fate worse than death. And then we have the clowning of clown and shepherd, the hilarious account of Antigonus's death, and the celebration of their "lucky day." In one hundred remarkable lines we have run the gamut from tragedy to comedy. We will span sixteen years in the next thirty-two, and leap from a winter's tale to a summer's. Only a playwright well-practiced in playing with the fragile, foolish conventions of his art would try so audacious a thing. Only a Shakespeare who has already discovered and exploited the humbling but joyous connections between the "insubstantial pageants" of lovers and playwrights would risk such aesthetic folly. That it works again is eloquent testimony to the coherence of Shakespeare's dramatic vision.

Of all the other plays by Shakespeare, *The Tempest* is most richly consonant with the Pauline and Erasmian visions of faith and folly we find in the romantic comedies. Like Richard II, Prospero has ruled badly and has been deposed for his inattention to that duty. But given the time that Richard was never vouchsafed, Prospero has been able to reflect on his imperfect rule and amend it. He has also forgiven his enemies as the years have passed, though he still remembers their treachery. Poised on his symbolic island between Caliban and Ariel, finitude and infinitude, flesh and spirit, and between Miranda's innocence and Antonio's reprobation, Prospero has also been given a complete vision of the positive and negative potentiality of man. Time has edified him, but it has also made him an edifier of others, a holy fool in the Festean tradition. Alonso, Caliban, Antonio, Sebastian, Stephano, and Trinculo are all potential recipients of his benevolent ministry. In this rigorously honest paradise some can benefit but more cannot. Alonso acknowledges his "trespass" (III.iii.99), and even asks his "child forgiveness" (v.i.198). That Prospero does not succeed too well with the others accounts in part for his own final humility. But surely that humble self-knowledge with which Prospero drowns his book and closes out his career is also a result of his years of self-scrutiny. He has tasted his finitude and his infinitude to the lees, and he has learned that he must be something of both to be a man.

His play, like *The Winter's Tale* or *As You Like It,* seems also to have absorbed its share of this comforting humility. For throughout, like Prospero, it makes fun of itself, and takes itself too seriously too, all at the same time. Think of the preposterous amount of exposition in Act I, Scene ii and of Prospero nervously nudging his audience,

Miranda, as it goes on. Late in the play Prospero beautifully sum-marizes for us these combined motifs of aesthetic, ethical, and epis-temological folly:

> Our revels now are ended. These our actors,
> As I foretold you, were all spirits and
> Are melted into air, into thin air;
> And like the baseless fabric of this vision,
> The cloud-capped tow'rs, the gorgeous palaces,
> The solemn temples, the great globe itself,
> Yea, all which it inherit, shall dissolve,
> And, like this insubstantial pageant faded,
> Leave not a rack behind. We are such stuff
> As dreams are made on, and our little life
> Is rounded with a sleep.     (IV.i.148–58)

This is justifiably one of the best-loved passages in Shakespeare. With simple eloquence it states once and for all the reason why the wisdom of folly has so persistently characterized his dramatic vision, and espe-cially the vision of his romantic comedies. "We are such stuff / As dreams are made on, and our little life / Is rounded with a sleep." The distinctly biblical sound of these words is not accidental, for their sub-stance is as solidly Pauline and Erasmian as anything in the romantic comedies. They share with simple eloquence the ultimate folly we all share, the folly of our mortality. We can know only in part; we can act only in that knowledge. But with faith such folly can be cause for great joy in the theater of the world. *The Tempest,* like several of the romantic comedies, ends with an epilogue in which Prospero com-bines this awareness of human weakness with the paradoxical blessings of humility and forgiveness:

> And my ending is despair
> Unless I be relieved by prayer,
> Which pierces so that it assaults
> Mercy itself and frees all faults.
> As you from crimes would pardoned be,
> Let your indulgence set me free.

He would be pardoned, as would his Renaissance audience, of these inevitable follies; with faith and forgiveness, it may be so. As these last plays return to the comic-Christian sense of human life as an insubstantial pageant with a benevolent, forgiving auditor, so they urge upon their Renaissance audience a comforting old response to the new scientific rationalism that may be threatening their composure. Remember the ethical and epistemological humility preached by St. Paul and Erasmus; set yourself free from contemporary philosophic despair. Such an attitude gives a profound wholeness to Shakespeare's dramatic canon.

But in a book about faith and folly in Shakespeare's comic vision, this is an awfully sombre ending. Perhaps Stultitia's epilogue to *The Praise of Folie* will tip the beam back toward the center:

> I perceive ye loke for an EPILOGE or knotte of my tale, but than sure ye are verie fooles, if ye wene that I yet remember what I have spoken, after suche a rablement of wordes powred foorth. The old proverbe saieth, *I hate a talebearer from the boorde:* But I saie, *I hate hym that remembreth what he hath sayd.* Fare ye well therfore, clappe your handes in token of gladnesse, live carelesse, and drinke all out, ye the trustie servantes and solemne ministers of Folie.
>
> (Pp. 128–29)

Stultitia's irreverent and joyous humility reminds us that Shakespeare's comic vision, like Erasmus's, can delight and edify whether we know the Pauline paradoxes it informedly alludes to or not. Still, these Pauline reversals of folly and wisdom are a vital part of both visions. For we are all, whether we like it or not, "trustie servantes and solemne ministers of Folie." And since we are, we might as well make the best of it.

# Notes

## PREFACE

1. Richmond Noble, *Shakespeare's Biblical Knowledge;* E. M. W. Tillyard, *The Elizabethan World Picture;* Walter Clyde Curry, *Shakespeare's Philosophic Patterns;* Alfred Harbage, *Shakespeare and the Rival Traditions;* Frank Kermode, *Shakespeare, Spenser, Donne;* Nevill Coghill, "The Basis of Shakespearian Comedy."

2. R. G. Hunter, *Shakespeare and the Comedy of Forgiveness;* Robert West, *Shakespeare and the Outer Mystery;* Roy Battenhouse, "Falstaff as Parodist and Perhaps Holy Fool"; Barbara Lewalski, "Biblical Allusion and Allegory in *The Merchant of Venice*"; idem, "Thematic Patterns in *Twelfth Night*"; Delora Cunningham, "Repentance and the Art of Living Well"; and J. A. Bryant, *Hippolyta's View,* are prominent recent exceptions, but most deal with the later plays.

3. See R. M. Frye, *Shakespeare and Christian Doctrine;* subsequent references to this work will be cited in the text. See also Frye's "Theological and Non-theological Structures in Tragedy," p. 134. In "St. Paul and Shakespeare's Romantic Comedies," *Thought* 46 (1971): 371–88, I began to consider the thesis of this book. Some of that material appears here in altered form.

4. Davies, *Worship and Theology in England,* pp. 219–20; see also pp. 173–78. Also documenting such pressures are G. Culkin, "England: The Early Tudors 1485–1558," and Thomas Fuller, *The Church History of Britain* 4: 263, 317–19, 333.

5. Williston Walker, *A History of the Christian Church,* pp. 389–96. Patrick Collinson, *The Elizabethan Puritan Movement;* H. G. Alexander, *Religion in England 1558–1662,* parts 3 and 4; and C. H. George and Katherine George, *The Protestant Mind of the English Reformation (1570–1640),* part 3, all discuss controversy and uniformity simultaneously.

6. L. A. Cormican, "Medieval Idiom in Shakespeare," p. 187.

7. O. B. Hardison, Jr., *Christian Rite and Christian Drama in the Middle Ages,* p. x; Muriel C. Bradbrook, *Shakespeare and Elizabethan Poetry,* pp. 34, 51; John Vyvyan, *Shakespeare and The Rose of Love,* pp. 39–40.

NOTES

8. A recent, interesting book is Robert Creeth's *Mankynde in Shake-speare.*

9. Alan Dessen, *Jonson's Moral Comedy,* argues this central thesis, especially pp. 37–42.

10. *The Christmas Prince,* p. 56.

11. Hardison, *Christian Rite ahd Christian Drama,* p. x.

12. Paul A. Jorgensen, *Our Naked Frailties,* p. 54.

13. Hardison, *Christian Rite and Christian Drama,* p. 291. The second chapter of Roy Battenhouse, *Shakespearean Tragedy: Its Art and Its Christian Premises,* also contains a learned defense of the possibility of such interpretation.

14. Included in this category should be Harvey Cox, *The Feast of Fools;* Wolfgang M. Zucker, "The Clown as the Lord of Disorder"; Nelvin Vos, *The Drama of Comedy: Victim and Victor;* William F. Lynch, *Christ and Apollo;* and Nathan A. Scott, *The Broken Center.*

CHAPTER I

1. The one exception to this chronological arrangement is *The Merchant of Venice;* its ironic relationship to these other plays is best understood after their normative, celebratory treatments of faith and folly have been established.

2. Northrop Frye, *Anatomy of Criticism,* pp. 184–85; Coghill, "The Basis of Shakespearean Comedy," pp. 1–28; Hunter, *Shakespeare and the Comedy of Forgiveness.*

3. See Massey Shepherd, *The Prayer-Book Commentary,* pp. 68–69.

4. *The Prayer Book of Queen Elizabeth, 1559,* pp. 54–60, 147–48, 42.

5. Alexander Nowell, *A Catechism,* pp. 149–50, 155, 199, e.g.

6. George and George, *The Protestant Mind,* p. 98.

7. Sig. A2. Fulke was a major doctrinal voice of the Anglican Church. See also George and George, *The Protestant Mind,* p. 98.

8. John Marbeck, *A Book of Notes and Commonplaces,* pp. 415, 644.

9. *The Prayer Book of Queen Elizabeth,* pp. 54–60, 48, 57.

10. Lynch, *Christ and Apollo,* pp. 97–98, 110; V. A. Kolve, *The Play Called Corpus Christi,* pp. 128–43; Scott, *The Broken Center,* pp. 109, 103; Hardison, *Christian Rite and Christian Drama,* p. 284.

11. John Hollander, "*Twelfth Night* and the Morality of Indulgence," pp. 220–38.

12. Zucker, "The Clown as the Lord of Disorder," pp. 312–14.

13. Russell Fraser, *The War against Poetry,* pp. 40–44; Jonas H. Barish, "Exhibitionism and the Antitheatrical Prejudice," pp. 6–7.

14. *The Prayer Book of Queen Elizabeth*, pp. 100–101, 106; see Davies, *Worship and Theology*, pp. 219–20.

15. *Certaine Sermons or Homilies*, pp. 264–68.

16. Since the seventh century a group of heretics called Paulicians have held St. Paul in excessive awe, naming their disciples after his. An even more extreme group, called *Paulins* but related to the Paulicans, are described in the *Dictionnaire des Hérésies* of M. L'Abbé J. Jh. Claris, 1:1079: "Ce nom fut donné à certains hérétiques de la Bulgarie, qui préféraient saint Paul à Jésus-Christ, et qui administraient le baptême, non pas avec de l'eau, mais avec du feu."

17. William Tyndale, *Doctrinal Treatises*, pp. 483–84.

18. John 14:6; all biblical quotations will refer to the *New Testament Octapla*, and will be taken from the Bishops' Bible that Noble suggests Shakespeare uses more often than the Geneva before 1600 (pp. 75–76). Ninety-five percent of the quotations will be very similar to the more familiar King James Authorized Version of 1611. Whenever significant variations occur, I shall note them.

19. John Colet, *An Exposition of St. Paul's First Epistle to the Corinthians*, p. 8.

20. *The Sermons of John Donne*, 1:286; see also 9:155–56.

21. *The Prayer Book of Queen Elizabeth*, p. 101.

22. *Sermons by Hugh Latimer*, p. 490.

23. G. Wilson Knight, *The Christian Renaissance*, mentions another of St. Paul's unique qualifications as primary doctrinal source of a predominantly secular drama: he relates the transcendental truth of Christ's revelation to current affairs and practical instrumentation (p. 187).

24. William Empson, " 'Fool' in *Lear*," pp. 177–78. See also *The Interpreters' Bible*, 10:29–31, for the uniqueness of this paradox.

25. *The Geneva Bible, a facsimile of the 1560 edition*.

26. Ibid.

27. *The Praise of Folie*, tr. Sir Thomas Chaloner, p. xxiv. Subsequent references to this work will be cited in the text. Preserved Smith, *Erasmus*, p. 124, mentions 20,000 copies of the work in print by 1522, and 40 editions during Erasmus's lifetime.

28. Barbara Swain, *Fools and Folly*, pp. 155, 158, and ch. 3. Cox, Zucker, Lynch, and Scott are similarly aware of the Erasmian dimensions of folly in western comedy, but do similarly little with its presence in Shakespeare's romantic comedies.

29. Kenneth Muir, "Shakespeare and Erasmus," pp. 424–25; Walter Kaiser, *Praisers of Folly*, part 3; Battenhouse, "Falstaff as Parodist," pp. 32–52; Empson, " 'Fool' in *Lear*," pp. 177–78.

30. Thelma N. Greenfield, "*A Midsummer Night's Dream* and *The Praise of Folly*," p. 243.

31. Willeford, *The Fool and His Sceptre*, pp. 131–32, 137–38.

32. Emrys Jones, *The Origins of Shakespeare*, p. 11.

33. Besides my frequent use of Pauline and Erasmian passages, there are several other respected and centristic English sources of Christian doctrine that are rather prominent in my discussions. The Bible itself is obviously the most important of these sources. The individual commentators—William Tyndale, John Colet, and John Marbeck—have been chosen as thoroughly representative of sixteenth century doctrinal commonplaces in England. The institutional sources—the *Book of Common Prayer,* Alexander Nowell's *Catechism,* and the two prescribed volumes, *Certaine Sermons or Homilies*—were well known and almost universally used. The sermons of John Donne and Lancelot Andrewes are also frequently cited, as they may share with Shakespeare's works the same court audience. The care with which I have selected such representative doctrinal voices is intended to guarantee that Shakespeare's generally recognized position as an enlightened Renaissance Christian (R. M. Frye, p. 9) remain sufficient to establish my case of pervasive general influence. Shakespeare was no more a disciple of Colet or Marbeck than he was of Erasmus or St. Paul. But like his contemporaries he would have absorbed a lot of Pauline doctrine directly through the commentaries and sermons of their most influential and representative English interpreters.

34. *The Prayer Book of Queen Elizabeth,* p. 127 ("Matrimony"). The material which follows originally appeared in slightly altered form in my "Shakespeare's Comic Epilogues: Invitations to Festive Communion," *Jahrbuch der Shakespeare-Gesellschaft West* 106 (1970): 60–69.

35. Northrop Frye, *Anatomy of Criticism*, pp. 163–64.

36. See Stanley Wells, "Happy Endings in Shakespeare," pp. 111–23; Robert G. Hunter, "The Function of the Songs at the End of *Love's Labour's Lost*," pp. 55–64; Cyrus Hoy, "*Love's Labour's Lost* and the Nature of Comedy," p. 39; and C. L. Barber, *Shakespeare's Festive Comedy,* pp. 117–18.

37. All subsequent citations of Shakespeare will refer to *William Shakespeare: The Complete Works,* ed. Alfred Harbage.

38. Most critics urge us to suspend our judgments between these perspectives: J. R. Brown, *Shakespeare and His Comedies*, pp. 83, 86; R. W. Dent, "Imagination in *A Midsummer Night's Dream*," pp. 115–29; Paul N. Siegel, "*A Midsummer Night's Dream* and the Wedding Guests," pp. 141–44; Frank Kermode, "The Mature Comedies," pp. 214–19. However, some readers insist that we must choose cool reason: H. B. Charlton,

*Shakespearian Comedy*, p. 122; Paul A. Olson, "*A Midsummer Night's Dream* and the Meaning of Court Marriage," pp. 101–2.

39. Of course he is also appealing for applause.

40. The motif of role-playing has been noticed frequently. The best studies are by D. J. Palmer, "*As You Like It* and the Idea of Play," pp. 237–38; and idem, "Art and Nature in *As You Like It*," p. 38. See also P. V. Kreider, "Genial Literary Satire in the Forest of Arden," p. 222; Bradbrook, *Shakespeare and Elizabethan Poetry*, p. 220.

41. Most critics agree that Feste's allusions to unpleasantness broaden the comic vision: Hollander, "Twelfth Night," p. 236; Clifford Leech, *Twelfth Night and Shakespearian Comedy*, p. 53; Enid Welsford, *The Fool*, p. 252; Brown, *Shakespeare and His Comedies*, p. 182; and Barber, *Shakespeare's Festive Comedy*, pp. 259–60.

42. The exposing of flaws is his most widely accepted function: Julian Markels, "Shakespeare's Confluence of Tragedy and Comedy: *Twelfth Night* and *King Lear*," p. 77; Harold Jenkins, "Shakespeare's *Twelfth Night*," pp. 32–33; R. H. Goldsmith, *Wise Fools in Shakespeare*, p. 53.

43. Leslie Hotson, *The First Night of Twelfth Night*, p. 167.

44. See S. L. Bethell, *Shakespeare and the Popular Dramatic Tradition*, pp. 31–32.

45. Vos, *The Drama of Comedy*, p. 112. Lynch, *Christ and Apollo*, p. 110; and Zucker, "The Clown," p. 314, would agree.

46. Cox, "The Feast of Fools," pp. 151–52.

47. Scott, *The Broken Center*, pp. 93–94.

48. "The Order for Holy Communion" states, "it is requisite that no manne shoulde come to the holye Communion, but with a ful trust in goddes mercy, and with a quiet conscience" (p. 99). Similarly, the "Exhortations" stress the futility, the blasphemy, of refusing communion on the grounds that "I am a grevous sinner, and therefore am afrayed to come" (p. 97).

## CHAPTER II

1. Walker, *A History of the Christian Church*, p. 302, focuses upon the medieval sacramental structures as the focus of Reformation energy; Davies, *Worship and Theology in England*, p. 23, finds the related faith-works issue "the central theological tenet of the Reformation." Both issues reverberate through the play. This chapter originally appeared in *Shakespeare Studies*, 10 (1977): 17–41, as "Love Versus Charity in *Love's Labour's Lost*."

2. David Bevington, *Tudor Drama and Politics*, pp. 197–202, 289–302, assigns a characteristic and unique delicacy to Shakespeare's handling of many controversial matters.

3. Geoffrey Bullough, *Narrative and Dramatic Sources of Shakespeare*, 1:427; Richard David, ed., *Love's Labour's Lost*, pp. l-li.

4. Noble, *Shakespeare's Biblical Knowledge*, p. 70. See also Henry Wheeler Robinson, ed., *The Bible in Its Ancient and English Versions*, p. 182.

5. Luther A. Weigle, *The English New Testament*, pp. 73–77. By the second edition of the Bishops' Bible, thirty-two of Tyndale's "loves" have reverted to "charity."

6. See, for example, Ranier Pineas, *Thomas More and Tudor Polemics*, p. 40; and W. E. Campbell, *Erasmus, Tyndale, and More*, p. 110. As before, I am using More and Tyndale because of their thoroughness, centrality, perception, and popularity, and not to suggest direct verbal sources.

7. Walker, *A History of the Christian Church*, pp. 307, 238, 240, 252.

8. See Henry Gough, *A General Index to the Publications of the Parker Society* (Cambridge: The University Press, 1855), p. 795.

9. Sir Thomas More, *The Dialogue Concerning Tyndale*, 2:208. Subsequent references to this work will be cited in the text.

10. See Davies, *Worship and Theology in England*, pp. 18–19.

11. William Tyndale, *An Answer to Sir Thomas More's Dialogue*, p. 21. Subsequent references to this edition will be cited in the text.

12. See Denis de Rougement, *Love in the Western World;* M. C. D'Arcy, *The Mind and Heart of Love;* Ceslaus Spicq, *Agape in the New Testament;* C. S. Lewis, *The Allegory of Love;* and Don Cameron Allen's study, *Mysteriously Meant*, for a variety of insights into the topic.

13. Weigle, *The English New Testament*, pp. 78–79.

14. See Campbell, *Erasmus, Tyndale, and More*, pp. 84–85, 128, 144, for a brief discussion of the paradoxical contradictions between this Lutheran tenet and the Christian assumption of human depravity.

15. William Fulke, *The Text of the New Testament of Jesus Christ . . . whereunto is added . . . a Confutation . . . of Manifest impietie, of heresie, treason, and slander, against the Catholike Church of God, and the true teachers thereof, or the Translations used in the Church of England*, title page. Subsequent references to this work are cited in the text. Also illustrating the political stakes are Alexander, *Religion in England*, pp. 82–83; and John Strype, *Documentary Annals of the Reformed Church of England*, 3:93ff.; Davies, *Worship and Theology in England*, pp. xv–xvii, 3–11; George and George, *The Protestant Mind*, pp. 174–256, 375–418.

16. Davies, *Worship and Theology in England*, p. 23.

17. John Calvin, *Commentaries on the Epistle of Paul the Apostle to the Romans*, p. 486. See also his *Commentaries on the Epistles to Timothy, Titus, and Philemon*, p. 27.

18. Fulke, *The Text of the New Testament*, fol. 290v; John Calvin, *Commentary on the Epistles of Paul the Apostle to the Corinthians*, 1:432.

19. Alexander, *Religion in England*, p. 123, assures us that Puritans and orthodox English churchmen were agreed on these basic issues until 1595: justification by faith, the fallen nature of man, and predestination. There can be ascertained, therefore, a Protestant position on these issues before that time.

20. Henry Bullinger, *Commonplaces of Christian Religion*, fol. 102. See also Tyndale, *An Answer to Sir Thomas More*, pp. 172–73; Fulke, *The Text of the New Testament*, fol. 258v; Herschel Baker, *The Wars of Truth*, pp. 204–5; Rom. 7:18–19; and *The Prayer Book*, p. 42.

21. Bullinger, *Commonplaces of Christian Religion*, fol. 112.

22. See chapter 7.

23. Martin, quoted in Fulke, *The Text of the New Testament*, fol. 290v.

24. Fulke, *The Text of the New Testament*, fol. 290v; Davies, *Worship and Theology in England*, p. 20.

25. Martin's words in William Fulke, *A defense of the sincere and true Translations of the holie Scriptures into the English tong, against the . . . cavils of . . . Gregory Martin*, p. 428, lead us to understand how *Love's Labor's Lost* can link the issue of faith and works with that of penance and repentance: "Upon the heresy of only faith justifying and saving a man, followeth the denial of all penance and satisfaction for sins." See Davies, *Worship and Theology in England*, pp. 17–25.

26. Campbell, *Erasmus, Tyndale, and More*, pp. 128, 144; Davies, *Worship and Theology in England*, p. 71. As is so often the case, the controversialists imply a much greater polarization than would have characterized moderate churchmen. See note 45.

27. Martin, in Fulke, *A Defense*, p. 71.

28. Walker, *A History of the Christian Church*, p. 317.

29. Gustav Ungerer, *Anglo-Spanish Relations in Tudor Literature*, pp. 120–21, argues that Armado was particularly apt because he would have suggested the notorious Spanish bisexual Antonio Perez. His famous gifts and linguistic extravagance might well have combined with his scandalously flippant and immoral sexuality to place the lords' abuses against love in a more serious light.

30. See Bullough, *Narrative and Dramatic Sources of Shakespeare*, 1:428–30; and the *Encyclopaedia Britannica*, s.v. "Navarra."

31. Robert G. Hunter suggested this first connection to me. For the second, see Thomas Fuller, *The Church History of Britain,* 5:72–73.

32. Marbeck, *A Book of Notes and Commonplaces,* p. 641. Martin Luther, *Lectures on Romans,* p. 245.

33. Spicq, *Agape in the New Testament,* pp. 140–41. The pattern of acknowledgement, repentance, and amendment is a common one. Probably the most frequently heard statement of it would have been in the "General Confession" of *The Prayer Book of Queen Elizabeth,* pp. 100–101. *Certaine Sermons or Homilies,* pp. 264–68, also articulated the pattern.

34. Even Malvolio is forgiven and sent for at the end, but no plan is outlined for his final enlightenment. E. M. W. Tillyard, *Shakespeare's Early Comedies,* pp. 176–81, thinks that the lords' regeneration and marriage is not at all certain at the end of the play.

35. Walker, *A History of the Christian Church,* p. 351.

36. *New Catholic Encyclopedia,* s.v. "Justification in Catholic Theology"; Fulke, *A Defense,* pp. 340–41, illustrates for us that *works, might,* and *merits* could be used synonymously in the debate.

37. Cunningham, "Repentance and the Art of Living Well," pp. 10–11, mentions the relationship between the controversy of faith and works and the lords' pact.

38. Barber, *Shakespeare's Festive Comedy,* pp. 88–93, focuses at length on the relationship between this speech and the tradition of Saturnalian misrule. He would agree that their freeing is only ironic. James L. Calderwood, *"Love's Labour's Lost:* A Wantoning with Words," p. 324, predicts verbal chaos and philosophic nihilism if perjury can replace charity. In his grotesque equivocation Berowne might also have suggested someone like the Jesuit Garnet.

39. Calvin, *Commentary on Corinthians,* 1:420, intriguingly resorts to another traditional Protestant evasion of this most difficult Pauline passage when he calls this faith which is less than love "special faith." Notice that Berowne talks about a "special grace" in his first allusion to the controversy.

40. See Lowell D. Stratton, "The Nine Worthies," pp. 67–91.

41. Frances Shirley, "Shakespeare's Use of Oaths," in *The Triple Bond,* ed. Joseph G. Price (University Park: Pennsylvania State Press, 1975), pp. 118–36.

42. Noble feels that two other allusions might be operative in the same scene, ii:292, where Boyet says of all them, "And leap for joy though they are lame with blows." Two biblical passages similarly exult in the coming of Christ, with his merciful, charitable forgiveness of all imperfect men in similar terms: "And leape ye for joy" (Luke 6:23) and "Then shall the lame man leape as an Hart" (Isa. 35:6). The second pas-

NOTES

sage is from the famous section prophesying Christ's coming, and is the same passage that Handel interprets in the *Messiah*.

43. Hoy, *"Love's Labour's Lost,"* p. 36, notices in this connection that the salutory experience of discovering such inevitable, natural folly is basic to Shakespeare's comic vision.

44. I.i.149, 199. Noble, *Shakespeare's Biblical Knowledge*, pp. 142–43. The Anglican litany reads, "That it maye please the to gyve all thy people encrease of grace, to heare mekely thy worde, and to receyve it wyth pure affection, and to bring furthe the fruites of the spirit." (*The Prayer Book of Queen Elizabeth*, p. 56.)

45. More, 2:207–9. Hooker, Book 4, defends sacraments and ceremonies against the more extreme reformist groups.

46. See my note, "Armado's Sexual Puns," pp. 7–9.

47. See note 45. See also *Certaine Sermons or Homilies*, "Of the Worthy Receiving of the Sacraments" and "Of Repentance and True Reconciliation Unto God," for further Anglican agreement.

48. According to the Council of Trent, merit was a gift of God, but also a reward for good works (*New Catholic Encyclopedia*, s.v. "Merit").

49. Herbert R. Coursen, *"Love's Labour's Lost* and the Comic Truth,"* pp. 320–22, is good on this point.

50. D'Arcy, *The Mind and Heart of Love*, p. 24, n.


CHAPTER III

1. Rashbrook, "Shakespeare and the Bible," p. 49.

2. Colet, *An Exposition of Corinthians*, pp. 1, 9–12. *The Geneva Bible, a facsimile*, "The Argument" to First Corinthians. See also Matt. 19:23–24. These traditional categories encompass all sins: the world, the flesh, the devil.

3. Colet, *An Exposition of Corinthians*, p. 19.

4. Feste says, "Those wits that think they have thee do very oft prove fools, and I that am sure I lack thee may pass for a wise man" (I.v.30–32). And St. Paul, "If any man among you seeme *to himselfe* to be wise in this world, let him become a foole, that hee may be wise" (1 Cor. 3:18). Interestingly, Touchstone also knows enough of St. Paul to become hopelessly confused over the same paradox (*AYLI* v.i.30–31).

5. Colet, *An Exposition of Corinthians*, p. 27.

6. Vos, *The Drama of Comedy*, p. 114.

7. Roy Battenhouse helped me formulate this specific theological interpretation of the possible significance of Bottom's dream.

8. Cox, *The Feast of Fools*, p. 140.

9. William E. Willeford, *The Fool and His Sceptre,* pp. 137–38. James L. Calderwood, *"A Midsummer Night's Dream:* The Illusion of Drama," similarly argues that although art in the play can express the inexpressible, with Bottom "the vision drifts into dream" (pp. 518–19).

10. Greenfield, *"A Midsummer Night's Dream* and *The Praise of Folly,"* pp. 236–44, discusses some other Erasmian and Christian implications of Bottom's profound folly. See also Battenhouse, "Falstaff as Parodist," pp. 32–52; Kaiser, *Praisers of Folly,* part 3, pp. 18–24; and Jones, *The Origins of Shakespeare,* pp. 9–12.

11. This discussion of their miraculous transformation from a Christian perspective is in no way meant to diminish or reject the attractive possibility that Ovid's *Metamorphosis* is also functioning here. These are but two of a number of interrelated cultural patterns Shakespeare is bringing into play outside of Athens. See Walter F. Staton, Jr., "Ovidian Elements in *A Midsummer Night's Dream,"* pp. 167–78.

12. Feste alludes much more obviously to this passage in his epilogue. See ch. 6.

13. Dante Alighieri, *The Divine Comedy,* p. 24. See Charles Singleton, *Dante Studies II: Journey to Beatrice;* much of *The Fairie Queene* and John Lyly's *Endymion* should illustrate how readily English Renaissance poets and dramatists could transform Truth and Christian idealism into a woman and vice versa.

14. Bullinger, *Commonplaces of Christian Religion,* fol. 104.

15. William Fulke, *A Comfortable Sermon of Faith,* sigs. A2, E3.

16. Colet, *An Exposition of Corinthians,* p. 26.

17. Called St. Paul's Hymn of Love. See *The Interpreter's Bible,* 10: 165.

18. Nowell, *A Catechism,* p. 188.

19. See Bryant, *Hippolyta's View,* for an interesting discussion of her "faith."


CHAPTER IV

1. Hunter, *Shakespeare and the Comedy of Forgiveness,* pp. 93ff.

2. James Smith, *"Much Ado about Nothing,"* p. 256; Bertrand Evans, *Shakespeare's Comedies,* pp. 84ff.; T. W. Craik, *"Much Ado about Nothing,"* pp. 313–14.

3. Hunter, *Shakespeare and the Comedy of Forgiveness,* ch. 4.

4. Kirby Neill, "More Ado about Claudio: An Acquittal for the Slandered Groom," pp. 97–102.

5. Hunter, *Shakespeare and the Comedy of Forgiveness,* pp. 103–5;

Barbara Lewalski, "Love, Appearance and Reality: Much Ado about Something," pp. 249–51.

6. *Certaine Sermons or Homilies,* pp. 264–68, passim; subsequent quotations from this homily will be cited in the text. *The Prayer Book of Queen Elizabeth,* pp. 100–101, provides the clear source for this homily. Thus the process of Claudio's regeneration would be liturgically as well as homiletically familiar. For convenience, I will quote the parts of the General Confession that correspond with the four parts of repentance in the notes. My discussion of Claudio and repentance originally appeared as part of "Sacraments and the Intentional Ambiguity of *Much Ado about Nothing,*" *Anglican Theological Review* 58 (1976): 330–45.

7. P. 264. Cf. the General Confession: "Almighty God father of oure Lorde Jesus Christe, maker of all thynges, Judge of all menne, we acknowledge and bewayle oure manifolde synnes and wyckednesse, whiche we from tyme to tyme moste grevously have committed, by thoughte, woorde and deede."

8. v.i.203–9. See *The Prayer Book of Queen Elizabeth,* pp. 41–43, 58, for other echoes such as "loke upon our infirmities."

9. P. 265. Cf. again the General Confession: "provokynge mooste justlye thy wrathe and indignation againste us: we do earnestly repente, and bee hartely sorye for these oure misdoings, the remembraunce of them is grevous unto us: the burthen of theim is intollerable."

10. Pp. 267–68. Cf. the General Confession: "have mercy upon us, have mercye upon us, mooste mercyfull father, for thy sonne oure Lorde Jesus Christes sake, forgeve us all that is paste."

11. Theodore Spencer, *Shakespeare and the Nature of Man,* pp. 12–13, 23, apprises us of this dominant thematic pattern, and demonstrates it to be a consistent Renaissance literary interest. Also discussing the epistemological theme in *Much Ado* are A. P. Rossiter, *"Much Ado about Nothing,"* p. 47; Donald A. Stauffer, *Shakespeare's World of Images,* pp. 71, 76; and Bradbrook, *Shakespeare and Elizabethan Poetry,* p. 180.

12. George and George, *The Protestant Mind of the English Reformation,* p. 46. Subsequent references occur in the text.

13. P. 268. Cf. the General Confession: "and graunte that we may ever hereafter serve and please the, in newenes of lyfe, to the honour and glorye of thy name throughe Jesus Christ our Lorde."

14. *The Prayer Book of Queen Elizabeth,* p. 126; *A Spirituall Wedding, wherein we are by similitudes taught, How Christ his bride, the faithful soule, is in this life prepared and adorned, . . .* (London, 1597).

15. Lewalski, "Love, Appearance and Reality," pp. 250–51. Lewalski has a nice discussion of reason and folly through the perspective of Bembo's discourse on love in *The Courtier,* Book 4.

16. See note 11 and Walter N. King, "Much Ado about Something," pp. 143–49. My "Donne's *Ignatius His Conclave* and the New Astronomy," pp. 329–37, discusses the practice of the "dismissal of reason." Brown, *Shakespeare and His Comedies*, pp. 109–18, predictably summarizes the thematic interest well, and concludes with an analogy between love, truth, and faith. Paul A. Jorgensen, *"Much Ado about Nothing,"* pp. 287–95, places "nothing" within the tradition of the triviality of the world. The pun "nothing-noting" enhances this epistemological context. Dorothy C. Hockey, "Notes, Notes, Forsooth . . .," pp. 356ff., expands the idea by discussing misnoting in the play.

17. Colet, *An Exposition of Corinthians*, p. 19.

18. See George and George, *The Protestant Mind of the English Reformation*, pp. 97–98, discussing the Protestant commonplace of such outward evidence of the inner man, the "new man," regenerate and cleansed.

19. See John Dover Wilson, *Shakespeare's Happy Comedies*, p. 137. Some critics find the command more sinister; see John Palmer, *Comic Characters of Shakespeare*, pp. 112–14, 126; and Thomas H. McNeal, "Shakespeare's Cruel Queens," p. 47. See also Lewalski, "Love, Appearance, and Reality," p. 245.

20. Hunter, *Shakespeare and the Comedy of Forgiveness*, chs. 1 and 2.

21. Ibid., pp. 103–5.


CHAPTER V

1. See ch. 1, pp. 9–15; ch. 3, pp. 53–63.

2. Richard Hooker, for example, devotes an entire book of his *Laws of Ecclesiastical Polity* (Book 4) to this topic. See Davies, *Worship and Theology in England*, chs. 1–3; and George and George, *The Protestant Mind of the English Reformation*, pp. 348–63, on the importance of this controversy.

3. Agnes Latham, among many others, notices this unusual humility in the green world in her introduction to *As You Like It*. She attributes it to the forest's magic (pp. lxx–lxxi), but banishment is itself humiliating enough to have achieved some natural magic among the foresters. Surprisingly little has been made of the important effects of this humility on the fools.

4. Morris Palmer Tilley cites 128 proverbs concerning fools and folly. That none of them contains this Pauline and Erasmian paradox illustrates its unique biblical context. See *A Dictionary of the Proverbs in England* (Ann Arbor: University of Michigan Press, 1950), pp. 226–34.

5. See Barber, *Shakespeare's Festive Comedy*, pp. 233–39; Kreider,

"Genial Literary Satire," p. 222; Peter G. Phialas, *Shakespeare's Romantic Comedies*, pp. 219, 254; Brown, *Shakespeare and His Comedies*, pp. 145–50; T. M. Parrott, *Shakespearean Comedy*, p. 168; and Sylvan Barnet, "Strange Events: Improbability in *As You Like It*," p. 120.

6. Plato *Republic* Book 10, 598e, 605b, trans. Paul Shorey, Loeb Classical Library.

7. Sir Philip Sidney, *An Apology for Poetry*, in *Criticism: The Major Texts*, ed. Walter Jackson Bate (New York: Harcourt, Brace & World, 1952), p. 97.

8. D. J. Palmer has written two excellent articles on this theme in *As You Like It:* "Art and Nature in *As You Like It*," and "*As You Like It* and the Idea of Play."

9. Nowell, *A Catechism*, pp. 142, 191.

10. PHEBE. Good shepherd, tell this youth what 'tis to love.
SILVIUS. It is to be all made of sighs and tears;
    And so am I for Phebe.
PHEBE. And I for Ganymede.
ORLANDO. And I for Rosalind.
ROSALIND. And I for no woman.
SILVIUS. It is to be all made of faith and service;
    And so am I for Phebe.
PHEBE. And I for Ganymede.
ORLANDO. And I for Rosalind.
ROSALIND. And I for no woman.
SILVIUS. It is to be all made of fantasy,
    All made of passion, and all made of wishes,
    All adoration, duty, and observance,
    All humbleness, all patience, and impatience,
    All purity, all trial, all observance;
    And so am I for Phebe.
PHEBE. And so am I for Ganymede.
ORLANDO. And so am I for Rosalind.
ROSALIND. And so am I for no woman. (v.ii.78–97)

11. G. Wilson Knight, *The Burning Oracle*, p. 21, intuits this metaphoric phenomenon when he suggests that dramatic action becomes sacramental when the audience participates in it.

12. Pico della Mirandola, *On the Imagination*, p. 6.

13. Although many critics mention role-playing as a motif in *As You Like It*, few consider it as central as I do. See especially Palmer, "Idea of Play," pp. 237–38. For other prominent statements see Bradbrook, *Shake-*

*speare and Elizabethan Poetry,* p. 220; Kreider, "Genial Literary Satire," p. 212.

14. Mark Van Doren, *Shakespeare,* pp. 127–35.
15. Palmer, "Art and Nature," p. 38.
16. Peter J. Seng, "The Forester's Song in *As You Like It,*" p. 249.
17. Barber, *Shakespeare's Festive Comedy,* p. 236.
18. Palmer, "Idea of Play," p. 235.
19. Fraser, *The War against Poetry,* pp. 40–44.
20. Bevington, *Tudor Drama and Politics,* p. 298.
21. Jonas A. Barish, "Exhibitionism and the Antitheatrical Prejudice," pp. 6–7.
22. Fraser, *The War against Poetry,* p. 79.
23. Bevington, *Tudor Drama and Politics,* p. 302. Jackson Cope's *The Theater and the Dream.* pp. 172–218, also comments on connections between drama and liturgy. He suggests that *As You Like It,* like Thomas Heywood's *Apology for Actors* (1612), defends theatrical illusion through the use of the theological topos of the theater of the world (pp. 173–74).
24. Mircea Eliade, "Methodological Remarks on the Study of Religious Symbolism," in *The History of Religions,* p. 98.
25. For Erasmian and Pauline statements, see chs. 1 and 3. See Pico della Mirandola, *On the Imagination,* pp. 5–6.
26. Vos, *The Drama of Comedy,* p. 114.

## CHAPTER VI

1. Barber, *Shakespeare's Festive Comedy,* pp. 3–35; John Hollander, "*Musica Mundana* and *Twelfth Night,*" pp. 55–82. Some of the material in this chapter originally appeared in expanded form in my book, *Renaissance Drama and the English Church Year.* On the "Festus" see Lewalski, "Thematic Patterns in *Twelfth Night,*" pp. 168–69. Hotson, *The First Night of Twelfth Night;* the critics are legion. See Phialas, *Shakespeare's Romantic Comedies,* p. 258.
2. Lewalski, "Thematic Patterns in *Twelfth Night,*" pp. 169–77.
3. Marion Bodwell Smith, *Dualities in Shakespeare,* p. 115. Subsequent references to Smith will be cited in the text.
4. *The Prayer Book of Queen Elizabeth,* pp. 25, 29, and 64, denote these as the proper passages for Epiphany: Isa. 49 and 60; Matt. 2:1–12; Eph. 3:1–12; Luke 3.
5. I cite the King James version here as Handel's text.
6. *The Sermons of John Donne,* 3:354. Subsequent quotations of Donne's sermons will refer to this edition and be cited in the text. Robert

NOTES

Nelson, *A Companion for the Festivals and Fasts of the Church of England*, p. 63, says of the Magi: "Lest they should expect a Prince accompanied with outward Pomp and Magnificence, the Angel describeth the Meanness and Obscurity of his Circumstances." And Donne in another Epiphany sermon adds, "He was God, *humbled in the flesh;* he was Man, *received into glory*" (3:206).

7. Andrewes, *Ninety-Six Sermons,* 1:204. Subsequent references to this edition will be made in the text.

8. Davies, *Worship and Theology in England,* p. 67. See also Lewalski, "Thematic Patterns in *Twelfth Night,*" pp. 176–77.

9. Virtually all comments about Feste recognize his regenerative efforts. None have placed him securely in this Christian context. Goldsmith, *Wise Fools in Shakespeare,* p. 53; Brown, *Shakespeare and His Comedies,* p. 176; and Jenkins, "Shakespeare's *Twelfth Night,*" pp. 32–33.

10. Hollander, "*Twelfth Night* and the Morality of Indulgence," pp. 224–25.

11. *Certaine Sermons or Homilies,* p. 201. John Foxe, *A Sermon Preached at the Christening of a Certaine Jew,* sigs. A4v–A5.

12. Smith, *Dualities in Shakespeare,* pp. 118–19, has some good comments on Malvolio's discomfort in an Epiphany setting. *Certaine Sermons or Homilies,* pp. 204, 257–58, 272.

13. See *The Sermons of John Donne,* 1:314; Davies, *Worship and Theology in England,* p. 36; see also Gregory Martin's marginal notes in *The New Testament,* p. 701.

14. *New Catholic Encyclopedia,* s.v. "Epiphany, Feast of."

15. L. G. Salingar, "The Design of *Twelfth Night,*" p. 118, suggests that Feste is "mumming it as a priest and attempting a mock exorcism in the manner of the Feast of Fools." Cf. Dr. Pinch in *The Comedy of Errors.*

16. William Tyndale, *Doctrinal Treatises,* p. 496.

17. William Tyndale, *The Work of William Tyndale,* p. 126.

18. Noble, *Shakespeare's Biblical Knowledge,* pp. 212–13. Robert E. Fitch, *Shakespeare: The Perspective of Value,* p. 77; and Lewalski, "Thematic Patterns in *Twelfth Night,*" p. 179, discuss this allusion with different but complementary readings. See also *The New Testament Octapla.*

19. Alexander Nowell, *A Catechism,* pp. 137, 216–17.

20. Ibid., p. 199.

21. See the excellent commentary on this in *The Annotated Book of Common Prayer,* p. 453.

22. *The Merchant of Venice,* II.vii.16.

23. In the third chapter of *Fools and Folly,* "The Fool Triumphs over the Wise Man," Barbara Swain gives many historical examples of these fools for Christ's sake: the Franciscan order of simplicity, Nicholas de

Cusa, Jean Gerson, Benedetti da Toda, and Gregory all wrote about or enacted this Christian paradox. Such characters were, incidentally, called "poor Toms" (pp. 40–46). Kaiser, *Praisers of Folly*, has a brief chapter on "The Fool in Christ." Like Swain, he has almost nothing to say about Erasmus's influence on Shakespeare's romantic comedies. Glenys McMullen, "The Fool as Entertainer and Satirist, on Stage and in the World," p. 12, mentions that Feste's role as curate is "like the French *sottises*, where priest and fool were identified with each other."

24. Colet, *An Exposition of Corinthians*, p. 19. See also J. Penry (?) *A Treatise*, sig. D1.

25. Fulke, *A Comfortable Sermon of Faith*, sig. A2.

26. Kaiser, *Praisers of Folly*, p. 87, states the commonly accepted observation that Stultitia abandons much of her irony in the final section.

27. Ibid., pp. 88–90. See also Cox, *The Feast of Fools*, ch. 10: "Christ the Harlequin."

28. Lewalski, "Thematic Patterns in *Twelfth Night*," (pp. 168–69) mentions from Barber's lead that Festus, the traditional Lord of Misrule, is played by Toby Belch in *Twelfth Night*. I would submit that Shakespeare also adapts this traditional name to indicate through Feste his innovative comic-Christian festivity of humility and good will.

## CHAPTER VII

1. *Extracts from the Accounts of the Revels at Court*, pp. 204–5. Some of this introductory material on Shrovetide and the play originally appeared in altered form in my book, *Renaissance Drama and the English Church Year*.

2. Frederick George Lee, *A Glossary of Liturgical and Ecclesiastical Terms*, p. 371.

3. Ethel Urlin, *Festivals, Holy Days, and Saints' Days*, pp. 41–42; Enid Welsford, *The Court Masque*, p. 12.

4. A. R. Wright, *British Calendar Customs: England*, 1:1.

5. *The Prayer Book Dictionary*, p. 749.

6. See marginal notes in *The Geneva Bible;* and *The Interpreters' Bible*, 1: 558–59, 582; *The Prayer Book of Queen Elizabeth*, p. 67.

7. *The Sermons of John Donne*, 7:73, spoken to James at Whitehall, Feb. 24, 1625/6. See also 2:165–67, 2:348, 3:348–51.

8. *The Interpreters' Bible*, 1:551–52; see also George and George, *The Protestant Mind of the English Reformation*, pp. 95ff., on the same dilemma. The fathers of the English Church frequently discuss this precarious Shrovetide balance of presumption and despair. See particularly William

Tyndale, *Doctrinal Treatises,* pp. 500–504; Hugh Latimer, *Sermons and Remains,* p. 182; John Hooper, *Early Writings,* pp. 415–26. See also Andrewes, *Ninety-Six Sermons,* 5: 513–15, 535.

9. These understandings are widely shared; they reflect particularly the work of Lewalski, "Biblical Allusion and Allegory," pp. 327–43; and Brown, *Shakespeare and His Comedies.*

10. See Thomas Fujimura, "Mode and Structure in *The Merchant of Venice,*" pp. 499–511, for a sensitive discussion of the mixed modes.

11. Noble, *Shakespeare's Biblical Knowledge,* pp. 162–65, lists other New Testament statements of the same commonplace.

12. John Colet, *An Exposition of St. Paul's Epistle to the Romans,* pp. 4, 23.

13. Ibid., p. 4.

14. Ibid., pp. 4, 23, 60–61.

15. The paradoxical concept of surfeiting is mentioned twice in the play, both times precepturally (I.ii.5–6; III.ii.113–14). The Christians seem unable to profit from it.

16. Welsford, *The Court Masque,* p. 12.

17. Davies, *Worship and Theology in England,* pp. 76–123. See George and George, *The Protestant Mind of the English Reformation,* pp. 348–63; Walker, *A History of the Christian Church,* p. 308, actually places the sacramental issue first in importance among Reformation controversies.

18. George and George, *The Protestant Mind of the English Reformation,* pp. 102–7. My "Antonio and the Ironic Festivity of *The Merchant of Venice*" was originally published in *Shakespeare Studies;* the material has been much altered here.

19. *The Interpreters' Bible,* 1:551–52.

20. Paul N. Siegel, "Shylock the Puritan," pp. 14–16.

21. Charles Mitchell, "The Conscience of Venice: Shakespeare's Merchant," pp. 214–25; Davies, *Worship and Theology in England,* p. 324, discusses the "razor edge between presumption and despair" in the Renaissance Puritan.

22. Graham Midgley, "*The Merchant of Venice:* A Reconsideration," pp. 119–33, discusses Antonio's "unconscious homosexuality" and concludes that Antonio and Shylock are essentially similar as outsiders, one to a Christian society, the other to a "blatantly heterosexual society." To me the implications of Antonio's imperfect love are more significant and more varied. See also Coghill, "The Basis of Shakespearian Comedy," p. 16.

23. On this point I strongly disagree with M. G. Deshpande, "Loneliness in *The Merchant of Venice,*" pp. 368–69.

24. See note 17. My discussion of Antonio and Shylock originally ap-

peared in much altered form in *Cithara* 13 (1974): 19–33, as "Frustrated Communion in *The Merchant of Venice*."

25. Davies, *Worship and Theology in England*, pp. 17–25.

26. Fulke, *The Text of the New Testament*, fol. 258v.

27. Luther, *Lectures on Romans*, p. 245; Fulke, *A Defense*, p. 429; Tyndale, *An Answer to Sir Thomas More*, pp. 172–73; Bullinger, *Commonplaces of Christian Religion*, p. 102; *The Prayer Book of Queen Elizabeth*, p. 42; and Rom. 7:18–19.

28. Alexander Nowell, *A Catechism*, p. 215. *The Prayer Book of Queen Elizabeth*, p. 103, similarly reads that Christ "made ther (by his one oblation of himself once offered), a ful, perfect, and sufficient sacrifice, oblation, and satisfaction for the synnes of the whole worlde."

29. *Certaine Sermons or Homilies*, p. 200.

30. *New Catholic Encyclopedia*, s.v. "Priesthood of Christ."

31. *The Prayer Book of Queen Elizabeth*, p. 104.

32. *New Catholic Encyclopedia*, s.v. "Sacrifice in Christian Theology, IV." The homily concerning communion stresses the "inward man" who must humbly share the reenactment of Christ's sacrifice, not "stand for" Christ (*Certaine Sermons or Homilies*, pp. 197–201).

33. Lewalski, "Biblical Allusion and Allegory in *The Merchant of Venice*," p. 334, mentions some aspects of the Christlike Antonio, but notes none of the pervasive irony or its doctrinal precedent. On the other hand, Fujimura, "Mode and Structure in *The Merchant of Venice*," p. 509, mentions Antonio's excessive pride and his lack of charity, and suggests that an ironic perspective is useful in understanding part of the comedy (pp. 499–500).

34. From John 15:13: "Greater love hath no man than this, that a man bestow his life for his friends."

35. Frye, *Anatomy of Criticism*, p. 176; on p. 45 Frye discusses how often the expulsion of the literary scapegoat creates ambiguous comic situations. He may embody the society's viciousness but his expulsion suggests its ironic continuance.

36. No other of Shakespeare's comic villains is excluded without the promise of reunification, albeit sometimes the reunion will contain "brave punishments." Even Malvolio is welcomed, but chooses his own exclusion; so, too, Jaques chooses a reflective society among the "convertites." Antonio in *The Tempest* is an extreme example of this inclusiveness.

37. Colet, *An Exposition of St. Paul's Epistle to the Romans*, pp. 60–61.

38. William Tyndale, *The Supper of Our Lord*, p. 227.

39. Marvin Felheim, *"The Merchant of Venice*," pp. 102ff., discusses the food imagery to suggest Shylock's unsuccessful absorption into the

Christian society; Isidore H. Coriat, "Anal-erotic Character Traits in Shylock," pp. 354–60.

40. See Paula Brady, "Shylock's Omophagia," pp. 229–33; and Robert Fleissner, "Review," p. 610, for two recent and brief anticipations of this general idea.

41. *Certaine Sermons or Homilies*, p. 203; see also Nowell, *A Catechism*, p. 216; and *New Catholic Encyclopedia*, s.v. "Agape." Vos, *The Drama of Comedy*, p. 110, suggests that eating in comedy is often to be associated with the Christian symbolism of reconciliation.

42. An elaborate debate concerning Shylock's salvation as a result of Portia's trickery may be pursued by glancing at Parrott, *Shakespearean Comedy*, pp. 139, 143; Wilson, *Shakespeare's Happy Comedies*, p. 106; and Bernard Grebanier, *The Truth about Shylock*, pp. 282, 291–92, all of whom believe that he was paradoxically saved by the ending. See also Coghill, "The Basis of Shakespearean Comedy," pp. 21–23; and Evans, *Shakespeare's Comedies*, p. 64, who suggest that our dissatisfaction at the trick is not an indictment of the Christians.

43. This final comparison between the controversy and the play suggests the completeness of Shakespeare's use of the material. According to Walker, *A History of the Christian Church*, "Luther criticized the denial of the cup to the laity, doubted transubstantiation, and especially rejected the doctrine that the supper is a sacrifice" (p. 308). All three issues have a prominent place in the play.

44. Quoted in A. R. Humphreys, *The Merchant of Venice*, p. 23.

45. Quoted in Grebanier, *The Truth about Shylock*, pp. 230–31.

46. See ibid., p. 231.

47. J. A. Bryant, *"The Merchant of Venice* and the Common Flaw," p. 618; Alan C. Dessen, "The Elizabethan Stage-Jew and Christian Example," pp. 242–43.

48. See Grebanier, *The Truth about Shylock*, pp. 250–54.

49. See note 42. Grebanier is clearly wrong on the second point, however (p. 292). The Christians will take his life as well as his wealth if he refuses to convert.

50. Dessen, "The Elizabethan Stage-Jew," p. 233.

51. See *The Prayer Book of Queen Elizabeth*, p. 99.

52. The sickness of the Christian society is usually attributed only to Venice. John Palmer, *Comic Characters of Shakespeare*, pp. 80, 86–87; Wilson, *Shakespeare's Happy Comedies*, pp. 108–14; Harold C. Goddard, *The Meaning of Shakespeare*, pp. 88–90; and Barber, *Shakespeare's Festive Comedy*, p. 169.

53. R. M. Frye, p. 180.

54. Coghill, "The Basis of Shakespearian Comedy," p. 23.

# NOTES

## EPILOGUE

1. I Cor. 1:20 (Genevan marginal notes).
2. See note 10, ch. 1.
3. Douglas Bush, *The Renaissance and English Humanism*, pp. 67, 80–81; see also pp. 17–33, 93–96.
4. Spencer, *Shakespeare and the Nature of Man*, pp. x–xi, chs. 1 and 2.
5. Mikhail Bakhtin, *Rabelais and His World*, pp. 16–29, discusses the place of these "base epithets" in the satiric and intellectual traditions. See Alvin B. Kernan, "The Henriad: Shakespeare's Major History Plays," pp. 107–15, for an instructive discussion of the conflict of historical and sacramental world-views in *Richard II*.
6. Maynard Mack, "The World of *Hamlet*," p. 49.
7. D. A. Traversi, *Shakespeare: The Roman Plays*, has obviously influenced my understanding of the play.

# Bibliography

## PRIMARY SOURCES

Andrewes, Lancelot. *Ninety-Six Sermons*. Reprint of 1843 edition. New York: AMS Press, 1967.

*The Annotated Book of Common Prayer*. Edited by John Henry Blunt. New York: E. P. Dutton and Co., 1908.

Bullinger, Henry. *Commonplaces of Christian Religion*. Translated by John Stockwood. London, 1572.

Calvin, John. *Commentaries on the Epistle of Paul the Apostle to the Romans*. Translated by John Owens. Grand Rapids, Mich.: William B. Eerdmans Publishing Co., 1955.

————. *Commentary on the Epistles of Paul the Apostle to the Corinthians*. Translated by John Pringle. 2 vols. Grand Rapids, Mich.: William B. Eerdmans Publishing Co., 1948.

————. *Commentaries on the Epistles to Timothy, Titus, and Philemon*. Translated by William Pringle. Grand Rapids, Mich.: William B. Eerdmans Publishing Co., 1948.

*Certaine Sermons or Homilies Appointed to be Read in Churches in the Time of Queen Elizabeth I*. Edited by Mary Ellen Rickey and Thomas B. Stroup. Gainesville: The University of Florida Press, 1968.

*The Christmas Prince*. Oxford: The Malone Society Reprints, 1922.

Colet, John. *An Exposition of St. Paul's Epistle to the Romans*. Edited by J. H. Lupton. Reprint of 1873 edition. Ridgewood: The Gregg Press, 1965.

————. *An Exposition of St. Paul's First Epistle to the Corinthians*. Edited by J. H. Lupton. Reprint of 1874 edition. Ridgewood: The Gregg Press, 1965.

*Criticism: The Major Texts*. Edited by Walter Jackson Bate. New York: Harcourt, Brace and World, 1952.

Dante Alighieri. *The Divine Comedy*. Translated by Dorothy L. Sayers. Edinburgh: R. and R. Clark, 1955.

Donne, John. *The Sermons of John Donne*. Edited by George R. Potter and Evelyn M. Simpson. Berkeley: University of California Press, 1953–62.

Erasmus, Desiderius. *The Praise of Folie*. Translated by Sir Thomas Chaloner. Oxford: Early English Text Society, 1965.

————. *Proverbes or adagies, gathered out of the Chiliades by Richard Taverner*. London, 1569.

*Extracts from the Accounts of the Revels at Court in the Reigns of Queen Elizabeth and King James I.* Edited by Peter Cunningham. London: The Shakespeare Society, 1842.

Foxe, John. *A Sermon Preached at the Christening of a Certaine Jew*. Translated by James Bell. London, 1578.

Fulke, William. *A Comfortable Sermon of Faith*. London, 1574.

————. *A defense of the sincere and true Translations of the holie Scriptures into the English tong, against the . . . cavils of . . . Gregory Martin*. Edited by C. H. Hartshorne. Cambridge: The Parker Society, 1843.

————. *The Text of the New Testament of Iesus Christ . . .* London, 1589.

Fuller, Thomas. *The Church History of Britain*. Edited by J. S. Brewer. 6 vols. Reprint of 1845 edition. Ridgewood: Gregg International Publishers, 1970.

*The Geneva Bible, a facsimile of the 1560 edition*. Introduction by Lloyd E. Berry. Madison: The University of Wisconsin Press, 1969.

Hooker, Richard. *Ecclesiastical Polity*. London: J. M. Dent and Sons, 1925.

Hooper, John. *Early Writings*. Edited by Samuel Carr. Cambridge: The Parker Society, 1843.

Latimer, Hugh. *Sermons*. Edited by G. E. Corrie. Cambridge: The Parker Society, 1844.

————. *Sermons and Remains*. Edited by G. E. Corrie. Cambridge: The Parker Society, 1845.

Luther, Martin. *Lectures on Romans*. Edited by Hilton C. Oswald. St. Louis: Concordia, 1972.

Marbeck, John. *A Book of Notes and Commonplaces*. London: Thomas East, 1581.

Martin, Gregory. Annotations and Notes of *The New Testament*. Translated by Rhemes. Antworp: D. Vervliet, 1600.

More, Sir Thomas. *The Dialogue Concerning Tyndale,* edited by W. E. Campbell. In *The English Works of Sir Thomas More*. Vol. 2. London: Eyre and Spottiswood, 1927.

Nelson, Robert. *A Companion for the Festivals and Fasts of the Church of England*. 19th ed. London, 1748.

*The New Testament Octapla*. Edited by Luther A. Weigle. New York: Thomas Nelson & Sons, 1962.

Nowell, Alexander. *A Catechism*. Translated by Thomas Norton, edited by G. E. Corrie. Cambridge: The Parker Society, 1853.

Penry (?), J. *A Treatise Wherein it is Manifestlee Proved . . .* [1590].

Pico della Mirandola. *On the Imagination.* Translated by Harry Caplan. New Haven: Yale University Press, 1930.

*The Prayer Book of Queen Elizabeth 1559.* London: Griffith Farran & Co., 1890.

*William Shakespeare: The Complete Works.* Edited by Alfred Harbage. The revised Pelican text. Baltimore: Penguin Books, 1969.

*The Stage Acquitted.* London: John Barnes, 1699.

Strype, John. *Documentary Annals of the Reformed Church of England.* Edited by Edward Cardwell. Reprint of 1844 edition. Ridgewood: The Gregg Press, 1966.

Tyndale, William. *An Answer to Sir Thomas More's Dialogue.* Edited by Henry Walter. Cambridge: The Parker Society, 1850.

———. *Doctrinal Treatises.* Edited by Henry Walter. Cambridge: The Parker Society, 1848.

———. *The Supper of Our Lord.* Edited by Henry Walter. Cambridge: The Parker Society, 1850.

———. *The Work of William Tyndale.* Edited by S. L. Greenslade. London and Glasgow: Blackie & Son, 1938.

Weigel, Luther A., ed. *The English New Testament.* New York: The Abingdon Cokesbury Press, 1949.

## SECONDARY SOURCES

Alexander, H. G. *Religion in England 1558–1662.* London: University of London Press, 1968.

Allen, Don Cameron. *Mysteriously Meant.* Baltimore: The Johns Hopkins Press, 1970.

Baker, Herschel. *The Wars of Truth.* Cambridge: Harvard University Press, 1952.

Bakhtin, Mikhail. *Rabelais and His World.* Translated by Helene Iswolsky. Cambridge: M.I.T. Press, 1968.

Barber, C. L. *Shakespeare's Festive Comedy.* Princeton: Princeton University Press, 1959.

Barish, Jonas A. "Exhibitionism and the Antitheatrical Prejudice." *ELH* 36 (1969): 1–29.

Barnet, Sylvan. "Strange Events: Improbability in *As You Like It.*" *Shakespeare Studies* 4 (1968): 119–31.

Battenhouse, Roy W. "Falstaff as Parodist and Perhaps Holy Fool." *PMLA* 90 (1975): 32–52.

———. *Shakespearean Tragedy: Its Art and Its Christian Premises.* Bloomington: Indiana University Press, 1968.

# BIBLIOGRAPHY

Bethell, S. L. *Shakespeare and the Popular Dramatic Tradition.* Durham: Duke University Press, 1944.

Bevington, David. *Tudor Drama and Politics.* Cambridge: Harvard University Press, 1968.

Bradbrook, Muriel C. *Shakespeare and Elizabethan Poetry.* New York: Oxford University Press, 1952.

Brady, Paula. "Shylock's Omophagia." *Literature and Psychology* 17 (1967): 229–33.

Brown, John Russell. *Shakespeare and His Comedies.* London: Methuen, 1957.

Bryant, J. A., Jr. *Hippolyta's View.* Lexington: University of Kentucky Press, 1961.

———. "*The Merchant of Venice* and the Common Flaw." *Sewanee Review* 81 (1973): 606–12.

Bullough, Geoffrey. *Narrative and Dramatic Sources of Shakespeare.* 7 vols. to date. New York: Columbia University Press, 1957–.

Bush, Douglas. *The Renaissance and English Humanism.* Toronto: University of Toronto Press, 1939.

Calderwood, James L. "*A Midsummer Night's Dream:* The Illusion of Drama." *Modern Language Quarterly* 26 (1965): 506–22.

———. "*Love's Labour's Lost:* A Wantoning with Words." *Studies in English Literature* 5 (1965): 317–32.

Campbell, O. J., and Edward G. Quinn. *The Readers' Encyclopedia of Shakespeare.* New York: Thomas Y. Crowell Co., 1966.

Campbell, W. E. *Erasmus, Tyndale, and More.* Milwaukee: The Bruce Publishing Co., n.d.

Charlton, H. B. *Shakespearian Comedy.* 4th ed. London, 1949.

Coghill, Nevill. "The Basis of Shakespearian Comedy." *Essays and Studies,* n.s. 3 (1950): 1–28.

Collinson, Patrick. *The Elizabethan Puritan Movement.* Berkeley: University of California Press, 1967.

Cope, Jackson. *The Theater and the Dream.* Baltimore: The Johns Hopkins Press, 1973.

Coriat, Isidore H. "Anal-Erotic Character Traits in Shylock." *International Journal of Psychoanalysis* 2 (1921): 354–60.

Cormican, L. A. "Medieval Idiom in Shakespeare: (I) Shakespeare and the Liturgy." *Scrutiny* 17 (1950): 186–202.

Coursen, Herbert R., Jr. "*Love's Labour's Lost* and the Comic Truth." *Papers on Language and Literature* 6 (1970): 316–22.

Cox, Harvey. *The Feast of Fools.* Cambridge: Harvard University Press, 1969.

# BIBLIOGRAPHY

Craik, T. W. *"Much Ado about Nothing." Scrutiny* 19 (1953): 297–316.

Creeth, Robert. *Mankynde in Shakespeare.* Athens: University of Georgia Press, 1976.

Cunningham, Delora. "Repentance and the Art of Living Well." In *Ashland Studies in Shakespeare.* Ashland, Or.: Oregon Shakespeare Festival, 1955.

Curry, Walter Clyde. *Shakespeare's Philosophic Patterns.* 2nd ed. Baton Rouge: Louisiana State University Press, 1959.

D'Arcy, M. C. *The Mind and Heart of Love.* New York: Henry Holt and Co., 1947.

David, Richard, ed. *Love's Labour's Lost.* London: Methuen, 1951.

Davies, Horton. *Worship and Theology in England.* Princeton: Princeton University Press, 1970.

Dent, R. W. "Imagination in *A Midsummer Night's Dream." Shakespeare Quarterly* 15 (1964): 115–29.

Deshpande, M. G. "Loneliness in *The Merchant of Venice." Essays in Criticism* 11 (1961): 368–69.

Dessen, Alan C. "The Elizabethan Stage-Jew and Christian Example." *Modern Language Quarterly* 35 (1974): 231–45.

———. *Jonson's Moral Comedy.* Evanston, Illinois: Northwestern University Press, 1971.

*Dictionnaire des Hérésies,* by M. L'Abbe J. Jh. Claris. 2 vols. Paris: J. P. Migne, 1847.

Eliade, Mircea. "Methodological Remarks on the Study of Religious Symbolism." In *The History of Religion,* edited by Mircea Eliade and Joseph M. Kitagawa. Chicago: University of Chicago Press, 1959.

Empson, William. " 'Fool' in *Lear." Sewanee Review* 57 (1949): 177–214.

Evans, Bertrand. *Shakespeare's Comedies.* Oxford: Clarendon Press, 1960.

Felheim, Marvin. *"The Merchant of Venice." Shakespeare Studies* 4 (1968): 94–108.

Fitch, Robert E. *Shakespeare: The Perspective of Value.* Philadelphia: The Westminster Press, 1969.

Fleissner, Robert. Untitled review article. *Journal of Human Relations* 19 (1971): 608–10.

Fraser, Russell. *The War against Poetry.* Princeton: Princeton University Press, 1970.

Frye, Northrop. *Anatomy of Criticism.* Princeton: Princeton University Press, 1957.

Frye, R. M. *Shakespeare and Christian Doctrine.* Princeton: Princeton University Press, 1963.

# BIBLIOGRAPHY

————. "Theological and Non-theological Structures in Tragedy." *Shakespeare Studies* 4 (1968): 132–48.

Fujimura, Thomas. "Mode and Structure in *The Merchant of Venice*." *PMLA* 81 (1966): 499–511.

George, C. H., and Katherine George. *The Protestant Mind of the English Reformation (1570–1640)*. Princeton: Princeton University Press, 1961.

Goddard, Harold C. *The Meaning of Shakespeare*. Chicago: University of Chicago Press, 1951.

Goldsmith, R. H. *Wise Fools in Shakespeare*. East Lansing, Mich.: Michigan State University Press, 1955.

Grebanier, Bernard. *The Truth about Shylock*. New York: Random House, 1962.

Greenfield, Thelma N. "*A Midsummer Night's Dream* and *The Praise of Folly*." *Journal of Comparative Literature* 20 (1968): 236–44.

Guardini, Romano. *The Spirit of the Liturgy*. Translated by Ada Lane. New York: Sheed and Ward, 1940.

Harbage, Alfred. *Shakespeare and the Rival Traditions*. New York: The Macmillan Co., 1952.

Hardison, O. B., Jr. *Christian Rite and Christian Drama in the Middle Ages*. Baltimore: The Johns Hopkins Press, 1965.

Hassel, R. Chris, Jr. "Armando's Sexual Puns." *Language Quarterly* 9 (1971): 7–9, 42.

————. "Donne's *Ignatius His Conclave* and the New Astronomy." *Modern Philology* 68 (1971): 329–37.

Haugaard, William P. *Elizabeth and the English Reformation*. London: Cambridge University Press, 1968.

Hockey, Dorothy C. "Notes, Notes, Forsooth . . .." *Shakespeare Quarterly* 8 (1957): 353–58.

Hollander, John. "*Musica Mundana* and *Twelfth Night*." In *English Institute Essays,* edited by Northrop Frye. New York: Columbia University Press, 1957.

————. "*Twelfth Night* and the Morality of Indulgence." *Sewanee Review* 67 (1959): 220–38.

Hotson, Leslie. *The First Night of Twelfth Night*. London: Hart-Davis, 1954.

Hoy, Cyrus. "*Love's Labour's Lost* and the Nature of Comedy." *Shakespeare Quarterly* 13 (1962): 31–40.

Humphreys, A. R. *The Merchant of Venice*. Oxford: Basil Blackwell, 1973.

Hunter, Robert G. "The Function of the Songs at the End of *Love's Labour's Lost*." *Shakespeare Studies* 7 (1974): 55–64.

# BIBLIOGRAPHY

————. *Shakespeare and the Comedy of Forgiveness.* New York: Columbia University Press, 1965.

*The Interpreter's Bible.* Edited by George Arthur Buttrick et al. 12 vols. New York: Abingdon Press, 1952.

Jenkins, Harold. "Shakespeare's *Twelfth Night.*" *Rice Institute Pamphlets* 45 (1959): 19–42.

Jones, Emrys. *The Origins of Shakespeare.* Oxford: Clarendon Press, 1977.

Jorgensen, Paul A. "*Much Ado about Nothing.*" *Shakespeare Quarterly* 5 (1954): 287–95.

————. *Our Naked Frailties.* Berkeley: The University of California Press, 1971.

Kaiser, Walter Jacob. *Praisers of Folly.* Cambridge, Mass.: Harvard University Press, 1963.

Kermode, Frank. "The Mature Comedies." In *Early Shakespeare*, edited by J. R. Brown and Bernard Harris. New York: St. Martin's Press, 1961.

————. *Shakespeare, Spenser, Donne.* New York: Viking Press, 1971.

Kernan, Alvin. "The Henriad: Shakespeare's Major History Plays." In *Twentieth Century Interpretations of Richard II,* edited by Paul M. Cubeta. Englewood Cliffs, N.J.: Prentice-Hall, 1971.

King, Walter N. "Much Ado about Something." *Shakespeare Quarterly* 15 (1964), 143–55.

Knight, G. Wilson. *The Burning Oracle.* London: Oxford University Press, 1939.

————. *The Christian Renaissance.* Revised edition. London: Methuen & Co., 1962.

Kolve, V. A. *The Play Called Corpus Christi.* Stanford: Stanford University Press, 1966.

Kreider, P. V. "Genial Literary Satire in the Forest of Arden." *Shakespeare Association Bulletin* 10 (1935): 212–31.

Latham, Agnes, ed. *As You Like It.* London: Methuen, 1975.

Lee, Frederick George. *A Glossary of Liturgical and Ecclesiastical Terms.* London: Bernard Quaritch, 1877.

Leech, Clifford. *Twelfth Night and Shakespearian Comedy.* Halifax, N.S.: Dalhousie University Press, 1965.

Lewalski, Barbara K. "Biblical Allusion and Allegory in *The Merchant of Venice.*" *Shakespeare Quarterly* 13 (1962): 327–43.

————. "Love, Appearance and Reality: Much Ado about Something." *Studies in English Literature* 8 (1968): 235–51.

————. "Thematic Patterns in *Twelfth Night.*" *Shakespeare Studies* 1 (1965): 168–81.

Lewis, C. S. *The Allegory of Love.* London: Oxford University Press, 1959.

# BIBLIOGRAPHY

Lynch, William F. *Christ and Apollo*. New York: Sheed & Ward, 1960.

Mack, Maynard. "The World of *Hamlet*." In *Twentieth Century Interpretations of Hamlet*, edited by David Bevington. Englewood Cliffs, N.J.: Prentice-Hall, 1968.

Manley, Frank, ed. *John Donne: The Anniversaries*. Baltimore: The Johns Hopkins University Press, 1963.

Markels, Julian. "Shakespeare's Confluence of Tragedy and Comedy: *Twelfth Night* and *King Lear*." *Shakespeare Quarterly* 15 (1964): 75–88.

McMullen, Glenys. "The Fool as Entertainer and Satirist, on Stage and in the World." *Dalhousie Review* 50 (1970): 10–22.

McNeal, Thomas H. "Shakespeare's Cruel Queens." *Huntington Library Quarterly* 22 (1958): 41–50.

Midgley, Graham. "*The Merchant of Venice:* A Reconsideration." *Essays in Criticism* 10 (1960): 119–33.

Mitchell, Charles. "The Conscience of Venice: Shakespeare's Merchant." *Journal of English and Germanic Philology* 63 (1964): 214–25.

Muir, Kenneth. "Shakespeare and Erasmus." *Notes & Queries,* n.s. 3 (1956): 424–25.

Neal, Daniel. *The History of the Puritans*. Portsmouth, N.H.: W. B. Allen & Co., 1816.

Neill, Kirby. "More Ado about Claudio: An Acquittal for the Slandered Groom." *Shakespeare Quarterly* 3 (1952): 91–107.

Noble, Richmond. *Shakespeare's Biblical Knowledge*. New York: The Macmillan Co., 1935.

Olsen, Paul A. "*A Midsummer Night's Dream* and the Meaning of Court Marriage." *ELH* 24 (1957): 95–119.

Palmer, John. *Comic Characters of Shakespeare*. London: Macmillan & Co., 1946.

Palmer, D. J. "Art and Nature in *As You Like It*." *Philological Quarterly* 49 (1970): 30–40.

———. "*As You Like It* and the Idea of Play." *Critical Quarterly* 13 (1971): 234–45.

Parrott, Thomas Marc. *Shakespearean Comedy*. Reprint of 1949 edition. New York: Russell and Russell, 1962.

Phialas, Peter G. *Shakespeare's Romantic Comedies*. Chapel Hill: University of North Carolina Press, 1966.

Pineas, Ranier. *Thomas More and Tudor Polemics*. Bloomington: Indiana University Press, 1968.

*The Prayer Book Dictionary,* ed. George Harford. London: Sir Isaac Pitman & Sons, 1912.

# BIBLIOGRAPHY

Rashbrook, R. P. "Shakespeare and the Bible." *Notes & Queries* 197 (1952): 49–50.

Robinson, Henry Wheeler. *The Bible in Its Ancient and English Versions.* Oxford: The Clarendon Press, 1940.

Rossiter, A. P. "*Much Ado about Nothing.*" In *Shakespeare: The Comedies,* edited by Kenneth Muir. Englewood Cliffs, N.J.: Prentice-Hall, 1965.

Rougement, Denis de. *Love in the Western World.* Translated by Montgomery Belgion. New York: Harcourt, Brace and Co., 1940.

Salingar, L. G. "The Design of *Twelfth Night.*" *Shakespeare Quarterly* 9 (1958): 117–39.

Scott, Nathan A. *The Broken Center.* New Haven: Yale University Press, 1966.

Seng, Peter J. "The Forester's Song in *As You Like It.*" *Shakespeare Quarterly* 10 (1959): 246–49.

Shepherd, Massey Hamilton. *The Oxford American Prayer Book Commentary.* New York: Oxford University Press, 1950.

Siegel, Paul N. "*A Midsummer Night's Dream* and the Wedding Guests." *Shakespeare Quarterly* 4 (1953): 139–44.

———— "Shylock the Puritan." *Columbia University Forum* 5, iv (1962): 14–19.

Singleton, Charles. *Dante Studies II: Journey to Beatrice.* Cambridge, Mass.: Harvard University Press, 1954–58.

Smith, James. "*Much Ado about Nothing.*" *Scrutiny* 13 (1946): 242–57.

Smith, Marion Bodwell. *Dualities in Shakespeare.* Toronto: University of Toronto Press, 1966.

Smith, Preserved. *Erasmus.* New York: Harper and Brothers, 1962.

Spencer, Theodore. *Shakespeare and the Nature of Man.* New York: The Macmillan Co., 1942.

Spicq, Ceslaus. *Agape in the New Testament.* Translated by Sisters Marie Aquinas McNamara and Mary Honoria Richter. St. Louis: B. Herder Book Co., 1965.

Stanley, Frances. "Shakespeare's Use of Oaths." In *The Triple Bond,* edited by Joseph G. Price. University Park: Penn State Press, 1975.

Staton, Walter F., Jr. "Ovidian Elements in *A Midsummer Night's Dream.*" *Huntington Library Quarterly* 26 (1963): 167–78.

Stauffer, Donald A. *Shakespeare's World of Images.* New York: Norton, 1949.

Stratton, Lowell D. "The Nine Worthies." In *Ashland Studies in Shakespeare.* Ashland, Or.: Oregon Shakespeare Festival, 1956.

Swain, Barbara. *Fools and Folly.* New York: Columbia University Press, 1932.

# BIBLIOGRAPHY

Tilley, Morris Palmer. *A Dictionary of the Proverbs in England.* Ann Arbor: University of Michigan Press, 1950.

Tillyard, E. M. W. *The Elizabethan World Picture.* New York: The Macmillan Co., 1944.

————. *Shakespeare's Early Comedies.* London: Chatto and Windus, 1966.

Traversi, D. A. *Shakespeare: The Roman Plays.* Stanford: Stanford University Press, 1963.

Ungerer, Gustav. *Anglo-Spanish Relations in Tudor Literature.* Madrid, 1956.

Urlin, Ethel. *Festivals, Holy Days, and Saints' Days.* Reprint of 1915 edition. Ann Arbor: Gryphon Books, 1971.

Van Doren, Mark. *Shakespeare.* Garden City: Doubleday, 1953.

Vos, Nelvin. *The Drama of Comedy: Victim and Victor.* Richmond, Va.: The John Knox Press, 1966.

Vyvyan, John. *Shakespeare and the Rose of Love.* London: Chatto and Windus, 1960.

Walker, Williston. *A History of the Christian Church.* Revised edition. New York: Charles Scribner's Sons, 1959.

Wells, Stanley. "Happy Endings in Shakespeare." *Jahrbuch der Deutschen Shakespeare-Gesellschaft West* 102 (1966): 103–23.

Welsford, Enid. *The Court Masque.* Reprint of 1927 edition. New York: Russell & Russell, 1962.

————. *The Fool.* London: Faber and Faber, 1935.

West, Robert H. *Shakespeare and the Outer Mystery.* Lexington: University of Kentucky Press, 1968.

Willeford, William E. *The Fool and His Sceptre.* Evanston: Northwestern University Press, 1969.

Wilson, John Dover. *Shakespeare's Happy Comedies.* Evanston: Northwestern University Press, 1962.

Wright, A. R. *British Calendar Customs: English.* 3 vols. London: Glaisher, 1936.

Zucker, Wolfgang M. "The Clown as the Lord of Disorder." *Theology Today* 24 (1967–68): 306–17.

# Index

# INDEX